HEADSTRAP

HEADSTRAP

Legends and Lore
from the Climbing
Sherpas of Darjeeling

Nandini Purandare and Deepa Balsavar
Foreword by Katie Ives

A LEGENDS & LORE TITLE

MOUNTAINEERS
BOOKS

MOUNTAINEERS BOOKS is dedicated to the exploration, preservation, and enjoyment of outdoor and wilderness areas.

1001 SW Klickitat Way, Suite 201, Seattle, WA 98134
800-553-4453, www.mountaineersbooks.org

Printed in the United States of America
27 26 25 24   1 2 3 4 5

Design and layout: Jen Grable
Cartographer: Erin Greb Cartography
All photographs by the authors unless credited otherwise
Cover photographs: *Nepalese Sherpa*, alexbrylov/123rf; *Mount Everest,* DanielPrudek/iStock; *Nawang Topgay's medals,* The Sherpa Project; *Tea plantations,* nevarpp/iStock; *Sherpas enjoying a rest break on an early Everest expedition,* Dorjee Lhatoo Collection

Library of Congress Cataloging-in-Publication Data is on file for this title at https://lccn.loc.gov/2023034461. LC ebook record available at https://lccn.loc .gov/2023034462.

Mountaineers Books titles may be purchased for corporate, educational, or other promotional sales, and our authors are available for a wide range of events. For information on special discounts or booking an author, contact our customer service at 800-553-4453 or mbooks@mountaineersbooks.org.

 Printed on FSC®-certified and 30% recycled materials

ISBN (paperback): 978-1-68051-640-1
ISBN (ebook): 978-1-68051-641-8

An independent nonprofit publisher since 1960

To the Climbing Sherpas of Darjeeling—
past, for the rich legacy they left behind,
present, for telling us their stories and opening their hearts and homes to us,
and future, for carrying forward this heritage with their heads held high.

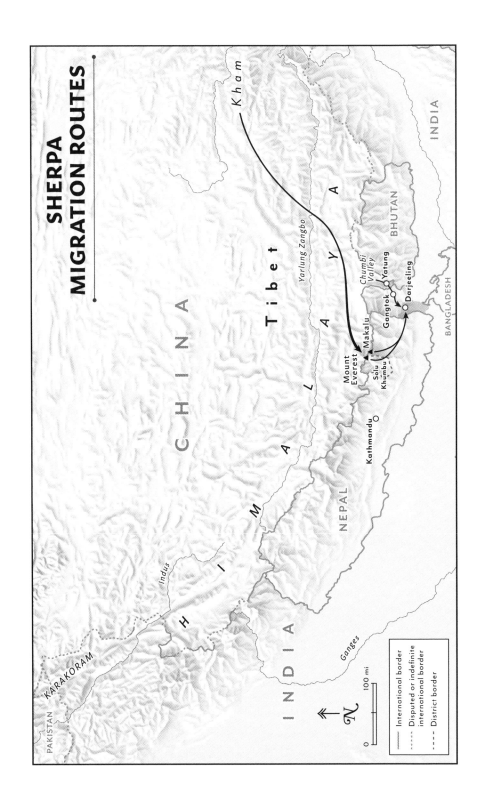

SHERPA
MIGRATION ROUTES

Kham

CHINA

Tibet

Yarlung Zangbo

KARAKORAM

PAKISTAN

H I M A L A Y A

Indus

INDIA

NEPAL

Kathmandu

Mount
Everest

Makalu

Solu
Khumbu

Chumbi
Valley

Gangtok Yatung

Darjeeling

BHUTAN

Ganges

BANGLADESH

INDIA

INDIA

N

0   100 mi

— International border
····· Disputed or indefinite
      international border
--- District border

CONTENTS

Part Three

THE FLIGHT OF THE GARUD

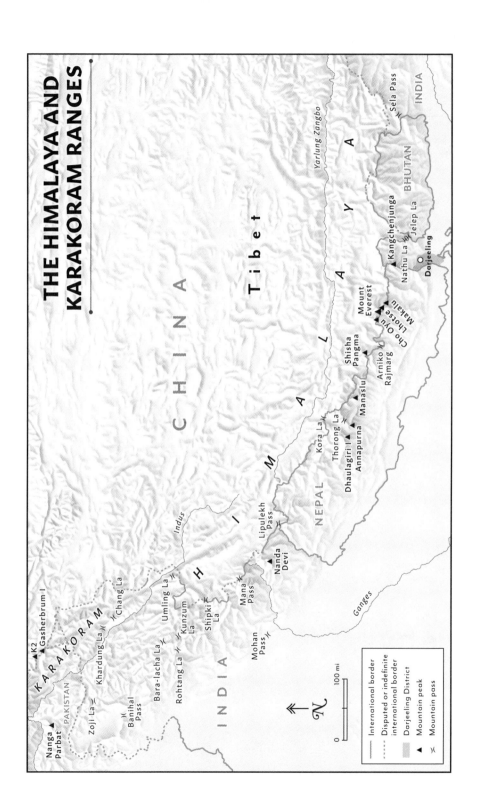

THE HIMALAYA AND KARAKORAM RANGES

CHINA

Tibet

HIMALAYA

NEPAL

BHUTAN

INDIA

PAKISTAN

KARAKORAM

Yarlung Zangbo

Indus

Ganges

Nanga Parbat ▲
K2 ▲
Gasherbrum I ▲
Zoji La)(
Banihal Pass)(
Bara-lacha La)(
Rohtang La)(
Khardung La)(
Chang La)(
Umling La)(
Kunzum La)(
Shipki La)(
Mana Pass)(
Mohan Pass)(
Nanda Devi ▲
Lipulekh Pass)(
Kora La)(
Thorong La)(
Dhaulagiri ▲
Annapurna ▲
Manaslu ▲
Shisha Pangma ▲
Arniko Rajmarg
Cho Oyu ▲
Mount Everest ▲
Lhotse ▲
Makalu ▲
Kangchenjunga ▲
Nathu La)(
Jelep La)(
Darjeeling ○
Sela Pass)(

N ⬅

0   100 mi

— International border
⋯ Disputed or indefinite
  international border
▨ Darjeeling District
▲ Mountain peak
)(Mountain pass

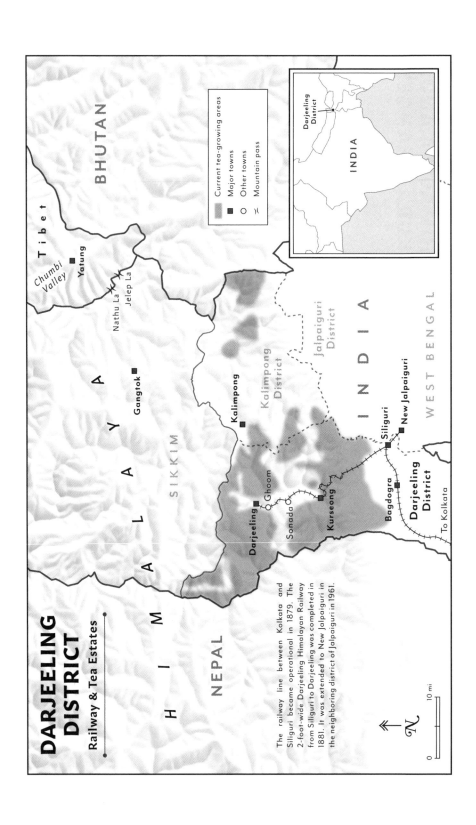

DARJEELING DISTRICT

Railway & Tea Estates

BHUTAN

Tibet

Chumbi Valley

Yatung

Nathu La
Jelep La

Gangtok

S I K K I M

H I M A L A Y A

Kalimpong

Kalimpong
District

Jalpaiguri
District

I N D I A

WEST BENGAL

New Jalpaiguri

Siliguri

Ghoom

Darjeeling

Sonada

Kurseong

Bagdogra

Darjeeling
District

To Kolkata

N E P A L

Current tea-growing areas
■ Major towns
○ Other towns
✕ Mountain pass

Darjeeling
District

INDIA

The railway line between Kolkata and Siliguri became operational in 1879. The 2-foot-wide Darjeeling Himalayan Railway from Siliguri to Darjeeling was completed in 1881. It was extended to New Jalpaiguri in the neighboring district of Jalpaiguri in 1961.

N

0   10 mi

Foreword
THE GIFT OF HISTORY

Katie Ives

May 29, 1953: More than seventy years before the publication of this book, with flags bound to his ice axe and raised against the dark-blue Himalayan sky, Tenzing Norgay posed on a crest of snow while his partner, Edmund Hillary, took the only summit photos. Within days, across the globe, front-page headlines proclaimed the first ascent of Mount Everest, or Chomolungma, as Sherpas call the peak. Countless readers gazed in awe at the picture of a man who, in that moment, stood above all others in the world.

In 1954, Prime Minister Jawaharlal Nehru helped found the Himalayan Mountaineering Institute in Darjeeling, India, hoping the school would produce "a thousand Tenzings." And a year later, when Tenzing Norgay published *Man of Everest*, with James Ramsey Ullman, he described how much it meant, at last, to have his own autobiography: "Here is my story. Here is myself."

Already, however, narratives by some Western writers appeared to try to push Tenzing Norgay away from the center of the Everest story, emphasizing Edmund Hillary's role instead. And expedition leader John Hunt had relegated struggles of high-altitude workers to the margins of his own memoir, Tenzing Norgay observed. "His is an official account," Tenzing Norgay reflected. "My story is not official. I am not an Englishman but a Sherpa." For years afterward, while great Sherpa mountaineers continued to arise, few had a chance to represent themselves in print. Often, even the most accomplished appeared in foreign climbers' books as mere supporting characters—seemingly devoid of personal lives, complex emotions, and aspirations of their own.

Maybe, in that mass-replicated, universal image of the oxygen-masked man in 1953—as Tenzing Norgay's biographer Ed Douglas suggested—the particulars got lost. Or perhaps colonialist attitudes remained too embedded in much of the international media and climbing communities for Sherpas and other Indigenous climbers to become frequent, well-rounded protagonists in tales other than that of the first ascent of the world's highest peak.

But there have long been innumerable, lesser-known stories, preserved in a few shelves' worth of books, but more often passed on orally from generation to generation in mountain villages and city neighborhoods—echoes, at times, of the vanished and the dead whose experiences reverberate through the lives and lore of loved ones and descendants.

A compilation of such oral histories—collected by Nandini Purandare and Deepa Balsavar, and narrated by Dorjee Lhatoo and other Darjeeling Sherpas—*Headstrap* features a body of adventure literature far more significant than the endless procession of I-Survived-the-Death-Zone and How-Climbing-the-Corporate-Ladder-Can-Be-Your-Personal-Everest accounts by Sherpas' Western clients that crowd bestseller lists and propel inspirational speaking tours. Here, instead, we read of young Sherpas who ran away from Khumbu during the early twentieth century, insulating their feet with bags of straw to cross snowy passes, chasing dreams of new opportunities in the booming hill station of Darjeeling. We follow their journeys through cold, high realms of avalanches and icefalls, intense winds and thin air, where they risked their lives as expedition workers—sometimes gaining hard-won futures of expanded choices for their children. Other times, losing their fingers, their toes, or even their lives.

We learn of people whose roles have all too often been ignored, including Sherpa women who bore loads "as heavy as carrying a man," as Ani Daku Sherpa, a 1953 Everest expedition worker, recounted. We are reminded of heroic acts off the mountains as well as on: of how Ang Tsering struggled down Nanga Parbat in a blizzard in 1934, snow blind and frostbitten, seeking help for his doomed companions. "For nine days I ate only ice," his family recalled him saying. And of how, in the aftermath, he took care of more and more children of Sherpas who perished in the mountains: "These are all my children," he told Dorjee Lhatoo. We hear of the fates of expedition staff who fell into poverty, rejected for work because of injury or age—such as Lewa Sherpa, who lost his toes to frostbite during the first ascent of Kamet and who later threw his Tiger Badge down a hill, protesting an industry that valued him so little and discarded him so easily.

"It is high time," Purandare and Balsavar write, "these stories are told." This collection—along with other books by or about expedition workers—represents far more than a crucial way of filling gaps in the historical record. It is also a call to action for more writers, editors, publishers, and readers to join a larger reckoning and reenvisioning of what mountain literature has been, should have been, and might yet become.

Such books have a particular resonance now, as the first winter ascent of K2 by a nearly all-Sherpa team once more expands the audience for their achievements, building momentum toward equity that must be supported well enough, this time, to endure. During an era when the rise of AI-generated content seems to threaten the future of literature, *Headstrap* reminds us of the importance of human storytellers and story collectors: the value of sifting for buried lore through tangible, nondigitized things—old journals, mementos, and artifacts; of traveling to speak with people in their homes; of listening to multiple voices weave in and out of each other, creating overstories and understories that offer deeper layers of perspective and truth.

While fights erupt over the teaching of history in the US and other parts of the world, this book provides yet more evidence that more inclusive accounts are also more accurate ones, and that issues of injustice cannot be resolved if their past and present-day realities are censored or suppressed. "A mountain is a metaphor," wrote the anthropologist Pasang Yangjee Sherpa in a 2021 essay for *Alpinist* that seems more urgent than ever. "To imagine a future of alpinism is to imagine the kind of future we, collectively as global citizens, want to create on and off the mountain. The gift of history offers us an advantage. The knowledge we have inherited orally or textually shows us what to leave behind and what to take forward. Each of us has a choice to make. I dream of a future that is just and fair. *What would that be like?*"

What will you, readers, do with this gift of history?

A NOTE FROM
THE AUTHORS

The seeds of this project were planted in early 2012 in a remote area of Arunachal Pradesh in the eastern Himalaya. We were hiking with our old friend and trekking companion Harish Kapadia, modern India's preeminent explorer. Travels with Harish are always filled with songs, stories, and anecdotes about the people he has met while traveling. He told us a fascinating story about the legendary climber Pasang Dawa Lama of Darjeeling—jumping naked into the icy waters of a Nepali river to advertise his having slept with one hundred women—that ignited our imagination about the community of Sherpa climbers in that hill town. We wanted to know more, and that's how it all began.

At the end of our first visit to Darjeeling, in April 2012, we made a promise that this book seeks to fulfill: to record and share Sherpa stories and histories from this region. We uncovered many tales over the coming years, in the narrow, often grotty lanes of Toong Soong, a Sherpa settlement in Darjeeling. We found them in the warm homes of the sons and daughters of Sherpa heroes from decades ago. We traced connections and attempted to chart family trees. We discovered that there are new Sherpa climbers in Darjeeling today, but they are separated geographically, historically, and technologically from those who came almost a century ago. We dug into forgotten papers and books published by The Himalayan Club, set up in India in 1928 to encourage climbing and exploration in the Himalaya, and met with climbers all over the world who shared their memories with us.

Many of the Sherpas and other people we wanted to meet had died without anyone hearing about their remarkable lives. Over the years we returned to Darjeeling for months at a time to learn about these men and women. We kept at it, gaining confidence, making friends, and listening. The experience was both humbling and uplifting.

During the hours we spent in different homes, we realized and learned many things. We realized that memory is fallible. More importantly, our memories are not linear; they emerge from emotion, not logic, and not necessarily from fact. We occasionally came across discrepancies, either between how two people recalled the same event or between an oral recounting and a written one. For example, we interviewed Kusang Sherpa in 2013 about his arrival in Darjeeling and entry into climbing, but in his autobiography published a few years later, he recounts different details. In such cases, we have done our best to determine and recount those versions most likely to be accurate.

It took time to understand that it was the memories, personal and intimate, rather than the written accounts, that should be the focus of our work—after all, memories let us into people's hearts and minds. Still, stories from memory are often left with gaps, which we worried about how to fill. It took time to understand that we could string together a narrative despite these imperfections, even as some facts have likely been lost along the way. We had to learn not to ask our interviewees questions that reflected our modern intellectual concerns and may be insensitive to our subjects' conditions and priorities at the time, like "Did you ever think of doing something else to earn your living?" or "What did the women feel when their men left for the mountains?" Most of all, we learned that many Sherpas who appear in expedition accounts, both written and oral, were legendary climbers, but had no family or heirs to their stories left in Darjeeling. We are sincerely sorry that we could not cover them.

We recorded hundreds of hours of conversations, which had to be painstakingly transcribed. Narrators spoke in Nepali, Hindi, and English. The interviews were filled with hesitation, self-contradiction, doubt, and gossip. A single hour of recording took many hours to simultaneously translate and transcribe. It took a few years to record and subsequently transcribe all those conversations and interviews.

Interspersed with our trips to Darjeeling were our home lives in Mumbai, our day jobs, and our family obligations. We also took trips to other cities and towns to meet other people who knew these Sherpas and to visit libraries for research. In the early years, we were also constantly writing grant proposals and meeting with potential donors to the project. A travel agency,

A Note on Headstraps

All across Darjeeling and Nepal, porters can be seen carrying heavy loads secured by straps across the head. Officially called tumplines, these are known locally as head-straps, or *namlo*. During Himalayan climbing's early decades, all loads were carried using the headstrap. Even today, porters carry loads up to basecamp this way.

There is no single origin story for the headstrap. Traditionally, it could be a strip of leather, fabric, or rope that was knotted, looped, or buckled around a load and worn across the top of the head. Although this technique is found in almost every culture, Sherpas are probably the most famous headstrap users today, using it to carry loads as heavy as their own body weight. Even when offered modern packs, they often prefer their cane baskets, called *doko*, secured with the simple strap.

Headstraps are known to be ergonomically efficient and physically healthy. They enable weight to be distributed evenly down the back and allow for lung expansion without restriction, unlike backpacks, which often restrict the chest. However, using them safely and comfortably requires years of training and spine strengthening.

Cox & Kings, bought our airplane tickets for a few years, but we worked on a shoestring budget for everything else.

The hardest part came later when we had to sift through accounts, facts, dates, and names, and verify and organize them. Over 150 interviews, representing hundreds of hours, had to be condensed into a cohesive, readable, interesting narrative. Much had to be left out, in order to let the diamonds emerge.

Over the years, place names have changed. For instance, Bombay became Mumbai in 1995, and Calcutta became Kolkata in 2001. For consistency, we have gone with the more modern, Indian names for each place regardless of the timeline of the events being described, unless the reference appears in a direct quote.

A decade is a long time to write a book. Many of our narrators have died over this period. Still, we hope to keep their memories alive on the pages of this book—not an anthropological work or an academic tome but a tale about a fascinating community of mountain people and climbers. Finally, we take full responsibility for any oversights, factual inaccuracies, or mis-interpretations.

The view down the road to Bhutia *basti* (settlement) in Darjeeling *(Photo by Dilip Banerjee)*

Introduction
GATEWAY TO HEAVEN

Between 40 and 50 million years ago, the Indian landmass collided with the Eurasian plate to give rise to a series of crumples and folds known today as the Himalaya. This massive mountain range extends in a 2,400-kilometer-long arc that separates the Indian subcontinent from the rest of Asia. The effects of that collision have shaped the lives of all the nations that developed in the region. This book features three of them: India, Nepal, and Tibet.

Our story concerns a community of people who migrated hundreds of years ago over the high mountain passes from windswept Tibet into Nepal, a small, landlocked country nestled in the lap of the highest peaks in the world. There they lived at altitudes above 3,000 meters, farming and herding until a new way of life beckoned, occasioned by the very range in which they dwelled. This second migration brought some of them over the lower ranges of the Himalaya into India, to Darjeeling. Darjeeling was a gateway in two senses: north from British India for early expeditions in the Himalaya and south from Tibet and Nepal for tribespeople seeking employment and a better life.

This small town lies in the foothills of the Himalaya, east of Nepal in the Indian state of West Bengal. The peaks of Kangchenjunga (8,586 meters), the third-highest mountain in the world, hover on the horizon to the northwest. On our first visit, we stayed at Dekeling Hotel in the center of town. Through the large plate-glass windows of the hotel's Lunar Restaurant, above the jumble of broken wires and antennae, we could see Kangchenjunga, the golden mountain and keeper of this chaotic town, suspended in the distance. In Tibetan, the name Kangchenjunga means Five Treasures of the Snow, and when the sun rises, the mountain peaks glow with a fiery light. Over the next few years, there would be several defining points in our journey, but the first one occurred on the very day of our arrival. We had just finished breakfast when the hotel owner rushed in all atwitter. The Clint Eastwood of Darjeeling had arrived to meet us, she whispered excitedly.

Sitting in the small hotel lobby was Dorjee Lhatoo, a dapper Sherpa wearing polished knee-length leather boots, a leather jacket, blue jeans, and a pink-and-white checked shirt. Wrapped around his neck was a silk cravat. Whatever we were expecting, it wasn't this. From that very first meeting, this famed mountaineer shared with us his store of memories and his immense knowledge about his community. We would spend many hours over the next few years in his wood-paneled living room, as he corrected our pronunciations, explained relationships, and wove an intricate historical tapestry of relived conversations and events. But all that was yet to come. On this first meeting, leaving his Bullet motorcycle at the hotel, Lhatoo took us on a long walk through Darjeeling. First we strolled down Mall Road, with its cafés and tourist shops, then along a beautiful path lined with deodar—the Himalayan cedar—and past the zoo and the Himalayan Mountaineering Institute (HMI), India's first climbing school, which opened in 1954. This route brought us to the rear entrance of the institute, where the prominent Sherpa Nawang Gombu had built his home. He had passed away exactly a year prior, and we had come to observe the one-year anniversary of his death.

ALMOST EVERY SHERPA HOUSE IN Darjeeling has a prayer room, as is the custom in Buddhist households. Even small, one-room homes devote an entire wall to the altar. In Nawang Gombu's house, the large prayer room had a table covered with butter lamps at the entrance and woollen rugs covering the floor. Each wall had *thangkas*, intricately painted Buddhist wall hangings garlanded with white silk scarves called *khadas*, while brightly painted wooden cabinets held an array of religious photos and figurines. Above the altar, which took up the back wall of the room, hung canopies of ruffled yellow silk.

A dozen monks sat opposite each other, clad in sleeveless yellow silk shirts and maroon robes, all playing instruments. Cymbals, two great telescoping Tsangdoh trumpets, short trumpets, drums, and hand bells boomed, shrilled, and clashed, rhythmically accompanying the rise and fall of the Buddhist prayers. Each monk had a teacup in front of him, which was constantly replenished by the young ladies of the house. Also on offer were Coke, Sprite, and water. Earlier the younger monks had crafted colorful figurines called *tormas* made of oil, flour, and food coloring that would be offered to the gods, then fed to animals.

Downstairs, away from the solemnity of the rituals, the kitchen teemed with women stirring pots of tea, shaping momos, boiling rice, and chopping vegetables. This ceremony continued nonstop for a week, during which time the monks and visitors had to be continually refreshed and fed. The mood was what—happy, sad, nostalgic? It felt a bit like all of these. Above all, it was a celebration of Nawang Gombu's life.

Part of the ritual, Lhatoo told us, involved religious appeasement, but mostly it was a reason for the community to gather and keep alive age-old traditions and bonds. And we were here as invited voyeurs.

We met Gombu's wife, Sita la (*la* has several meanings, but in this context, it is used as a title of respect for women). She was busy with the cooking and serving for the celebration, but she stopped to smile warmly and implored us to eat. We met her brother Phursumba, surely the tallest and lankiest Sherpa in Darjeeling. He had lived in America most of his life, teaching climbing at Rainier Mountaineering, Inc. in Washington State. In 1967, he had gone on a National Geographic trans-Arctic expedition to the North Pole. "I thought I was there to climb a mountain," he chuckled.

After the expedition, he stopped in Seattle for a night and stayed on for forty-six years. He had come to Darjeeling for the ceremony, and would return permanently in 2013 to carry on the community work started by his dearest friend and brother-in-law, Gombu daju (*daju* is a term of respect that translates as "older brother"). And we met Nawang Gombu's daughters— Rita, a mountaineer herself; Yangdu; and Ongmu—educated, working women living in Delhi.

"When you read books," said Ongmu, "they romanticize the entire Sherpa concept. For them climbing was a livelihood, pretty much a way of life. During my dad's funeral, Norbu—Tenzing's older son—and I were talking. We thought what was really amazing was that Tenzing Norgay, as well as my dad, did not know how to read or write. They grew up learning Tibetan. Then they came to Nepal and learned Nepalese, and then came to Darjeeling and then travelled abroad! This was all in one generation, not two." She reflected on how that decision affected her life: "We always talk about it. My dad had a choice to put us either into a Nepalese medium school or an English medium school ['medium' refers to the language of instruction in school, i.e., whether subjects are taught in Nepalese or English]. The reality is if we had gone to a Nepali school, we would still have been in Darjeeling."

In the garden sat a row of middle-aged Sherpa women (Sherpanis), most of whom were dressed in traditional clothes: a long inner shirt called *wan ju*, covered by a wraparound robe, or *baku*. A couple of them were smoking surreptitiously. Some had local government jobs, some had shops in the market, and others volunteered with regional political parties or at the Sherpa monastery. Almost none of them were stay-at-home women.

Chatting with them was another Sherpa who would soon guide us to people and take a keen interest in our work. Phurtemba Sherpa, a loved and respected local leader, had made it his mission after retiring from the army to help Sherpas get the recognition they deserve. Though not a climber he took greater pride in the achievements of Sherpa climbers than many did themselves. From petitioning for a Bharat Ratna—the highest civilian honor bestowed by the Republic of India—for Tenzing Norgay to getting scholarships for Sherpa children, to wanting to start Sherpa language classes, to working tirelessly at the local Buddhist temple (the *gompa*), this spirited man works ceaselessly on behalf of his people. He soon became another dear friend.

On our third day in Darjeeling, Lhatoo took us to the locality called Toong Soong. More than a century ago, Toong Soong was where the Sherpas came and settled on its thickly forested hillsides. Today, it is overcrowded, with narrow roads and rickety houses piled precariously on bare slopes.

Lhatoo told us, "I heard from the early Sherpas that Toong Soong is a corruption of Thung Soom. Thung is *shankh* [a conch shell]. There were three prominent rock features on this road. One is still there. From Chong Rinzing's house"—Chong Rinzing was Lhatoo's friend and the son of a prominent Sherpa climber—"if you look up, there's a big rock. We used to do our rappelling on that. That looks like a shell. There was one rock close to the Sherpa gompa. And there was one where the three roads meet. They have blown that up and built a big house there. *Soom* in Tibetan is 'three.' Thung Soom—Three Shells. The old Sherpas still say, 'Thung Soom.'"

When we interviewed Chong Rinzing at his home, we could indeed see the big rock. Rinzing's family had migrated to Darjeeling in 1947 when he was a young boy. He remembered being caught up in the excitement of

Indian Independence and waving the Indian tricolor with Dorjee Lhatoo, the first friend he made.

The middle lane in Toong Soong is called Tenzing Norgay Road. Past the Sherpa gompa, the packed houses have a little more breathing room, and we soon came upon a flight of stairs that led down to an open courtyard and a lovely green cottage. The sign on the cottage wall read "Ang Tsering Sherpa, H. No. 10/1, Ganesh Gram, Toong Soong Basty, Darjeeling." We didn't yet know it, but this house would soon become our favorite place to put our feet up whenever we came to Darjeeling.

On the way to Ang Tsering's cottage is the home of PemPem, Tenzing Norgay's daughter, and her husband, Thendup. We rang their doorbell one afternoon and went down stone steps to a small, flower-filled garden surrounded by various rooms. Inside, the house was like a burrow. With its several dark, interconnected rooms built more than a century ago, it was like entering the past.

We introduced ourselves and asked PemPem, "So is this Tenzing Norgay's house?"

"Actually, this is Thendup's house," she replied. "We used to live just below this house when my father came to Darjeeling. Thendup's parents were our landlords, and his grandparents built this house in 1902." PemPem said that both Thendup and his father were born in that home. "Thendup's grandfather owned half of Toong Soong, but everything is now sold," she continued. "It was the time when the Sherpas were coming—they used to live all around this house."

And on yet another sunny afternoon, at the central meeting place in town called Chowrasta, we met 101-year-old Lhakpa Diki, Dorjee Lhatoo's aunt. Her husband had been a celebrated porter, and she was a load bearer when young. Her thoughts were garbled, but her eyes shone as she remembered fragments of her life.

Some days later, we made a trip north from Darjeeling to the town of Gangtok in the state of Sikkim to meet another woman porter. *Ani* (aunt) Daku was in her nineties, but remained nostalgic about her climbing years. As the days drew to an end on our first visit, the prayer flag at Nawang Gombu's house was hoisted after the one-year mourning period. We took a high road to the house known as Ghang-la, built for Tenzing after his historic Everest ascent. (Ghang-la was both the name of Tenzing's father and that of the village the family came from.) We met and interviewed Jamling, Tenzing Norgay's eldest son, who has a private museum dedicated to his illustrious father. We also took a low road down another hillside to visit Nawang Topgay, the last surviving Sherpa Tiger (a term used to honor the most accomplished Sherpa climbers), in his meager dwelling.

Our meetings had been interspersed with visits to the gompa, the Oxford bookshop for its wonderful selection of mountaineering books, and the Das Studio, where photographs of early climbers still hang on the walls. We met many more people—Sherpas and their friends—and took copious notes and recordings. We had slurped Tibetan noodle soup (*thukpa*) in the local eateries, drunk many cups of Darjeeling tea, and eaten more than one momo. It was not going to be easy to leave this town.

On our way to the airport, we made one last stop at the house of Tenzing Tharkay, son of legendary climber Ang Tharkay. We were accompanied by Dorjee Lhatoo, whose stories swallowed up the miles.

These are just some of the remarkable people we met on that first trip to Darjeeling. Over the years that followed, we met many more amazing characters across India and abroad as we chased anyone who had anything to tell us. From Kolkata, Bengaluru, Delhi, Nagpur, Dehradun, and Mumbai in India, to England, France, and America, people were generous with their time and help. Eventually, we also met the current Sherpa climbers of Darjeeling, who had remained elusive to us, in the newer Sherpa enclaves of Alubari and Ghoom and at the Himalayan Mountaineering Institute.

Many of the storytellers we met have passed away since this project began: Lhakpa Diki, the spirited centenarian, whose face we wanted to capture again and again; Nawang Topgay, nephew of Tenzing Norgay and a celebrated yet misunderstood Sherpa; Chong Rinzing, who featured in so many of Dorjee Lhatoo's childhood remembrances; Tenzing Tharkay, aesthete, gentleman, and chef, who cooked memorable Japanese meals; Sangye Sherpa, who died with dreams unfulfilled; Pemba Sherpa, victim of a tragic mountaineering accident; Colonel Narendra "Bull" Kumar, who tackled all problems head-on; Nalni Jayal and Gurdial Singh, friends and mountaineers who were so intricately linked with early mountaineering; Chanchal Mitra, pioneer climber from Kolkata; Daku Sherpa, who at ninety-two could teach the world about living life on your own terms; Colonel Paul, whose thoughts dwelt so much on the past; and PemPem, defender of her father, Tenzing Norgay, until the very end. It is high time these stories are told.

PART ONE

HISTORY

The founding of the Sherpa Association in Toong Soong in 1952 *(Dorjee Lhatoo Collection)*

CHAPTER 1

Who Is the Sherpa in the Word *Sherpa*?

Nawang Gombu's brother-in-law Phursumba stands out in the Sherpa community, not only for his remarkable height but also for his decidedly American accent when speaking English. "I went to America in 1967," he told us during our first trip to Darjeeling. "In '68 I started guiding and bought a car." One day, Phursumba was stopped by an American policeman for speeding. When the policeman noticed on Phursumba's license that he was a Sherpa, he let him off with a warning. Phursumba recalled with a laugh, "I was the first Sherpa to go [to America]. When Tenzing and Hillary climbed in 1953, every man and woman, young and old, all around the world, knew the word 'Sherpa.' I thought, oh, I'm glad that I am a Sherpa; I didn't have to pay the fine!"

The name Sherpa certainly carries cachet. A cursory search on the internet reveals a host of products and services named Sherpa, from synthetic yarn to dog and cat baskets; from adventure gear to business programs; from food products to metal connectors, all conjuring visions of durability, fidelity, and high performance. But what does the word *Sherpa* really mean? Who can call themselves a Sherpa? And, where do they come from?

The term *Sherpa* with a capital "S" usually refers to members of a specific community; *sherpa* with a lowercase "s" denotes high-altitude load carriers and personal guides regardless of the community they belong to. Although the Sherpas are very identity conscious and would like to be referred to as Sherpas with a capital *S*, they are equally conscious about the fact that they have become synonymous with personal assistants, route openers, high-altitude porters (HAPs), high-altitude friends (HAFs), Icefall Doctors (who prepare the route through the Khumbu Icefall each season on Mount Everest), and general guides in Nepal and some parts of India. Some of these are ethnic Sherpas and others are from other communities, often using the surname Sherpa. In that sense, the true Sherpas are generous about others appropriating their name, though very clear about who belongs to the Sherpa community and who is an outsider. We have used the word *Sherpa* throughout this book to avoid confusion.

THARCHEN, SON OF LEGENDARY CLIMBER Ang Tsering, gave us a lesson in pronunciation during one of our many chats with him. "It's not 'Sherpa'; it's *Sheaar-wa*. *Sheaar* means 'east,' and *wa* or *pa* means 'people.' So *Sheaarwa* or *Sheaarpa* means 'people who came from eastern Tibet to Nepal.' That is where the clan originally came from."

PemPem, daughter of Tenzing Norgay, offered an explanation based on her own research. Bordering the province of Sichuan in China is a region of Tibet called Kham. "The Sherpas come from the west [portion] of Sichuan and the east [portion] of Kham," she said. "The origin of Sherpas is from there. Another proof is—do you know Sichuan pepper? We call it *ermung*. Sherpa people treat ermung like chili. We eat ermung with butter and potato bread. You grate a potato, make a pancake, put butter and Sichuan pepper [on it], and eat. It's yummy.

"How did the Sherpa bring this pepper? From where? Their ancestors brought it from Sichuan. They used to live there. But their arrival, their movement to the foot of Everest on the Nepal side, has different explanations. Some say there was a war; Ghengis Khan massacred people, and so people started running away. Some moved north, some east, some west, and some south. Those who moved southwest crossed Nangpa La"—a 5,790-meter mountain pass between Tibet and Nepal—"and descended into huge green valleys. They thought this is a place for our yaks, for living. History says it was in the early 1500s. This is how the Sherpas spread."

The region south of the great peaks of Mount Everest, Nuptse, and Ama Dablam is known as Khumbu and is home to a village called Namche, or as the Sherpas say, Nauje Bazaar. This region, according to legend, was the first area in Nepal settled by the ancestors of the current Sherpas. From here, some families then started migrating south to the valley of the Solu Khola River and to the area separating Khumbu and Solu called Pharak, meaning "difference" or "divide." When talking about their homes, most Sherpas use the term Solu Khumbu, combining the entire area into one.

The anthropologist Christoph von Fürer-Haimendorf made several visits to the Khumbu region through the 1950s and early 1960s, staying for months at a time in all the main villages and following several groups of families to their high pastures. Nepal before the 1950s was closed to foreigners, so when he traveled there, almost nothing was known to the outside world about the local tribes. In *The Sherpas of Nepal*, he too wondered about the name "Sherpa." He writes:

> The name Sherpa is derived from the Tibetan word *shar-pa*, which means "easterner," but it is not clear in what manner this term came to be associated with this particular group. From the Tibetan point of view Sherpas are southerners rather than easterners, and even within a purely Nepalese setting the term has no real justification for other Bhotia groups dwell to the east as well as the west of the Sherpa country. Yet, the term has gained wide currency and must be accepted as the name of an ethnic group with a pronounced sense of separateness from other Bhotia groups.

Lhatoo explained that the name Bhotia, or Bhutia, "comes from the term *Bhot*, meaning 'Tibet.' For generations, Tibetans have migrated over the high passes and settled all along the lesser Himalayan range, from Ladakh in the west to Arunachal Pradesh in the east—not down in the plains where it is too hot, but up in the highlands where they can graze their cattle, cultivate crops, and make a living. At first the term *Bhutia* must have been a casual one to refer to all these people with Mongoloid features who settled on the southern slope of the Himalaya, but gradually it became formal nomenclature, accepted for administrative purposes in the classification of different tribes. In Darjeeling when you say, 'Bhutia,' you are of Tibetan stock. Sherpas are also of Tibetan stock. Specifically, they are the Tibetans who migrated to Solu Khumbu in Nepal."

So Bhutia is a broader term and Sherpa is narrower. All Sherpas are Bhutia, but a Bhutia is not necessarily a Sherpa. How did they come to Solu Khumbu? There is no written history. It's all theory, and the theories vary.

Sherpa celebration in Darjeeling circa 1940s *(Dorjee Lhatoo Collection)*

One theory, Lhatoo told us, was that the Sherpas were a group of clans who fled from a religious churning that took place in Tibet. There are four major schools of Tibetan Buddhism—Nyingma (the oldest), followed by Kagyu, Sakya, and Gelug. Sherpas are mainly Nyingmapas—followers of the Nyingma sect, which combines Hinduism with Buddhism in a form of highly ritualistic practices called Tantra. Sometime in the 1500s when the other three groups adopted a series of reforms, the Nyingmapas fled their traditional lands and came to Nepal.

Lhatoo explained, "Some also say they were actually nomadic. They moved with their cattle to greener pastures. For them in those days until the Chinese came to Tibet, all these borders were open: Sikkim, Nepal, Tibet, India. Only since my time—I have seen it happen—they quickly put check posts and restricted the crossing of borders. Earlier, these people just came and went. They came with their cattle as nomads and they found more fodder on this side of the Himalaya. Then they settled there and realized that this is another country and not Tibet, because immediately government people came to collect taxes. It is like my family's history."

Dorjee Lhatoo pointed to his face. He smiled and said, "So if you go to Bhutan, Sikkim, China, Arunachal, Ladakh, or Central Asia, you will see people of my face. I am that face." On another day, Lhatoo's niece Ongmu told us the same thing: "After all, we are all Genghis Khan's descendants!" she said with a laugh.

Anthropologist and writer Stanley F. Stevens explains in *Claiming the High Ground* that the tribes along the Himalayan belt that came from the same homeland have a great deal in common:

> Across this Tibetan culture region there are scores of peoples whose languages, religions, systems of social organization, economies, land-use practices, architecture, and styles of dress and ornamentation share strong resemblances. These similarities include Tibeto-Burman languages closely related to Tibetan; adherence to sects of Tibetan Buddhism; domestic and religious architecture featuring white, stone-walled structures with characteristic window patterns and other distinctive features; settlement sites at altitudes of more than 2,000 meters; cultural preferences for raising yak, sheep, and barley; distinctive traditional woolen dress consisting of a black or brown, extremely long-sleeved cloak for men and a dark, woolen dress with a striped apron for women; and special value put on certain types of jewelry, including silver amulet boxes and necklaces featuring coral, turquoise, *zi* stones, and silver.

But of all the Bhutia people, it was the Sherpas who became famous. Was it only because of Darjeeling and the Sherpas' association with early mountaineering expeditions? When did the Sherpas come to Darjeeling? And did none of the other tribes from the Himalayan region (like the Khampas, Kerompas, Walungpas, and the Kagatays) make their way to Darjeeling as the Sherpas did? All the ethnic Tibetans we met in Darjeeling called themselves Sherpa or Bhutia. No one introduced themselves as a Kerompa, say, or as a Khampa.

"Aah," said Lhatoo, "that is a long story." He then continued with a phrase we often heard from him:

> To make a long story short, in India, when lists of scheduled tribes, scheduled castes, and OBCs were drawn up, Bhutias and Sherpas—as a separate grouping—found themselves part of the listing. This made them eligible for concessions and reservations. Kerompas, Khampas, Walungpas, and the rest were not listed. This meant that to be eligible for concessions they had to declare themselves Bhutias or Sherpas.
>
> Here [in India], Sherpas and Bhutias enjoy an equal status. But in Nepal, while Sherpas are considered sons of the soil (not least for the tourism they have been bringing in), Bhutias are considered Tibetan refugees or migrants and they are not wanted.
>
> Ani Lhakpa Diki [Lhatoo's 101-year-old aunt] had two sons. One of them, who died, was called Ang Phurba Sherpa. He was in the British army. The one who is still alive is called Ang Norbu Bhutia.

"So, two sons—one Sherpa and one Bhutia," Lhatoo concluded. "It doesn't matter here."

Thus Sherpas are comfortable in both India and in Nepal. They have retained their title as Sherpa and they are respected in both countries, but the Bhutia subgroups have had to choose between being called Bhutia or Sherpa. In Darjeeling, though, everyone knows who everyone is, and ethnic Sherpas are quick to point out those who carry the name but actually belong to other tribes.

Existing sources provided some corroboration for Lhatoo's statements. The British undertook the first census of India between 1865 and 1872; it was considered defective because many people fled when the census takers came, suspicious of their intentions. The first synchronous all-India census was conducted in 1881, and has been repeated every ten years ever since. (The last census was in 2011, with the 2021 census cancelled due to the COVID-19 pandemic.) The 1881 census showed that there were 78,555 Buddhists in the province of Bengal (the majority of the Buddhist population would likely have been from Tibet and Nepal; however, there is no further information on the communities the Buddhists represent or of the languages they speak). This figure is noted, however, as showing a 93.29 percent increase over the number of Buddhists enumerated in the 1872 census.

The figures do not indicate whether Sherpas were included in the immigrants from Nepal or counted as Bhotias from Tibet. However, it is clear that by 1881, there was already a substantial exodus from across the border to the Darjeeling District in search of work.

In 1907, the *Bengal District Gazetteers: Darjeeling* was published. The author, L. S. S. O'Malley, was part of the great machinery of the Raj, in which British civilians undertook the preparation of district, provincial, and imperial Indian gazettes. O'Malley wrote several volumes of the gazette. In the 1907 publication, he noted for the first time the presence of 9,300 Bhutias in Darjeeling. These consisted of four classes: Sikkimese Bhutias (formed through intermarriage between Tibetans and the indigenous people of the Darjeeling District and nearby Sikkim called Lepchas); Sherpa Bhutias, who came from Solu Khumbu in Nepal; Drukpa Bhutias, who hailed from Bhutan; and Tibetan Bhutias, who came directly from Tibet. There is no mention of other clans. O'Malley writes:

> As a race, the Bhotias have been described as rude, turbulent and quarrelsome, but this seems an unfair estimate of their character. On the whole, they are a merry, cheerful people, quick to enjoy a joke, and the most willing workers, not so pushing as the Nepalese nor so law-abiding as the Lepchas. Powerfully built and of great natural strength, they are capable of carrying the heaviest burdens—there is a story current that in the days before the railway a single Bhotia carried a grand piano up the hills to Darjeeling, 50 miles distant and 7,000 ft [2,134 meters] in elevation; but their natural love of display and an inordinate love of gambling soon dissipate the sums which they could easily earn by labour.

O'Malley, of course, was making no distinction between the different kinds of Bhutias, and had lumped them all together in one undifferentiated group.

In the 1921, 1931, and 1941 censuses, Sherpas continued to find mention within the larger classification of Bhutia, a classification later ratified by the government of free India for the purposes of identifying and providing policies of positive reinforcement to communities needing political, social, and economic protection.

In 1961, the *West Bengal District Census Handbook Darjeeling* recorded that Nepali was the first major mother tongue in the Darjeeling District.

After Hinduism, the second major religion in the district was Buddhism, with 13.13 percent of the population of Darjeeling being Buddhists. Table 13.4 showed the percentage of certain scheduled tribes comprising the total tribal population, and listed "Bhutia *including* [emphasis added] Sherpa, Toto, Dukpa, Kagatay, Tibetan and Yolmo." These tribes were all originally from Nepal and Tibet. No other tribes were mentioned.

When Western adventurers started their first climbs in the Himalaya in the last two decades of the nineteenth century, they employed men from various local tribes on their expeditions. By the first decade of the twentieth century, however, the climbers had come to realize that the best and hardiest porters were those who had lived at the highest altitudes in the Khumbu and the Tibetan Highlands: the Sherpas and the Tibetan Bhutias. Both groups became equally valued on those early expeditions, but when Tenzing chose to identify himself as a Sherpa just before his historic summit of Mount Everest in 1953, he sealed the fame of the community. It is not difficult to understand, therefore, that in the context of official record keeping and job opportunities, many took to calling themselves Sherpas.

It's curious that in all the various census reports, with their detailed listings of jobs and professions, not one of them mentions porter work or climbing. The 1961 census of the independent India–Darjeeling District, while highlighting various points of interest in Darjeeling, has a note on the founding of the Himalayan Mountaineering Institute. The note acknowledges Norgay's contribution thusly: "Tenzing Norgay's ascent of Everest (29,028 ft.), along with Sir Edmund Hillary, in 1953 provided a great impetus and fillip to mountaineering as a sport in India, and it was to commemorate this signal success that the Himalayan Mountaineering Institute (H. M. I.) was founded in Darjeeling in 1954." Despite this, climbing or sherpa work do not appear anywhere as a profession. India's 2015 *National Classification of Occupations* is mind-bogglingly detailed, listing thousands of occupations including some that are extremely niche. And yet, the words *mountaineer, climber, Sherpa*, and *coolie* (often pejorative these days) appear nowhere in its many pages. The only listing for "porter" is Baggage (Hotel and Restaurant).

Finally, after a tiresome hunt, the only possible clue emerges in the group Travel Guides, in particular Listing 5113.0200 for Tourist Guide: "One who guides people to places of interest and explains historical, cultural, religious, social, architectural features; answers questions, may act as interpreter and takes tourists shopping." Meanwhile, Listing 5113.9900 refers to Guides, Other: "Travel guides and Ground Hosts, other include all other workers, engaged in guiding, ground hosting and assisting excursion parties in their travels and visits not elsewhere classified." Is this what the wheels of bureaucracy have reduced the climbers' contributions to?

It is quite clear that the profession existed. In 1951, The Himalayan Club listed 175 *climbing* porters on its rolls. Many more would have been involved as cooks, load carriers for treks, and in doing other peripheral carrying jobs for expeditions. It is true that for many, even up to the mid-1950s, climbing would have been seasonal work. Construction work, particularly road building, and the selling of milk, firewood, and other produce would have been the jobs that men did between expeditions. Perhaps that explains why high-altitude work does not appear in census after census and in the Listing of Occupations: porters instead offered these other occupations to census takers. Or perhaps the porters weren't enumerated due to travel back and forth across the Nepali border.

No matter what the records reflect, Sherpa migration grew exponentially from 1900 through 1950. For migrants who came from the bleak alpine landscapes to the bustle of Darjeeling, everything was new—the land, the people, and the occupations, along with their dreams.

One early Sherpa immigrant to Darjeeling was Gyalzen Kazi, who came from a rich landlord family in Sikkim. The term *Kazi* is an honorific title, indicating his high status. Information about him is scant, but British expedition records revealed that he was well read in Tibetan scriptures and could speak English and possibly Nepali. He was interpreter to the 1921 British Everest reconnaissance expedition and *sardar*/interpreter in 1922 and 1924. None in the British teams those three years knew Tibetan, so Gyalzen and Karma Paul, another prominent interpreter of the time, became the bridge between the mountain tribes and the Englishmen.

In 2012, we met Gyalzen Kazi's son, Nima Tsering. Searching for him in Toong Soong, we were directed to a plot covered in dense vegetation. The small gate at pavement level led to a series of moss-covered steps down to a fairy-tale but decrepit house screened almost entirely from street view.

Hidden within an adjacent grove of towering bamboo we saw a giant *maane* (revolving prayer wheel) in a small temple.

Nima Tsering, seventy years old at the time, took us around the home his father had built. He told us that Gyalzen Kazi had constructed the small gompa to give the Sherpas somewhere to worship. It had remained a place of

Nima Tsering in the house built by his father,
Gyalzen Kazi, over one hundred years ago
(The Sherpa Project)

congregation and celebration until Darjeeling's Sherpa population grew, and a large temple was constructed next door.

In a small room on the home's first floor, Nima Tsering recounted his story. "My father was among the earliest Sherpas who came to Darjeeling. Toong Soong was a remote area. Where this house is now and where all those houses are up there, was nothing. It was all jungle! There were only three houses," he said. Nima Tsering had grown up with six siblings, all of whom he'd outlived. At a time when no one knew the way from Darjeeling to Everest, his father became a guide and porter to British expeditions all the way to basecamp.

On a trip to Thyangboche gompa, in his birthplace in Solu Khumbu, Gyalzen showed a lama his horoscope. The lama told him that Everest was the seat of Lord Shiva and that he would die if he tried to climb it. With that, he gave up his job as a climber and became a lama himself. Gyalzen still needed an income so he became a contractor, getting other Sherpas jobs on Everest expeditions. Although he'd stopped taking part in the expeditions, he apparently still felt that he was violating the lama's advice by sending others to climb Everest. Eventually, he started a transportation business instead. "My parents bought a car," recalled Nima Tsering. "At that time there were no more than four or five cars in Darjeeling. It was from the transportation business that we made a living. All the Europeans who came would order the car; it would pick them up and bring them to Darjeeling. They would travel all over and then be dropped back at Siliguri [a nearby city]. With the money that was earned this house was built. When this maane was made, my father had six cars!"

As Nima Tsering stopped talking, his eyes teared up from nostalgia. He looked at the bustling area that was Toong Soong—home of the Sherpas. The settlement had begun with men like his father coming to fulfill their dreams. For many, those dreams had come true.

Darjeeling in the early 1950s *(Malati Jhaveri Collection)*

CHAPTER 2

Coming to Paradise

There are various stories of how Darjeeling (pronounced Dard-*zi*-lin in Nepali) got its name. According to popular opinion, the name comes from the combination of two Tibetan words: *dorje*, which means "thunderbolt," and *ling*, which means "place." It refers to the monastery that once stood on Observatory Hill in the city and was built in 1765 by a sect of Buddhists from Sikkim. The Nepalese Army looted and destroyed the monastery in 1815, leaving a small Hindu temple called Mahakal on the site. The monastery was later rebuilt in the nearby Bhutia *basti* (settlement). Both places of worship are in use to this day.

Another likely explanation is that the name is from the Limbu language, a Sino-Tibetan language with four dialects. Limbus were the original residents and rulers of the villages that later turned into the Darjeeling cluster. Limbus refer to themselves as Yakthung and their language as Yakthungpan. A local historian said that the name Darjeeling is derived from the Yakthungpan word Tajenglung, which means "Stones that talk to each other."

THE EAST INDIA COMPANY (EIC; also called the Company) was formed in 1600 by a group of British merchants and investors to trade in the Indian Ocean region. At the time, India was a collection of individual princely states. The Company started forming alliances, forging treaties, and attaching itself to various courts in a bid to gain the most favorable trading rights, only slowly revealing its real intentions of colonization and control.

By the 1800s, through skullduggery, subversion, and warfare, kingdoms were taken over and crippling laws and taxes introduced so that the EIC ruled large sections of India directly or by proxy, with its own military and administrative services. Other colonizing powers like the Dutch and Portuguese were aggressively driven out or restricted to small pockets of land.

The process of expansion continued unabated until the mid-1800s; Darjeeling was acquired in 1835 as part of this expansion. In 1857, violent opposition to the British flared across the country in what was called the First Indian War of Independence. Its aftermath led to the British parliament dissolving the Company in 1874 and taking direct control of its assets, administration, and army. Thus began the British Raj, under which India became the richest colony under imperial rule, the jewel in Queen Victoria's crown. It was to hold that power until India finally gained independence in 1947.

At the time of its acquisition, Darjeeling was part of Sikkim, an independent state ruled by a king known as the Chogyal. Sikkim shared borders with China, Tibet, Bhutan, India, and the Gurkha kingdom to the north—a collection of twenty-four states we know as Nepal. Since 1780, the Gurkhas had been making inroads into Sikkim in a series of ongoing skirmishes. Sensing opportunity, the EIC intervened to prevent the Gurkhas from overrunning the whole of the northern frontier. Thus began the Anglo-Nepalese War, which lasted from 1814 to 1816. Defeat of the Gurkhas led to the Treaty of Sugauli (1816), in which Nepal was forced to cede territories the Gurkhas had annexed from the Raja of Sikkim to the EIC. The EIC restored all the tracts of land, reinstated the Chogyal, and guaranteed his sovereignty. With this intervention, the Gurkhas were prevented from turning the whole of Sikkim into a province of Nepal, and Sikkim (including Darjeeling) was retained as a buffer state between Nepal, Bhutan, and Tibet.

Ten years later, when a dispute arose again between Sikkim and Nepal, the matter was referred to Lord William Bentinck, the Governor General of India. Accordingly in 1828, a Captain Lloyd was deputed to settle the dispute along with Mr. J. W. Grant, the commercial resident at Malda, a district in West Bengal. (The commercial resident was a senior British official who indirectly ruled a princely state assigned to him. His role included advising in governance, intervening in succession disputes, and ensuring that the states did not maintain military forces other than for internal policing.) On their visit they found Darjeeling attractive enough to recommend to the Governor General that the British acquire it. Its primary advantage was its strategic position. As it commanded an entrance to Nepal and Bhutan, it was perfect as a British outpost in the Himalaya and could serve as a base for the defense of the trade route to Tibet through Sikkim. Besides, from its commanding height, the whole of Sikkim and the neighborhood could be observed and protected.

Darjeeling was also perfect as a summer resort for British officials to escape the intense tropical heat and related diseases in the plains. The colonists were always on the lookout to develop sanatoriums—spaces for rest and recuperation. Moreover, as the empire consolidated, officials on long stints in India wanted their families to visit and even settle. So, they developed what we now know as hill stations, towns situated higher than the nearby plains or valleys. The term was used mostly in colonial India, for towns founded by European colonialists as refuges from the summer heat. Most hill stations are at an altitude of approximately 1,000 to 2,500 meters.

In *The Magic Mountains: Hill Stations and the British Raj*, Dane Kennedy writes:

> Lord William Bentinck, then governor general of India, was favourably disposed to the recommendation, noting in a minute "the great saving of European life and the consequent saving of expense that will accrue both to individuals and to the state." He was restrained, however, by the restrictions of Charles Metcalfe and other members of the governor general's council, who feared the response of the Nepalese to this encroachment on their eastern border.

Kennedy further writes that having enjoyed stays at Simla and Mussoorie, two other hill stations in North India, and failing to establish a satisfactory sanatorium at Cherrapunji in the east, Bentinck authorized Captain Lloyd to persuade the Chogyal of Sikkim to cede Darjeeling to the British, regardless of "the satisfaction or dissatisfaction of the Nepauli Durbar [the Nepali court]."

The government's letter to the Chogyal sought to assure him that "it is solely on account of the climate that the possession of the place is deemed desirable, [because] the cold . . . is understood . . . as peculiarly beneficial to the European constitution when debilitated by the Heat of the plains."

The British obtained the lease from the Chogyal on February 1, 1835. In *A Concise History of the Darjeeling District since 1835*, E. C. Dozey wrote that the aged ruler "handed over a strip of hill territory, 24 miles long and about

5 to 6 miles wide, stretching from the northern frontier of the district to Pankabarie in the plains, which in its trend included the villages of Darjeeling and Kurseong, as a mark of friendship for the Governor-General (Lord William Bentinck) for the establishment of a Sanatarium for the invalid servants of the East India Company."

Jeff Koehler, in *Darjeeling: A History of the World's Greatest Tea*, provides a more critical account of the handover. Koehler writes that another border dispute between Sikkim and Nepal erupted in 1834. Taking advantage of the situation, Lloyd went to negotiate and insisted on the Darjeeling tract in return for his services. The Chogyal, though reluctant, finally relented. Koehler notes:

> What had been a request for land to house a sanitarium became a generous 138-square-mile tract, an unconditional gift. In exchange, the rajah [king] received one rifle, one double-barrelled shotgun, twenty yards of red broadcloth, and two pairs of shawls, one of superior quality, the other inferior. A few years later the government granted the rajah an allowance of Rs 3,000 [$36] per annum for compensation, then doubled it to Rs 6,000 [$72].

This compensation, though, was not to last very long. The hill station of Darjeeling began life in 1835 as a collection of about twenty huts with a population of one hundred souls. In 1839, when Dr. Archibald (Arthur) Campbell was made superintendent of the place, development of the hill station really began. Apart from managing the administration of the district, this energetic Scotsman also controlled station funds, acted as postmaster, and was the marriage registrar. He introduced various crops, including chinchona for the production of quinine to treat malaria, and commissioned roads and bridges.

In 1849, Dr. Campbell and the botanist Joseph Dalton Hooker made a trip into Tibet. They were arrested in Sikkim on their way back. It was just the sort of situation the Company was always looking for, to expand its territories.

The following year, as punitive measures, the EIC withdrew the Chogyal's allowance and annexed the whole of the District of Darjeeling, covering an area of 1,030 square kilometers. E. C. Dozey in *A Concise History* concluded, "Thus did the district of Darjeeling pass into our possession, and that too without a shot being fired!"

Joseph Dalton Hooker

Near the Himalayan Mountaineering Institute in the center of Darjeeling there is an unpretentious path with a name that amuses people seeing it for the first time: Hooker Road. The name, of course, refers to Joseph Dalton Hooker, a key figure in the history of Darjeeling.

Hooker was a plant collector, one of the new breed of botanists, geologists, surveyors, and finally adventurers who came to Darjeeling. He spent three years during the late 1840s in the surrounding hills and in neighboring Sikkim and Nepal recording the region's abundant flora. The son of the director of London's Kew Gardens (he would go on to succeed his father in that role), and a lifelong friend and collaborator of Charles Darwin, it was Hooker who first discovered that the local tribe of Lepchas were not only willing companions and carriers of loads, but had a deep, intrinsic knowledge of the forests, which he exploited fully. Hooker called them "this merry troupe . . . ever foremost in the forest or on the bleak mountain, and ever ready to help, to carry, to cook."

When the plant collector decided to expand his exploration into Nepal, he found that Lepchas were not suited for high-altitude work. Instead, he discovered that the trading nomads of Tibetan origin fared much better. When Darjeeling became a British settlement, they came in search of markets for barter. They were simply perfect to help Hooker launch his explorations to the highlands on the horizon.

On November 11, 1865, the British annexed land from Bhutan, increasing the area of the district to 3,014 square kilometers—its current shape and size.

WHILE THE TERRITORY WAS BEING expanded, two things led to a population explosion in Darjeeling: tea and the railway.

Chinese tea had arrived in England in the early 1600s. At first it was badly transported, stored, and brewed, making it a bitter, expensive drink. But by the mid-eighteenth century, as Jeff Koehler writes in *Darjeeling*, "the price had dropped from the dearly unaffordable to the merely expensive, and soon the drink moved from being a luxury of the aristocracy and upper class to a necessity of the working class."

In 1850, annual consumption of tea in Britain was already around one kilogram per person. Even as Victorian England demanded its brew, English traders were wary of having to depend upon China as a sole supplier. They wanted their very own source. Tea had already been discovered growing wild in Assam, so in 1841, only two years after arriving in Darjeeling, Campbell planted both the Assam variety and seeds from stock smuggled out of China. The Chinese plants proved highly successful, thriving in the misty climate of Darjeeling. Soon, land was cleared and burned, and virgin forests were destroyed. By 1852, the district's first commercial tea gardens of Tukvar, Steinthal, and Alubari were established.

By 1866, there were 39 tea gardens in Darjeeling. By 1895, 186 tea estates covered more than 48,000 acres across the district, injecting large amounts of capital into Darjeeling and neighboring districts.

All this industry required huge amounts of labor—for the clearing of land and building of roads, the transportation of material and erection of houses and public buildings, the provision of fodder and of wood for fuel, the tending of nurseries, the plucking and processing of tea, and seeing to the welfare of the *sahab*. (*Sahab* or *sahib* loosely translates as "master," and was the term the Indian populace used for its British masters. The mistress is called *memsahib* or *memsahab*.) Much of the initial labor force was sourced locally—often coerced—but the demand gradually spread to more distant parts of the country.

While people from the low-lying areas or plains of Bengal and the neighboring regions of India came to work in construction and road building, ethnic Nepali tribespeople like the Tamangs, Rais, Limbus, and Gurungs flocked to the tea gardens.

The 113 tea gardens existing in 1874 employed more than 19,000 workers (including women and very young children), and at the end of the century the labor force had risen to 64,000, a third of the district's population and consisting almost entirely of Nepalis.

Although arterial roads were built, the terrain did not allow for roads to every nook and cranny of Darjeeling. So, all the jobs that required the carrying of goods on backs and of people on chairs attached to poles and supported on shoulders went to the hardy Bhutia and Lepcha men so accustomed to ferrying loads over mountain passes, while their women were prized as ayahs (maids or nannies).

Furthermore, as Dane Kennedy writes in *The Magic Mountains*, "One guidebook told its readers, in a telling turn of phrase, that the Bhutias and Lepchas, 'when caught young, make excellent cooks and khitmatgars [butlers], and they have the advantage of having no caste prejudices, and of being able to turn their hands to any kind of work.'"

The second big fillip to Darjeeling came from the railways. Until the end of 1854, a journey up to Darjeeling was what E. C. Dozey described as an arduous trek requiring "leisure, a heavy purse and any amount of stamina." Travellers could plod on foot or travel by horseback (or even be carried by litter) the 645 kilometers from Kolkata by road, of which 64 kilometers was an uphill climb; or they could take a slow river journey part of the way before continuing by road.

In 1855, the first leg of the rail line was opened between Kolkata and Raniganj, approximately 193 kilometers to the northwest of the city, considerably reducing the road journey to Darjeeling.

The line continued to be pushed forward until July 4, 1881, when a narrow-gauge track was completed between Siliguri and Darjeeling, officially becoming the Darjeeling Himalayan Railway.

This made Darjeeling the first hill station to be linked directly to the plains by rail. "As a result," writes Dane Kennedy, "a Calcutta resident could arrive in Darjeeling in as little as twenty-one hours by the end of the century and in less than fourteen hours by the 1940s."

Chai

Everyone drinks chai (tea) in Darjeeling. In every house we visited, we were served cups of chai with a little something on the side—biscuits or a slice of cake. At all the main tourist areas and around Chowrasta you can sit watching the world go by through plate-glass windows and sip the golden fluid from a clear glass cup. To buy the tea leaves themselves, we were directed to the end of a narrow path in the main market, to the little shop of Baliram Prasad, which sells wares from the surrounding estates: Chamong, Makaibari, Margaret's Hope. There are three main seasons: First Flush (plucked from late February through mid-April), Second Flush (May through June), and Autumn Flush (July through September).

You state your preference, depending on the delicacy or robustness of the flavor you crave, and the boxes come out. The proprietor places a large pinch of tea on your palm. You make a loose fist around the leaves and gently blow air into the opening where your thumb wraps around your index finger. Then you shove your nose into that opening and breathe in a deep lungful of the fragrant aroma.

While there are no definitive records for the total labor involved in the building of the railway lines, the figures would have been immense. Records show that Campbell employed 1,200 laborers in 1839, for the building of local roads in Darjeeling. And no less than 24,000 men were at work building the 1.8-kilometer-long Hardinge Bridge—now a part of Bangladesh—over the Padma River during February 1912.

According to Dozey, the railway train boasted nine cars accommodating 59 first-class, 63 second-class, 104 intermediate, and 158 third-class passengers. Each first-class cabin had a shower bath and a spray bath with jets along its walls. Lavatories had paper towels (in rolls), and the basins were fitted with receptacles for liquid soap. The train was lit throughout with electricity, and the fans in the dining room were positioned to waft gentle air at the heads of the sitting passengers instead of on their food.

What set Darjeeling and other hill stations apart from the rest of British India was that these were family stations. British administration in the plains consisted of male officials who either visited their families in Britain once a year or brought them on short trips to India. It was only when the hill stations were established that memsahabs and children began to accompany the men. Hill stations were chosen for their cooler climate, which suited the British constitution well, as well as for their natural beauty and cleaner air; soon families weren't coming just on holiday, but also to settle. What had started as places for British soldiers to recuperate became permanent British settlements. And the resident population would swell every summer when unbearable heat closed down offices in the plains and visitors—other British families and affluent Indians—arrived in Darjeeling seeking respite and a prolonged holiday, creating a need for a whole host of other services.

The first church (Saint Andrew's, Church of England) came up as early as 1843. Loreto Convent, established in 1847, was the first to have an attached school for vernacular—mainly Nepali and Lepcha—students. By 1917, Dozey was able to list a total of 245 educational establishments (from primary to high school level, as well as special trade schools) for local students and 12 institutions offering education to the children of Europeans and Anglo-Indians.

At the time, the town already boasted nine hotels and twelve boarding houses for visiting Europeans, a botanic garden, a natural history museum, and hospitals and cemeteries for the different communities. Clubs were set up to satisfy the social and recreational needs of European tea planters. The Darjeeling Planter's Club was the first of these in 1868, followed by the Darjeeling Shooting and Fishing Club, the Darjeeling Gymkhana, the Darjeeling Golf Club, Rink Theatre, and the Jalpaiguri European Club. Visitors were encouraged to enjoy the natural beauty that Darjeeling had to offer and sample the curiosities of local tribespeople. In *The Magic Mountains*, Dane Kennedy writes:

> What sustained the hill stations was their image of aloofness. It was no less essential to their public than to their private purposes that they present themselves as exclusively European enclaves, isolated from the pressures and perils of India and its inhabitants. Yet the British were not alone: they were surrounded by Indians. One of the paradoxes of the hill stations is that their success as places where the British imagined it possible to get away from Indians depended on the contributions of Indians.

Take domestic life, for example, made comfortable by:

> a heavy demand for domestic servants, including khitmatgars (butlers or head waiters), khansamahs (cooks), malis (gardeners), dhobis (washermen), bheestis (water carriers), jhampanis (coolies who carried sedan chairs and later pulled rickshaws), mehtars (sweepers), and others. While many visitors brought personal servants with them from the plains, all but a few depended on local peoples for menial tasks. According to Charles Dilke [a minor official with the British administration], a "small family" in Simla [the summer capital of British India] required the services of "three body servants, two cooks, one butler, two grooms, two gardeners, two messengers, two nurses, two washermen, two water-carriers, thirteen jampan-men, one sweeper, one lamp-cleaner, and one boy . . . or thirty-five in all."
>
> When the *Times* war correspondent William Howard Russell and a friend rented a house in Simla, they felt obliged to employ thirty servants, including ten wood-cutters. Even transport within the station had surprisingly large labour ramifications. Mrs. Robert Moss King marvelled at the sight of two hundred dandies [chairs suspended between two poles and carried by four men], six hundred coolies (to carry the dandies), one hundred ponies, and one hundred syces (grooms) crammed together outside the Anglican church in Mussoorie on Sunday.

While the Britishers flocked to enjoy everything these mountain retreats, including Darjeeling, offered, communities of immigrants continued flocking in for what the Britishers had to offer—employment.

One such immigrant was Tenzing Wangdi, who came to Darjeeling from Tibet as a boy with his father probably in the early 1880s, to sell musk in Darjeeling. On the return journey they were robbed, so they turned back to Darjeeling and worked the 50-odd-kilometer long Phalut trek that was then being made, a spectacular trekking route with views of four of the 8,000-meter giants—Everest, Kangchenjunga, Makalu, and Lhotse. They became useful as interpreters and settled in Darjeeling. Wangdi went on to become a sardar—a leader of porters on expeditions.

Joan Townend, who was to have a close association with the Sherpas and Bhutias of Darjeeling in the 1930s and 1940s, met Wangdi and wrote his story in an article for *The Himalayan Journal* in 1947. Wangdi told Townend that the first Sherpas came to Darjeeling in about 1902 or 1903. They came to trade and, finding they could earn good wages, stayed through the summer season. One of them was called Norbhu Jhau, "The Bearded Man." This fact would be likely to fix itself in the memory, as it was rare to see anyone of Tibetan blood with a beard. Another Sherpa who came to Darjeeling was named Choktuk. When Norbhu Jhau and Choktuk returned to Solu Khumbu in Nepal, the people left their work and ran from their fields to see who these two grandly dressed strangers could be. Their account of Darjeeling inspired several of their fellow countrymen to follow their example. The following year, the original two plus six others journeyed to Darjeeling to work as laborers and rickshaw pullers.

Once the Sherpa migration from Solu Khumbu started, the trickle became a flood. Young men and women, hearing of employment, ran away from home. Traveling solo or in small groups, they would set out with nothing but the clothes on their backs and a handful of tsampa to eat on the way. They crossed high passes, their feet wrapped in straw and covered in bags.

The early migrants would have passed through dense forests in remote valleys, moving at altitudes between 600 and 3,500 meters. There would have been no *serais* (traveller lodges) for them to halt at. And even Sherpa villages were few and far between, situated only on the higher ridges.

How did they know where to go? "They followed the sun," say older Sherpas in Darjeeling. "They knew that Darjeeling was in the east, so they traveled in that direction, walking for days and days."

In Darjeeling, they would seek out the communities they knew. Everyone knew an uncle or clan brother who would give them shelter until they could find a small room of their own—the Sherpas to Toong Soong, the Bhutias to Bhutia basti, the Sikkimese Bhutias to Geen, where the Lepchas had a settlement of their own. These settlements in Darjeeling were out of sight of the British areas, facing the valleys, on forested, unlit slopes teeming with wildlife. At night, the women would wait in groups to scuttle through the darkness, and even the men avoided going home alone.

Newcomers to Darjeeling did the jobs that were identified with their communities. Dorjee Lhatoo told us that the early settlers brought their traditional occupations with them. There were communities of meat sellers called Shingsawas, traditional bakers called Yolmos, and skilled paper makers called Kagatays. They belonged to small tribes that soon integrated into the larger groupings of Sherpas or Bhutias. The ethnic Bhutias and Sherpas themselves were load carriers of different kinds, pulling rickshaws, carrying the chair-like *dandis*, and portering luggage and heavy loads.

Picture this: A memsahab alights from the first-class cabin of the gaily colored Darjeeling Himalayan Railway. She is perhaps newly married or has come with her children to join her husband, who is an officer or manager of a tea estate. With her she has brought a few personal servants (expecting to hire the rest in Darjeeling), who emerge from the third-class carriage and proceed to put together the boxes and trunks, the portmanteaus and bags containing the essentials and fripperies of English life. The hotel at which the mem will stay until her new house is put together and fully staffed has sent a troop of porters—mainly women—to carry the luggage up, while the dandi bearers jockey to transport the mem herself. She looks around and sniffs the clean mountain air and the flowers in the gardens that look so decidedly English, sighing with contentment.

The leader of the porters admonishes a young woman hoisting a heavy crate and balancing it precariously on her back with the help of the head-strap. The girl is new to the job, having come to Darjeeling only a week earlier. Carrying loads is hard work, but she has been doing it since she was little. What she is unused to, however, is the hustle and bustle, the curiosity of English clothes, the color of their eyes and hair. She looks sideways at the foreign woman shyly and sighs deeply. At least she is working and will get paid!

This new land holds promise for them both—they have come to paradise.

Assembling loads before an expedition, circa 1950 *(Photo by Jill Henderson)*

CHAPTER 3

The Night Before
the Expedition

For centuries, journeys to the Himalaya were undertaken only by pilgrims seeking salvation or enlightenment, or by Christian priests trying to convert the far corners of the world. They were also made by traders and shepherds, who accepted crossing passes as a way of life or as necessary for business. Other reasons for interest in the Himalaya began to emerge only much later.

As you may recall, the East India Company was founded in 1600 to establish trade in the Indian Ocean region, and eventually came to dominate large areas of the Indian subcontinent, exercising military and administrative control. In 1802, the EIC launched the Great Trigonometrical Survey (GTS), whose goal was to measure India with scientific precision. The story of this mapping is a fascinating tale, one involving the lugging of half-ton theodolites and thirty-meter-long collapsible metal chains that required bullock carts to transport. The survey gave rise to a breed of trained Indian surveyors who traversed the length and breadth of the country, charting, calculating, and mapping; many died of illness, heat, dehydration, contaminated food, or cold during their efforts.

The first triangulations were done from Madras on the east coast to Mangalore on the west and then Kanyakumari, on the southernmost tip of India. From here, they proceeded slowly up the great subcontinent. In 1833, the mappers reached Dehradun near the Himalayan foothills, establishing the Survey Office there. Two cousins, Nain Singh Rawat and Kishen Singh Rawat, were part of an elite group called Pandits, given the job of exploration and mapping in the border regions of Sikkim, Nepal, and Tibet. Disguising themselves as lamas, they used their rosaries to count off steps so that they covered one mile of ground in 2,000 paces. Crossing the disease-harboring marshes at the Himalayan foothills known as the Terai, these Pandits reached the vast, open deserts of Tibet. They hid the maps they made in their prayer wheels, and smuggled them back into India.

Using the measurements taken by the surveyors and Pandits, it was human computers who triangulated and accurately calculated the area that the British had dominion over. They also calculated the exact heights of all the peaks in the Himalaya and the adjoining Karakoram Range. Radhanath Sikdar was one such computer. As Rajesh Kochhar, former director of the National Institute of Science, Technology, and Development Studies in New Delhi, wrote, Sikdar was a student of the Hindu College, Kolkata, in 1831 when he was appointed to the newly established computing office. His mathematical abilities were recognized by George Everest, the first surveyor general of India, who took him to the survey office in Dehradun, where he remained for the next fifteen years. In a letter written to the government in 1838, Everest called Sikdar "the cheapest instrument that Government ever could employ in a task of this kind." In 1845, he was made chief computer. Kochhar writes:

> The GTS commenced its 'North-Eastern Himalayan Series' in 1845 and completed it in 1850. It spanned 2,720 km [eastward] from Dehradun to Sonakhoda, in Purnia, [in the state of] Bihar. The mightiest of the Himalayan peaks are visible from the principal stations of this series. Everest's successor, Andrew Waugh, the surveyor-general from 1843 to 1863, ordered that every visible peak, great and small, should be observed from every observing station, but that the identification of peaks must be left to the computers.
>
> Under normal circumstances, Sikdar's mathematics department would have carried out the computations. But in 1849, he along with his computing office was moved to Calcutta. And as soon as he retired, in 1862, the office was brought back to Dehradun. It is in this period that the heights of various Himalayan peaks were calculated.

As observational data came in, it must have become evident that these would be among the highest peaks in the world. Kochhar concludes that

Sikdar's banishment was motivated by racism, to prevent this historic information from being announced by a native. Immediately after Sikdar and his team were vacated, a new team was set up in Dehradun under the superintendence of J. B. N. Hennessy, with new native surveyors and sub assistants.

Under Hennessy, this office carried out computations for the snowy peaks, including Mount Everest. True to form, none of the native sub assistants associated with the computations was ever named.

At first, the surveyors did not assign individual names to the mountains but designated them by letters and Roman numerals. Everest was known as "H," which changed to "Peak XV" in 1850. Its height was observed from six different stations and independently calculated from each observation. The numbers when put together yielded a mean value of 8,839.8 meters. A Karakoram peak named K2 was calculated to have a height of 8,610 meters, and Kangchenjunga II a height of 8,474 meters. They were declared the three highest peaks in the world. In 1865, the Royal Geographical Society named the highest peak "Everest" for Sir George Everest, surveyor general of India from 1830 to 1843. By 1862, more than forty peaks with elevations exceeding 5,500 meters had been climbed for surveying purposes.

ONCE THE BRITISH GOVERNMENT TOOK control of India, the mid- to late nineteenth century became a period of intense international intrigue. Britain was in a bid to expand its empire but so was Russia, seeking to push its boundaries outward into Central Asia. It was in the Himalaya that these massive powers clashed. The imperialists, traveling both openly and in disguise, scouted the movements of their enemies, bribed and threatened local chieftains, planted flags claiming land, and waged diplomatic confrontations in a cat-and-mouse chase that came to be known as the "Great Game of Asia." The key goal was political and economic gain, despite the spirit of adventure with which these intrigues played out.

In 1848, when Joseph Dalton Hooker started his pioneering study on the plant life of the Sikkim Himalaya, it opened a pathway for a whole host of scientific studies other than mapping, such as natural history, geology, and anthropology. There were also the hunters. When he was laying the groundwork for The Himalayan Club in 1927, Sir Geoffrey L. Corbett admitted that it was shikar (hunting) that compelled nine-tenths of those who visited the Himalaya, and regimental mess halls were filled with the heads of ibex, markhor (wild goats), and *Ovis poli* (wild sheep). It was only in the last two decades of the nineteenth century that people began exploring the high Himalayan regions solely for the sport of it. These earliest attempts were undertaken by Europeans who had already climbed in the Alps and were searching for new adventures. Accompanied by surveyors, geologists and botanists, map experts, and members of the British military, these adventurers would hire local help from the region and along the route to carry loads and cook. The age of climbing in the Himalaya had begun!

As writer and teacher John Martyn wrote in an epic article for *The Himalayan Journal (THJ)* in 1979:

> The first person who admitted that he came to the Himalaya simply for the sport of climbing was W. W. Graham, who visited Sikkim and Garhwal in 1883 with his Swiss guides, but there is some doubt about what he climbed. Sir Martin Conway took a much-publicized expedition (for which he was knighted) to the Karakoram in 1892 but it was for exploration rather than for climbing. In 1895 [Albert F.] Mummery, Norman Collie and [Geoffrey] Hastings came out with the intention of attempting Nanga Parbat and Mummery perished in the attempt. In 1899 Douglas Freshfield, an eminent member of the Alpine Club, came out with a geologist, Professor Garwood, to make a high-level tour of Kangchenjunga and in 1902 an Englishman called [Oscar] Eckenstein had a look at K2 with an idea of climbing it. In 1905 [Tom] Longstaff, probably inspired by Graham, came out to explore the approaches in Nandadevi bringing two Swiss guides, the Brocherel brothers, with him. In 1909 Longstaff visited the Karakoram.

The year 1907 saw the first visit of Dr. Alexander M. Kellas, a scientist and one of the finest exploratory Himalayan mountaineers, to Darjeeling. This Britisher specialized in studying the effects of altitude on the human body. He came to India because of its high mountains, particularly to access Everest, where he could conduct rigorous tests on the value of supplemental oxygen for climbing at altitude. Between 1907 and 1921, Kellas undertook no fewer than eight Himalayan expeditions and spent more time above 6,000 meters than any Westerner had previously done.

In *Prelude to Everest: Alexander Kellas, Himalayan Mountaineer*, Ian Mitchell and George Rodway quote from Kellas's letter to the Alpine Club, the world's first mountaineering club (founded in London in 1857), established to facilitate exploration of the European Alps: "I have made three journeys to Sikkim in the years 1907, 1909, and 1911. In 1907 Swiss guides were taken but they proved unsatisfactory and in 1909 and 1911 only natives were employed. The natives were either Nepalese, Lepchas, or Bhutias. The Sherpas, who come from Eastern Nepal, were found to be the best, and they can safely be recommended to travellers."

In 1907, around the time that Kellas started climbing, two Norwegians, Carl Rubenson and Monrad Aas, attempted the first ascent of Kabru, a 7,284-meter peak on the ridgeline extending off Kangchenjunga on the India-Nepal border. In a talk to members of the Alpine Club, Rubenson particularly mentioned his satisfaction with the capabilities of the Sherpa porter, especially when properly equipped and well treated. Whether he had heard or merely read Rubenson's speech, Kellas took the advice on Sherpa porters to heart. Mitchell and Rodway tell us that Kellas provided his porters with adequate food, as well as the same tents, down quilts, and sleeping bags he himself used. He treated them with dignity, learning their names at a time when most mountaineers did not make such efforts to differentiate among them. Mitchell and Rodway wrote that Kellas also learned from them: when the porters feared incipient frostbite, they removed their shoes, rubbed their feet, and as insulation put "dry grass, of which they carried a small supply, into their boots." The experiences that Kellas had with his porters and the results of his field studies on high-altitude physiology proved invaluable when the first attempts were made on Everest, in the 1920s.

Then World War I happened, and everything changed in its wake. Its horrors seemed to imbue a generation of climbers with bravery and recklessness, rendering them sometimes foolishly stubborn in the face of defeat.

Terms such as *attack, assault*, and *conquest* entered the climbing parlance. Expeditions looked like small armies, and cost as much to outfit. These expeditions needed hundreds of porters to carry, cook, and support, and thus a new profession was born. Soon, the number of expeditions coming to climb in the Himalaya doubled and then trebled.

The man who arguably lent the most fame and color to Himalayan climbing in the early days was Brigadier General the Honourable Charles Granville Bruce. Born in Wales in 1866, he came to India in 1888 and was posted to the infantry regiment of the 5th Gurkha Rifles in Abbottabad. He

Porters on the 1922 Everest expedition led by General Charles Bruce (far right). (*Photo courtesy of Noel Odell*)

soon fell in love with the Himalaya, and spent all the time he could wandering about in them with two or three of his beloved Gurkhas—soldiers native to Nepal and northeast India—recruited into special units in the British Army. Labeled a "Mad Mountain Machine" in his obituary, he had— according to Sir Francis Younghusband, an explorer and lieutenant colonel in the British Army—"an extraordinary aptitude for entering into the lives of mountain peoples, learning their fables and even singing their songs. He so obviously liked being with them that they would open out their hearts to him, and as he sang to them, they would roar with delight."

Bruce perceived the value of the Baltis in Kashmir and the Bhotias in Garhwal, and he fully realized the worth of the Sherpas, which had already been identified by Dr. Kellas and the Norwegians. In the introduction to

Bruce's book *The Assault on Mount Everest, 1922,* Younghusband wrote that one of the chief features of expeditions to the mountain was:

> the organization of a corps of porters specially enlisted from among the hardiest men on that frontier for the particular purpose of carrying camps to high altitudes." This idea originated with Brigadier General Bruce himself. Prior to Bruce, Himalayan climbing expeditions had been dependent upon coolies collected at the highest villages and taken on for a few days, while the climb lasted. But this was never very satisfactory, and coolies so collected would be of no use on Mount Everest, clearly a much longer, more involved climb. General Bruce's plan was different: months before an expedition, he would select thirty or forty of the very best men to be found in the higher mountains, promising to enlist them for some months, pay, feed, and equip them well, and above all to instill in them a real esprit de corps.

For Bruce and all subsequent expeditions before the opening of Nepal in 1949, this corps of men was found among the Sherpas and Bhutias of Darjeeling.

What happened in the early days in Darjeeling when news of an Everest expedition got out? The sahabs would arrive with their loads and equipment and usually stay at one of the tea plantations or the grand Hotel Mount Everest. Each sahab would have his own duties, and on one or two of them would fall the task of recruiting porters for the expedition. Some accounts paint vivid pictures of what transpired.

On the day of interviews and hiring, the recruiters would appear on the verandah of the Planters' Club—what they called the quarterdeck—in the center of the town, the hopefuls gathered below. Many would be from Darjeeling, but there would be others from Khumbu who had traveled the ten days to Darjeeling as quickly as they could. Those who had been on expeditions before would clutch in their hands the chits provided by previous expedition leaders. These were "letters" of recommendation, sometimes consisting of just a line or two stating that the bearer of the paper had been on such and such an expedition and proved satisfactory, or had shown himself to be good at higher altitudes when kept in tight control, or was reliable until he got his hands on drink—to which he was not averse. Though the

porters could not read what was written, each paper nonetheless represented communication from one sahab to another, and carried the promise
of employment. Aspiring porters without chits depended on good luck and
their ability to impress with their keenness alone. Old hands often picked up
a smattering of words in different languages, and above the din of Nepali and
Sherpa might be heard a few words of English or perhaps a "ja ja" learned
from the Bavarians.

Hugh Ruttledge wrote in *Attack on Everest:*

> Yet you can size up a man pretty well, however imperfect your means of
> communication. Previous experience has shown that the big, muscular
> man who is capable of great feats of strength, usually of short duration,
> at moderate altitudes, is apt to fail on the high mountains. He has to
> carry too much tophamper in the shape of his own burly person, and an
> additional load is his undoing. We went out for the wiry, active, clean-
> bred type, reasonably intelligent and with the indefinable stamp of "qual-
> ity," as a horse-dealer would say.
>
> For this particular expedition, once the men were selected, they were
> sent to hospital to be medically examined and relieved of internal parasites.
>
> We used to visit the men in hospital, where there was much merriment
> over our attempts to re-identify recruits last seen in their grubby working
> clothes. Each man had had a bath and was clothed, for the first time
> in his life, in beautiful blue-and-white striped pyjamas. It was a wonder-
> ful transformation, and they were delighted by the admiration of their
> friends.

It is unlikely that most expeditions displayed such concern about
their porters' health (albeit to save themselves aggravation later on). In
many cases, selection would be left to a local British agent or a sardar who
appointed men they knew. Sometimes, the first time that most members
would see their porters would be at the start of the expedition itself.

Once selections had been made, the porters would help in the packing
and weighing of loads. Advances on salary would be given so that families were looked after while the men were away. Affairs would be put
in order, and finally one last and important ceremony would take place:
the Sherpas would seek the blessings of the head lamas of the nearby
monasteries.

Chang: Nepalese/Tibetan Beer

Chang is a beer brewed by Nepali and Tibetan people. It is made of rice, millet, or maize, has an alcohol content of between 5 and 7.5 percent, and is drunk at all social and religious gatherings. As Nima Tsering told us, "Earlier there used to be general meetings near the Sherpa gompa. The women would take along their home-made chang. The men would sit and drink and discuss, until they fell unconscious. The women drank too, and much earlier, children also drank." He added that when a batch turned out well, it was taken as a good auspice for the year, and the men would take it with them on expeditions. "We used to make batches to last six or seven months and keep it until it became really strong," he said. "There were never domestic fights after drinking. Sherpa men never raised a hand to their wives or children. Drinking was always done; no ganja, just chang and *rakshi*."

To make chang, first cook rice in plenty of water, then put it in a plastic tub to cool down. When the ricewater reaches room temperature, grate a local dry yeast called *madsa* or *phaap* into it, add more water, and pour the mixture into a vessel covered with several layers of cloth tied tightly. In three days, the chang is ready to be strained out and drunk. Add water each time the liquid is decanted until the chang loses its potency.

For *rakshi*, a stronger drink, add jaggery to the cooked ricewater. The addition of this unrefined sugar makes the alcohol stronger. Rakshi takes about four to five days to mature.

Dorjee Lhatoo makes his own chang. We watched as he carefully filtered the clear liquid from a larger pot. It had been freshly brewed and tasted pleasantly sweet. The drink was dangerously deceptive, though: after a few glasses, Lhatoo's kitchen, where we were sitting, began to sway.

While Sherpa and Bhutia men were the core of the high-altitude porters, women were also employed. At basecamp, with their loads deposited, the women and the bulk of the porters coming from the villages along the route would be paid in coin and would then leave the expedition.

In *The Assault on Mount Everest, 1922*, Brigadier General Bruce wrote:

> One girl, about eighteen years of age, actually carried a 160 lb tent by herself from Sakiathang to Chokarbo, over the top of the Chog La. More-over, this tent had been wet for the last ten days, and although we did our

best to dry all our camp as much as possible before starting, it must have been at least 20 to 30 lbs heavier than it ought to have been.

Back in Darjeeling, with everything in order, the porters in Toong Soong would have a night-long party. Dorjee Lhatoo shared with us his memories of the night before a typical expedition:

When we came down to Darjeeling, we lived below Ajeeba's [a prominent porter in the 1940s and 1950s] house. We had one room. At one side was the cooking area, another side the altar and one bed—we all slept on that one bed. My mother was Ajeeba's cousin. When the men were to leave on expeditions the next morning, the whole night there would be a marathon Sherpa dance with boots on—mountain boots! In those days there were clinkers. And when they danced up there, all the dust would fall on our faces. We were kids then, six or seven years old, and had just come from Tibet. We would cover our faces, and, in the morning, it was as if there had been a snowfall—dust fall actually! Early in the morning, before we got up, [the men] would be gone. They didn't sleep.

Celebration and dance were an important part of Sherpa life, accompanying weddings, engagements, clan meetings, and particularly expeditions. Expeditions meant work and money. A good performance on the mountain would be noticed and ensure employment next time; upon returning, you could also sell any equipment. But there was also fear. For the next three or four or five months, it would be left to the women who stayed behind to keep the family going until the men returned. Would everyone return? How many would come back frostbitten and incapable of work? The celebration, then, encompassed both happiness and the acknowledgment of an unknown future. Some women made and sold *chang* (rice beer) surreptitiously, or did a little trade in milk and vegetables, or other produce. They made and sold sweaters and visited the gompa to pray.

Harish Kapadia tells the story of a young Sherpani who sent a message to her husband on an expedition that she was very sick and that he should return home immediately. The husband rushed home from basecamp, doing in one day a journey that normally took three. He burst into the house to find his wife calmly cooking the evening meal. His fear gave way to astonishment and then anger. "Do you have any idea what you put me through?"

he screamed at her. "Now you know what I go through every time you leave on expedition," she replied. Her husband, apparently, never reproached her again. Another Sherpani explained the feelings she had in her husband's absence as a *dil mein jham-jham*, best described as an upheaval or a quickening of the heart, an anxiety, and a tumult.

ONE HUNDRED YEARS LATER, TECHNOLOGY has changed and with it, the way expeditions are organized and run. Expeditions don't last so long, and mobile phones make communication easier. The emotions, however, remain the same. Phuri Yangtze, daughter of a current Darjeeling climber named Pasang Phutar, told us this about her father:

> At first, he goes and for two to three days he is on the phone. He calls us up constantly at dinner, breakfast, lunch. Then after some time he says that he is going up. After that he won't be able to call. So, we are tense till he calls. We are always praying. If anyone is sick, we get very worried. And sometimes he calls to say, "I have my summit today," and then everyone prays that they summit. We hope that the weather is good, and sometimes mom even cries because it is very risky out there . . . It is not easy because sometimes somebody calls up and says there is an avalanche or something. Everyone gets worried. We call here and there, hoping that he is fine until we find out for sure.

And sometimes, no news can be very bad news—as young Sherpanis, daughters and sons, sisters and brothers, mothers and fathers wait in vain for at least bodily remains to help them find closure.

Unidentified Sherpas on an expedition in the 1930s *(Ang Tsering Collection)*

CHAPTER 4

The Men with No Names

In 1856, the Great Trigonometrical Survey of India officially confirmed Mount Everest (on the border between Nepal and Tibet) as the highest peak in the world. At 8,848 meters, it remained a daunting dream for adventurers for decades. It was only in 1921 that the British sent a team to explore possible routes to the top. Nepal had closed its borders to the outside world, so this reconnaissance expedition traveled from Darjeeling through Tibet to approach Everest from its north side. All subsequent expeditions to Everest, until Nepal finally opened its gates, were to take this route.

The next year, in 1922, the British made their first serious attempt to climb Everest. The expedition was led by Brigadier General Charles Granville Bruce of the Royal Gurkha Rifles, an old India hand. On June 7, sixteen men—three sahabs and thirteen porters—were on their way to the North Col, a 7,020-meter-high saddle dividing Everest from Changtse at the head of the East Rongbuk Glacier. Just after 1:30 p.m., they heard "an ominous sound, sharp, arresting, violent, and yet somehow soft like an explosion of untamped gunpowder." None of them had heard such a sound before, but they knew instinctively that it was an avalanche. When the snow settled, seven men, all porters, had died.

George Mallory, the British climber who was present when it happened, wrote a detailed account of the tragedy that appears in Bruce's book *The Assault on Mount Everest, 1922*. Several other expedition members, including Captain George Finch, Mr. Howard Somerwell, and Dr. Tom Longstaff, also contributed sections, and yet nowhere in the book is there a list of those who died. In fact, except for Mallory's servant Dasno, Somerwell's man

Narbu—who numbered among the dead—and a cook called Pou, *none* of the porters are ever mentioned by name (and judging by reports from later expeditions, the expedition would have employed anywhere between twenty and forty porters for several months).

This was a time when the notion of the superior white man was openly on display, along with the mistaken belief that Asians valued life less than Westerners did because of their religious belief in karma and rebirth.

The 1922 team was definitely a team of sahabs imbued with a sense of empire, notwithstanding Charles Bruce's paternalistic fondness for his Gurkhas in the regiments he commanded and his ability to lark around with the hired help. Mallory may have felt upset at the deaths, but he was quick to absolve himself of any guilt. He wrote, "More experience, more knowledge might perhaps have warned us not to go there. One never can know enough about snow. But looking up the corridor again after the event, I wondered how I ever could be certain not to be deceived by appearances so innocent." And again:

> The regret of all members of the Expedition for the loss of our seven porters will have been elsewhere expressed. It is my part only to add this: the work of carrying up our camps on Mount Everest is beyond the range of a simple contract measured in terms of money; the porters had come to have a share in our enterprise, and these men died in an act of voluntary service freely rendered and faithfully performed.

The names of the porters who died in the avalanche were subsequently etched on a memorial cairn built in 1924 to honor the deaths across three expeditions. That cairn no longer stands, but the names of the dead porters of 1922 were recorded on it as follows: Lhakpa, Narbu, Pasang, Pema, Sange, Dorje, and Temba.

Although the cairn memorial was lost, almost a century later, in 2012, The Himalayan Club received a letter from one Richard Robinson. The Summer Olympics were being held in London that year, and Mr. Robinson was the director of the "Olympic Games Pledge," an expedition that aimed to summit Mount Everest to fulfill an old pledge that Great Britain made during the closing ceremony of the 1924 Winter Olympics in Chamonix, France. That was the first year that medals had been given for "Alpinisme." Thirteen gold medals were awarded to the members of the British Himalayan expedition of 1922; one was earmarked for a Nepali soldier serving with the Gurkha Rifles, and seven for the men who died on the expedition. The pledge Great Britain had made was that it would put one of these gold medals on the summit of Everest in recognition of this pioneering expedition, a pledge that remained unfulfilled in 2012. Even as he wrote, Robinson informed us, the well-known climber Kenton Cool waited at Everest Basecamp to begin his tenth ascent of the mountain. He carried with him the gold medal awarded to the British climber and 1922 expedition medic Dr. Arthur Wakefield. Cool planned to lay the medal on top of the peak for a few minutes in fulfillment of the pledge and to honor the porters who had died.

Continued Robinson in his letter, "What we do know as fact is that the medals were awarded; what we have never been able to prove beyond doubt are the names and nationalities of the six men (*sic*) who received these medals." Could the club locate, he wanted to know, the family members of the dead porters, and could any of the medals still be found in Darjeeling?

Lhakpa, Narbu, Sange, and Pasang are common names; without their full names or other identifying details, tracing their families was impossible.

Even Dorjee Lhatoo, so immersed in Darjeeling Sherpa history, could not identify them, nor had he heard of any Olympic medals. His uncle Lobsang had been a prominent high-altitude Sherpa on a subsequent expedition in 1924. Whether he was on the 1921 and 1922 expeditions, Lhatoo was not sure. He had never tried to find out.

There is a solitary reference to an Olympic medal in E. F. Norton's book, *The Fight for Everest 1924*. While talking about Narbu Yishe, one of the porters on that 1924 expedition, he wrote, "He decided to return to his home in the Solah Khombu district of Nepal, where, I believe, he now wears with all honour a bronze medal presented by the Committee of the 8th Olympiad [i.e., the 1924 Winter Olympics]." Now this presents something of a mystery. Norton writes of it being a bronze medal, while records mention only gold medals. Furthermore, how did Narbu Yishe come to possess a medal that was given to the families of the dead porters? Were bronze medals given to other porters on the 1922 expedition—of whom Narbu Yishe could have been one—in recognition of their service? Or were bronze medals rather than gold ones awarded to the families of dead porters, and Narbu Yishe received his as a family member of a porter who had died? It is entirely credible that while the British expedition members were awarded gold Olympic medals, the porters were awarded the lesser honors.

This attitude has been witnessed right up to and including the awards given to Tenzing Norgay when Everest was climbed. Nonetheless, Kenton Cool placed the gold medal on top of Everest; the Olympic Games were celebrated in London; and we continue to hope that somewhere, possibly even in Toong Soong, at the bottom of a forgotten box, one day a medal will be found and the descendants of Lhakpa, Narbu, Pasang, Pema, Sange, Temba, or Dorje might hear the story that connects the medal to their family.

E. F. Norton's book on the 1924 Everest expedition included a host of Sherpa and Bhutia names, along with character sketches of many of them. For example, Norton wrote about his march to basecamp, "These marches also afforded a good opportunity of getting to know the porters … They were the most cheerful, friendly fellows imaginable and responded instantly to

Karma Paul

One of the most interesting individuals to straddle the world between the foreign climbers and the porters of Darjeeling during the 1920s and 1930s was the interpreter Karma Paul, born Karma Palden in 1894.

We met his daughter, Colonel Paul, an ex-army nurse, at the home of Dorjee Lhatoo. She told us that Karma had lost his parents at the age of twelve or thirteen, and, like many young orphans in Darjeeling at the time, was sent to work for a group of evangelists. In return for work, Karma received an education—and his name was changed from Palden to Paul because the missionaries could not pronounce it. Although he received the catechism, Karma remained a devout Buddhist all his life. After his education, he spent a brief period in Kolkata, where he learned how to operate a cinema projector. Colonel Paul told us that her father returned to Darjeeling, claiming cinema work was "not my cup."

It was then, being fluent in English, Nepali, and Tibetan, that he started interpreting for foreign expeditions. "He was a great acquisition to the [1922] Expedition," wrote General Bruce in *The Assault on Mount Everest, 1922*, "always good company and always cheerful, full of a quaint little vanity of his own and delighted when he was praised." He was zealous in pursuing his duties, an attitude that at times inspired an odd derisiveness in the British climbers. Describing an encounter with the lama of Rongbuk Monastery, Bruce wrote, "We were received with full ceremony, and after a joke. One Mingma, a baby-faced lad whose character belied his innocent expression, had distinguished himself earlier in the march by biting off one of his friend's fingers—so he became Mingma Kukar (the dog) and we used to bark and growl at him when we passed him on the road." No fewer than twenty-three porters appear in Norton's narrative, while an examination of *The Himalayan Journal's* porter list revealed twelve more names, including six who had been on the earlier expedition.

What happened between 1922 and 1924 to cause this important shift to recognizing Sherpas by name? One explanation is that by now, several porters were on their third expedition with the British. Some like the sardar Sanglu had been climbing even earlier with Alexander Kellas. At the beginning, the Sherpas were seen as a group—stout-hearted and loyal, they functioned above and beyond expectations—but they were not seen

compliments had been exchanged in the usual way by the almost grovelling interpreter, Karma Paul (who was very much of a Buddhist here), the Lama began to ask us questions with regard to the objects of the Expedition."

Despite the derision, Karma Paul's negotiating skills were unmatched, and he was interpreter, recruiter, and general go-between for all the large expeditions between 1922 and 1938. In group photographs he appears as a diminutive, dapper young man in a suit, his pillbox hat tilted at a slightly rakish angle.

As he made some money, Karma Paul bought a few cars and started a taxi service. "But he was not good at all at repairing," Colonel Paul added. He also acquired race horses and made and lost a small fortune on the race course. In his later life, Karma Paul started delivering talks on his expedition experiences at the hotels where foreigners stayed. Some offered to sponsor his travel abroad. "But my father thought it below his dignity and self-respect," said Colonel Paul. "He said, 'Why should we go? If anything happens here, this is our government. There, what is the surety?'" A fire at the family home in 1971 reduced the family to poverty and destroyed all of his mountain memorabilia. "If I had known about the offers, I would have forced my father to go," said Colonel Paul, who was away in the army at the time.

Karma Paul died an almost forgotten man in 1984. Colonel Paul retired from the army to look after her mentally challenged sister and passed away herself in 2019.

as individuals. They were counted among the pieces of equipment needed to scale a mountain. Now, however, the broad Mongolian features had started becoming identifiable. Then, during the 1924 Everest expedition, Mallory started calling those who climbed consistently better and higher than others "Tigers"—a name that stuck. Bonds that would last the next few decades were beginning to be forged. The reconnaissance expedition of 1921 cemented the Sherpas' reputation as climbers; the deaths in 1922 led to their recognition as individuals.

Toward the end of his book, Norton articulated two essentials for anyone climbing in the Himalaya. The first was a basic knowledge of the porters' language. "In addition," he wrote, "every climber should know every porter by name—here again I speak with certainty when I say that it is perfectly easy to know fifty or sixty men by name in a week or two; and more, not only must he know the men, the men must know and trust him."

This is not to say that attitudes toward the porters changed overnight. The Sherpas and Bhotias did not suddenly become friends or equals to the British. The British habit of identifying their own people as the very best and bravest while being quick to point out the inadequacies of others continued. For instance, Norton wrote of a young Sherpa, Lhakpa Tsering, after a fall: "It was indeed an instructive sight to see this superior young gentleman, who had climbed all day in excellent style and rather scoffed at our solicitude for his inexperience on snow and ice, suddenly converted into the veriest worm, clinging like a wet towel to steep ice slopes where safety is only found in an upright position." Norton described having to send down the porter Nema, who was complaining of mountain sickness: "It is wonderful how soon that strange malady, so often described as 'mountain sickness,' seems to disappear not only with descent, but when the decision to descend has been made: at any rate I have noticed it time and again with these native porters." It is worthwhile to remember at this point that only the expedition members—the British—were climbing for glory. While the porters were happy enough to push themselves as far as they could, to help the expedition achieve success, death or accidents on the mountain meant not only the end of their own lives, but incredible hardship for their families as well. It would take a long time for climbers to admit to wearing goggles tinted by prejudice. Still, acknowledging the Sherpas' names was a start.

Frank Smythe's expedition to the Valley of Flowers, Garhwal, India, in 1937. From left to right are Nurbu, Tewang, Frank Smythe, Wangdi Norbu, and Pasang. (*Frank Smythe Collection*)

BETWEEN 1924 AND THE OUTBREAK of World War II in 1939, there were at least thirteen large-scale expeditions—to Kangchenjunga, Everest, Nanga Parbat, Nanda Devi, Kamet, and Kabru—and tens of smaller explorations and travels across the Himalayan ranges. It was a busy time for the porters of Darjeeling. The population of Toong Soong swelled as more Sherpas abandoned their farms in Khumbu for the exciting possibilities that climbing and a life in Darjeeling had to offer.

Expedition accounts of this period reveal a growing familiarity as European climbers repeatedly sought out men they had climbed with earlier. Not only did the climbers over time know their porters by name, but they also came to know them as people. Foremost among these were men like Frank Smythe, Eric Shipton, and Bill Tilman, who wrote as much of the men they traveled with as of their climbs.

In 1934, Shipton and Tilman embarked on a seven-month exploration of the Kumaon-Garhwal mountains. They had three Sherpas with them, and traveled on a shoestring budget. In his autobiography, *Upon That Mountain*, anthologized with other works of Shipton's in *The Six Mountain-Travel Books*, Shipton wrote of the adventure:

> One of the things I enjoyed most was the opportunity of getting to know the Sherpas intimately, which was impossible on either of the two previous Himalayan expeditions I had known. Sharing with them the same life, the same camp fire, the same food and, later, the burden of load-carrying, we soon came to regard them as fellow mountaineers rather than servants and they felt with us the excitement of anticipation and the joy of success. We were admitted to their endless jokes and their occasional philosophical talk. We relied upon their judgment as much as upon our own.

Perhaps the most evocative sign of the changes that were happening appeared in Frank Smythe's book *The Spirit of the Hills*, published in 1935, at the end of a chapter called simply "Friendship." Smythe wrote about his first encounter with Sherpa Nima Tendrup and their growing association over several years and numerous expeditions. Sadly, Nima Tendrup likely never knew of these words that had written about him:

> It may be that you who read these lines may go one day to Darjeeling. Possibly, you may hire a rickshaw. If among those drawing it there is a broad-shouldered, solemn-faced man with a brightly polished medal suspended from his breast, you may be quite certain that it is Nima Ten-drup, the "Old Soldier." You will know that you are being drawn along by one who has been on four expeditions to Everest, two expeditions to Kangchenjunga, and expeditions to Kamet, Nanga Parbat and other of the greatest peaks in the world. You will know that beneath that polished medal and its stained and dirty ribbon, and the ragged jacket to which it is pinned, beats a brave heart, endowed with qualities of faithfulness and loyalty; a heart which responds instinctively to the call of comradeship and adventure, that exists in close communion with the noblest aspects of nature, that strives in the cause of others, upwards and onwards,

through sweat and weariness, through heat and cold, through hardship
and peril. A man to admire, respect and love as a friend.

There it is. Some wheels had slowly started turning. Could we say that
recognition had finally come to the porters? Unfortunately, there was still
some way to go. What happened next is linked to other events taking place
in the world of mountaineering. They involve a club and two remarkable
women we shall meet shortly.

EXPEDITIONS -

1924. Everest. Norton.
1929. Kanch: Bauer.
1930 " Dyrenfurth
1931 " Bauer.
1933 Everest Rutledge.
1932 Nanda Gavi "
1934 Nanga Parbat. Merkl.
1933 Lhasa Williamson
1939 Lahoul Krenek.
1952 Rathong
1952 Everest
1952 Kamet.
1953 Dhauligiri.
1954 Nepal
1955 Kulu.
1958 Chamba - Lah

Received the ade
Cross for Bravery
on Nanga Parbat

Date of Photograph. SEPT. 1958.

ANG TSERING.
H.C. No. 36.

Date of Birth 1904
Book Issued. 2 SEPT. 1958 (second)

Pages from the porter book of Ang Tsering I (*The Sherpa Project*)

CHAPTER 5

Two Women and a Club

Sherpas continued to gain recognition in the 1930s and beyond, due in large part to the efforts of two remarkable women who worked for The Himalayan Club, founded in 1928 and modeled after the Alpine Club founded nearly three-quarters of a century earlier. On the Alpine Club's 150th anniversary, George Band, an eminent mountaineer and president of the club, wrote, "The first half of the 1860s proved to be a golden age for the Club, when many alpine peaks were climbed for the first time. Leslie Stephen, President 1866–68, famously asserted, 'The number of unaccomplished feats may be reckoned on the fingers.' It was time to look further afield, to what we now term the Greater Ranges. Early choices were the Pyrenees, the Caucasus, Norway, the Rockies, and the Southern Alps of New Zealand. But the highest of all was the Greater Himalaya and its adjacent ranges."

From the late nineteenth to the first decade of the twentieth century, a flurry of activity brought Western explorers to the Himalaya for the first time. After World War I, the climbers returned in larger numbers. During the 1920s and 1930s, large expeditions dominated British climbing, but people like Eric Shipton and Bill Tilman proved that cheap and small expeditions, using local porters, could also accomplish a great deal.

The time was now ripe for a club to be established in the very lap of the Himalaya. Not one but two mountaineering clubs cropped up almost simultaneously: the Mountain Club in Kolkata and The Himalayan Club (THC) in Simla, in the northern state of Himachal Pradesh. Both clubs were started by British explorers, hunters, and adventurers. The first meeting of

The Himalayan Club took place in Delhi on February 17, 1928, and at this meeting club members decided to invite the Mountain Club to amalgamate with it, a proposal that was accepted. The first Annual General Meeting of this united Himalayan Club took place in February 1929. Out of 250 members, the sole Indian on the rolls was the King of Jubbal, a principality in Himachal Pradesh.

Sir Geoffrey L. Corbett, the first honorary secretary of the club, wrote in the 1929 introductory volume of *The Himalayan Journal*, "The idea must have occurred to many but it never took shape, not because a Club was not wanted, but because in this land of endlessness it is only now and then that the two or three are gathered together." Sir Corbett went on to pay a generous tribute to the Alpine Club, from which The Himalayan Club's objectives had been adapted: *To encourage and assist Himalayan travel and exploration, and to extend the knowledge of the Himalaya and adjoining ranges through science, art, literature, and sport.*

He continued, "We owe much to the Alpine Club, and in particular to Colonel E. L. Strutt, the editor of the *Alpine Journal*, who is also one of our founder members . . . Members of the Alpine Club who come to the Himalaya may be sure of a warm welcome and all the assistance that [The] Himalayan Club can give." Sir Geoffrey concluded his piece saying:

> And so [The] Himalayan Club is founded, and we hope great things of it: the geographer that the blank places on his map may be filled in; the scientist that our knowledge of the Himalaya, its rocks and glaciers, its animals and plants, its peoples and their way of living, may continually expand; the artist that its glories may inspire fine pictures. The mountaineer may dream of the first ascent of a thousand unclimbed peaks, the shikari [hunter] of record heads shot in nalas [ravines] yet unknown. My own hope is that it may help to rear a breed of men in India, hard and self-reliant, who will know how to enjoy life on the high hills.

How prophetic these words were, in a way that Corbett could never have dreamt. The Himalayan Club did very much rear a breed of such men. They were the hardy Sherpas based in Darjeeling who in the years to come would forge a lasting connection with this club.

By this time, important peaks had come to be associated with certain nationalities. Mount Everest belonged to the British, and Nanga Parbat became known as the German mountain. Nanga Parbat, meaning "Naked Mountain" in Hindi and Urdu, is at 8,126 meters the ninth-highest mountain in the world. After a German attempt in 1932 under the leadership of Willi Merkl—an engineer by profession and an avid mountaineer—in which the local Balti and Hunza porters were blamed for the ascent's failure, the Germans returned to Nanga Parbat in 1934, again with Merkl as their leader. This time, Merkl decided that the services of the Tigers of Darjeeling "had to be secured at all costs in order to avoid the disappointments of 1932." He arranged with The Himalayan Club for the supply of thirty-five Sherpa and Bhutia porters. Despite the presence of the Sherpas, the expedition turned into a nightmare. Four climbers, including Merkl, and six porters died on the slopes; some of the Sherpas still hung on the ropes. It was said that Sherpa Gaylay could have saved himself, but chose to stay and perish with Merkl.

A nine-member German team returned to Nanga Parbat in 1937. Eleven Darjeeling Sherpas were recruited under the leadership of Sardar Nursang, including Jigmi and Pasang "Picture" Norbu, both of whom had also been on the 1934 expedition. The disaster that struck this expedition was even larger than the one before. While sixteen people were fast asleep at Camp 4 on June 14, a massive serac broke off 300 meters above them and buried the tents. No one escaped alive.

Jigmi, Pasang "Picture" Norbu and his brother Mingma Tsering, Gyalzen Monjo III, Karmi, Nima Tsering, Nim Tsering, Pintso Norbu, Ang Tsering II, and Chong Karma perished. Only two Sherpas survived: the veteran Sardar Nursang and Man Bahadur Sherpa. When Pasang "Picture" Norbu was discovered beneath ten feet of ice, he was lying peacefully in his sleeping bag. Death had caught all the climbers unaware. On the advice of Nursang, the search was suspended for the rest of the porters—he suggested that it would be more in keeping with their faith to let them rest where they had fallen.

Out of the terrible events on Nanga Parbat arose two initiatives that were to prove extremely beneficial to the Sherpas: the issuing of porter books (also known as chit books), and a few years later the awarding of Tiger Badges, bestowed on exceptional Sherpas. THC members Joan Townend and Jill Henderson were to play an important role in formalizing these practices. Although the women are now remembered as "a fascinating footnote" in mountaineering history, they meant much more in the Sherpas' lives, and they found a permanent place in their hearts.

Joan Townend

Lettice Joan Bevington was born in Essex in 1892. She married Herbert Townend of the Indian Civil Service (ICS) in August 1913, and soon after they sailed for India. Herbert's work took him between Kolkata and the country districts in West Bengal. Joan Townend loved the mountains. She was an avid trekker and took a keen interest in the work of the botanists busy identifying all the species of flora in the Sikkim Himalaya.

Joan Townend was elected to The Himalayan Club in 1933, and became honorary secretary in 1934. She served for seven years on the Committee of the Club, and was vice president from 1939 to 1940. Club members in those years were regaled with the lectures and dinners that she arranged in the Lawn House of the stately United Services Club in the Chowringhee neighborhood of Kolkata, enabling members to meet visiting expeditions from all parts of the world. Climbers who passed through the city partook of her

Wangdi Norbu

The renowned porter Wangdi Norbu's illustrious career encompassed many of the early-twentieth-century expeditions to the great Himalayan peaks: Kangchenjunga in 1930; Kamet in 1931; Fluted Peak in 1932; Everest in 1933, 1936, and 1938; Nanga Parbat in 1934; and several expeditions to the Garhwal and Assam. His porter book is filled with glowing testimonials from some of the biggest names of the time, like these two from the British climbers Frank Smythe and Hugh Ruttledge:

> Wangdi Nurbu accompanied the 1931 Kamet expedition. On this he did excellent work and carried to the highest camp at 23200 ft. He is a tremendous worker and thoroughly trustworthy in every way. He sets a splendid example by his tenacity of purpose under the most adverse circumstances.
>
> —F. S. Smythe

> A real "stilt." Nearly died of pneumonia at the Base Camp, but turned up for work the moment he could. A hard case who will work splendidly for those who understand him, but he wants holding. Very strong.
>
> —Hugh Ruttledge, Leader, Everest 1933

In 1947, Norbu's career was cut short at the peak of his prowess by a horrific accident on Kedarnath (6,940 meters) in India. It was the first post-war Swiss expedition to explore the southwest part of the Garhwal Himalaya, and Wangdi was the Sherpa sardar. He fell while approaching the summit and slipped down an icy slope, carrying his ropemate, Alfred Sutter, with him. Their fall was arrested when the slope eased off but Wangdi suffered a broken leg, a fractured skull, and a knee severely damaged by the point of a crampon. The other climbers were unable to bring him down that day, so they injected him with morphine and left him bivouacked on an ice bridge just inside a crevasse.

A rescue team sent up the next day was unable to locate him. When the Swiss climber René Dittert along with the Sherpas Tenzing Norgay and Ang Norbu finally reached Wangdi a day later, they discovered a horrible sight. Thinking himself abandoned, in terrible pain, thirsty, and hungry, Wangdi had cut his own throat. There was blood everywhere, but he was alive. In an epic effort, the team first dragged then slid Wangdi down, and finally the Sherpas carried him to basecamp. Wangdi recovered from this accident but was never able to climb again.

Wangdi Norbu's son Dawa Tsering recalled that a year or two later Andre Roch and other members of the expedition came to Darjeeling. They brought with them an expedition documentary made using footage filmed during the climb. Dawa remembered seeing the film at The Everest Hotel though its name escaped him. He did remember, however, that Roch gave his father a table clock and him some chocolates. Upon returning from other expeditions, Dawa Tsering told us, his father sometimes brought home good boots or a sleeping bag or leftover fruit. Other than food, everything else was soon sold because the family needed the money.

Dawa proudly showed us the relics left from his father's career: a Tiger Badge, a porter book, a few letters, and a single photograph. When his father died, in 1952, Dawa was eleven. "After my father died, my mother burned everything. Even my father's pictures," he said, noting that this is a Tibetan custom. When we met him at Dorjee Lhatoo's house, he had just entrusted his precious legacy to Lhatoo. He told us, "I gave all this material to Lhatoo because I want it to be displayed in the HMI mountaineering museum. It is very valuable."

The porter book is the key. It helps build the story of who Sherpas such as Wangdi Norbu were. It reveals how they were perceived by the men they carried loads for, and provides a résumé of sorts of their careers.

hospitality and her unstinting help with their arrangements. It was largely due to her enthusiasm that the club thrived to such a remarkable degree in those pre–World War II years.

The Nanga Parbat tragedy in 1934 deeply distressed Townend. The Himalayan Club held a service of remembrance. Though Townend was keen that individual Sherpas be suitably honored, she was unable to find any details about their careers. She quickly realized how important it was to compile a record of all the Darjeeling porters, and her work was reported on in the Club Proceedings published in volume 7 of *The Himalayan Journal* in 1935: "The compilation of a register of Darjeeling porters has been begun and is going forward as information is collected. In conjunction with this, 'chit books' are being prepared to issue to each man whose name is on the register. The books are small with a photograph of the owner on the first page and each is wrapped in a mackintosh wallet."

Leaders were expected to review the work of each porter at the end of their expedition and write a brief note on the porter's performance in his chit book. They also wrote testimonials for porters who had been with them on previous expeditions. The books would serve as a record of employment and as a reference guide for future employers, while also providing an incentive to porters to do their best. General Bruce arrived in Darjeeling in December 1934 to throw a feast for his old friends and distribute the new porter books, but the person behind it all was Joan Townend. She wrote on The Himalayan Club register that there are "about an equal number of Sherpas and Bhotias, or true Tibetans. Both nationalities have distinguished themselves on mountaineering expeditions, and it would be impossible to say that one has outdone the other."

THE START OF WORLD WAR II inevitably meant a suspension of large expeditions, but volume 12 of *THJ* appeared in 1940 with a note by Joan Townend on the creation of Tiger Badges for Sherpas. The tragedy on Nanga Parbat in 1937 was still fresh in people's minds, and perhaps had something to do with this decision. George Mallory had coined the name "Tigers" for Sherpas who went high during the 1924 Everest expedition. It was now felt that the strongest and most skilled Sherpas should be identified and rewarded with better pay, which was to apply only when their special skills were required; otherwise, these higher rates might preclude them from getting employment on ordinary expeditions. These specially selected Sherpas would be officially called "Tigers" and awarded Tiger Badges. The Himalayan Club Committee was to take great pains in the years to come to ensure that the correct porters got the badges.

Herbert Townend retired from the ICS in 1942, and the couple left India. However, Joan's connection with the club was not severed. After returning to England, she became assistant editor of *The Himalayan Journal* in 1947, a position she held until 1949. She passed away on November 20, 1966, at the age of seventy-four. In a heartfelt obituary in 1966, THC President CEJ Crawford (1948–1953) wrote, "Much of Joan's interest centred round the Sherpas. 'Towney memsahib' was concerned with them as people, for their livelihood and welfare, and at the same time strove to see that the standard of 'Club Porters' was kept high. (The Porters) Register was a work of loving care, for it was compiled in her own hand, with a photograph and a climbing record of each man."

During the time that Mrs. Townend was secretary, The Himalayan Club became the fulcrum for mountaineering in the Himalaya. The club not only assisted in the hiring of Sherpa and Bhutia porters for large expeditions, but also provided information and informal liaison services with regard to government policies, permissions, and customs regulations. Foreign climbers swelled the club's membership list, and the organization even had a representative on the British Mount Everest Committee.

After World War II ended, expeditions slowly started to return to the Himalaya. In March 1950, THC local secretary Ludwig Krenek compiled a list of 175 Sherpa porters, with each man's, name, date of birth, unique Himalayan Club number (for easy identification), main expeditions, and relevant remarks. After Joan Townend's handwritten porter register, Krenek's list was—and has remained—the only other attempt to enumerate the climbing Sherpas of Darjeeling.

Jill Henderson

Nine years after Joan Townend left India, another woman took center stage in the lives of the Sherpas of Darjeeling. In 1951, Jill Henderson became THC honorary local secretary, Darjeeling, a post that she held for six years. It was a heady time, when Europeans were "knocking off" 8,000-meter peaks, and the Henderson home—then known as the Rungneet Tea Estate—became the center of Himalayan mountaineering. The croquet lawn was always filled with containers—loads and rations to be packed or unpacked—while sheds were constructed for porters to live in and work from, prior to leaving on expeditions. The Henderson bungalow was perched among the tea gardens on the side of a steep ridge. From the lawn in front of the house, when it was clear, you could see Kangchenjunga, seventy-four kilometers away as the crow flies.

Jill Henderson became a friend of the Sherpas. She recognized and encouraged individual talents, helped women run home businesses, and was ready to listen to any problem small or big. Ang Tsering once said, "Mrs. Henderson was a very good lady. Once a week she would come and see everybody—every Sherpa house—and ask how everyone was. And if anyone was sick, she would arrange for a doctor. For a long time, every Sherpa house would have a picture of her in their homes."

Ang Tharkay and his wife, Ang Yangje, were close friends of Jill's, as were Tenzing Norgay and his wife, Ang Lhamu. Trevor Braham, a British mountaineer and active member of THC, wrote, "I am certain that without Jill Henderson's gentle but wise persuasion Tenzing would not have agreed to join the 1953 Everest expedition, finding himself utterly spent both physically and in spirit after two determined attempts to climb Everest with the Swiss in 1952."

Tenzing had set his heart on climbing Everest with his good friend, the legendary mountaineer Raymond Lambert, and the Swiss expeditions of 1952. In the first attempt, the two had come tantalizingly close to the summit, while the second, post-monsoon expedition had to be aborted due to intensely cold weather conditions. On that latter expedition, Tenzing lost sixteen pounds on his thin frame and was racked with fever afterward as he lay convalescing in a hospital bed in Patna, India. While there he got a letter from Major Charles Wylie inviting him to go on a new British expedition to Everest the following year, led by John Hunt. Tenzing was inclined to refuse, while his wife, Ang Lahmu, presented a formidable barrier between her husband and anyone who would tax his fragile health.

Jill Henderson was the only person in the world who could break down the resistance. She plied the climber with Ovaltine until he regained his strength, knitted him a warm jersey, took him to the doctor for vitamins, and convinced him that he would get the best advantage, payment-wise, for his fellow Sherpas if he went as sardar. He negotiated a spot on the summit team as a condition for acceptance, and the rest as they say, is history. On

May 29, 1953, Tenzing wore the sweater Mrs. Henderson had knitted when he stood on the summit with the New Zealand beekeeper Edmund Hillary and picked up a stone for her from the top. Around his neck, he wore the red scarf belonging to Raymond Lambert—a tribute to the man who deserved a place by his side.

In January 1954, Jill Henderson organized a tea party for all the Everest 1953 Sherpas, their wives, and families, at which THC President Charles Crawford, representing the Queen of England, presented Coronation Medals to twenty-two select Sherpas who had carried loads to the South Col. In addition, twelve Sherpas were awarded the coveted Tiger Badge for outstanding service during the expeditions of 1952 and 1953.

Jill Henderson left India in 1958 upon her husband's retirement. After a short spell in East Africa, she and her husband returned to England. It is said that Ang Tharkay gifted Mrs. Henderson the Lhasa apso, Jiggy, that she took back with her. Jill Henderson finally settled in America, where she died in 1991.

A Club Transformed

The last few years of Mrs. Henderson's time in Darjeeling before her departure in 1958 coincided with many events that impacted the fortune of the Sherpas and consequently the importance of The Himalayan Club. Wrote Trevor Braham, in a letter to *THJ*, "By then a big change was on the way with the opening up of Nepal, the migration of Sherpas to the new center for expeditions in Kathmandu, and the dissolution of the Club's activities in Darjeeling as a recruiting agency for Sherpas. Of course, a few Sherpas never left Darjeeling, such as Tenzing, Pasang Dawa, even Ang Tharkay, who stayed until the end of the 1950s; and many others, encouraged by the establishment of the HMI." THC had begun a transitional phase during which three things happened that, while of advantage to the mountaineering world in general, diminished the importance of THC in Darjeeling, in its current avatar.

The first thing was the change in recruiting procedures. In 1954, *THJ* announced in the section on Club Proceedings and Notes:

> It will be of interest to members to know that in addition to Tensing Norkay, G. M., the following climbing Sardars will assist in arranging teams if applied to direct:

1. Ang Tharkay Sardar, 'West View,' Clark Road, Darjeeling.
2. Angtsering Sardar, Toong Soong Busti, Darjeeling.
3. Ajeeba Sardar, Toong Soong Busti, Darjeeling.
4. Gyalzen Mikchen Sardar, Toong Soong Busti, Darjeeling.
5. Pasang Dawa Lama, 'West View', Clark Road, Darjeeling.

As it was never the intention of the Club that the Honorary Local Secretary in Darjeeling should permanently become responsible for organizing
Sherpa porters for expeditions and as there are now Sherpa *sardars* able
themselves to accept this responsibility, the Committee recommends that
even when the Darjeeling Local Secretary is available, members should
apply direct to the *sardars*. The Darjeeling Local Secretary will continue
to maintain the Club's register of porters and will always be glad to ren-
der advice and assistance to members.

The Sherpas of Darjeeling post-1953 had discovered their ability to
take charge. Instead of THC, which often worked as a representative of the
sahabs, negotiating terms suited to *them*, the Sherpa Climbers' Association
was set up, led by Tenzing Norgay, to look out for Sherpa interests. This
organization negotiated better compensation for and financially supported
Sherpas in times of need.

Additionally, *The Statesman* newspaper of Kolkata had set up a fund to
help Tenzing Norgay build a house in Darjeeling, and it had been oversub-
scribed. After some of the money was used to pay for the house, the balance
was put into a Sherpa Trust, administrated by THC. But now this money,
along with all the papers relating to the running of the trust, was transferred
to the Sherpa Climbers' Association.

The second event that lessened the club's influence was the establishment, in 1954, of the Darjeeling-based climbing school, the Himalayan
Mountaineering Institute (HMI). Each year, the HMI ran both Basic and
Advanced courses, charging only moderate fees. It soon began to turn out a
steady stream of well-trained climbers who would change the character of
mountaineering in India. Within a decade, two other climbing institutions—
the Nehru Institute of Mountaineering (NIM) and the Western Himalayan
Mountaineering Institute (now called ABVIMAS)—were also set up in the
northern hill towns of Uttarkashi and Manali, respectively. These three

institutions had a considerable influence on mountaineering, and a community of mountaineers developed who did not feel the need to join THC.

The third factor was the founding of the Indian Mountaineering Foundation (IMF) in 1961. With the object of organizing mountaineering expeditions, encouraging the indigenous manufacture of equipment, and rewarding and helping Indian mountaineers, the IMF became the government of India's representative body to grant permissions for expeditions, provide liaison officers, and offer logistical support.

With this development, the final link in the formal chain between the Darjeeling Sherpas and THC was severed. The relationship did not end but was rather transformed. The Himalayan Club was no longer involved in expeditions, but its role as a repository of information on the Himalaya now assumed vital importance. It was just as well. In its earliest form, when the glories of this club were sung, it was essentially an extension of the Alpine Club. The work THC did and decisions it took, while pushing forward the boundaries of mountaineering, reflected its origins as a British club in a colonial setting. The events that occasioned changes in THC helped it transition into a truly independent club in an independent India.

The Sherpas of Darjeeling always found friends and mentors in THC. Discontinued after 1965, the Tiger Badge was reimagined as the Garud Medal for outstanding support staff; it is as coveted today by contemporary climbers of Darjeeling as the Tiger Badge once was by their forebears.

PART TWO

The Age of the Tigers

Ang Tharkay with his fellow instructors at the Himalayan Mountaineering Institute in 1954. From left to right are Nawang Topgay, Gyalzen Mikchen, Ang Tharkay, Principal Nandu Jayal, Tenzing Norgay, Da Namgyal, Ang Temba, and Nawang Gombu. (*Himalayan Mountaineering Institute Collection*)

CHAPTER 6

Big Little Man: Ang Tharkay

Perched on an outcrop, jutting out over a steep drop that eased into the forest below, was a tarpaulin that Ang Tharkay had fashioned into a tent, secured with climbers' knots against the wind and rain. One morning, when his wife, Ang Yangje, was inside the tent cooking breakfast, the flap lifted and a grinning, handsome face peeped in. "Yangje la, I brought you some rakshi and momos from Darjeeling. Daku sent them." It was Tenzing Norgay, with a gift from his wife on his way to the HMI basecamp in Sikkim, where field training took place. Tenzing dropped the packet and marched on, not listening as Yangje shouted after him, "How are my boys?" But she could hear the unkind laughter when he said something to the other HMI instructors as they walked by.

It had not always been like this. There was a time when Tenzing's previous wife, Ang Lahmu, would have visited Yangje bearing eggs as a gift, to ask whether Ang Tharkay had any jobs for her husband. But the tide had turned and Ang Tharkay, acknowledged by most climbers as the greatest Sherpa of his time, was now an impoverished road contractor. His wife accompanied him on his job in distant Sikkim while their four children were left in the care of others in Darjeeling.

OUR STORY BEGINS WITH A rickety ride, in 2012, in an old SUV taxi. Whatever could fall off already had, never to be replaced. On the way to the airport at Bagdogra to catch our flight back to Mumbai, we stopped at Tenzing

Tharkay's house in Siliguri. After thirty years of teaching the Nepalese language in Japan, he had retired to this quiet cottage a few hours from Darjeeling. We had many questions, but all would have to wait as the oldest son of the legendary Ang Tharkay showed us around his garden and then fed us a pretty Japanese meal.

We said to him, "Your father was one of the greatest."

He responded, "He was always on expeditions, and they were always unsuccessful."

What struck us most, as we went over the meeting later, was how little Tenzing Tharkay knew about his father. He had talked a lot, but like many children of those early porters, his tales of valor featured his strong mother, not his absent father. We tried our best to piece together a narrative of this legendary couple using the information we had.

When we began to research Ang Tharkay, we heard about his autobiography, written in French: *Ang Thrace, Memoirs d'un Sherpa*. A frantic search for it led nowhere, until a chance email from M. Laurent Padoux in France on quite another matter had us sending this kind gentleman in search of the elusive book. He found a copy in a public library and obligingly made several trips there to send us a detailed synopsis. Subsequently, we managed to source a secondhand copy of the publication and commissioned a working translation. Imagine our delight when just a few months later we heard that an English translation had been published.

Ang Tharkay was born in 1907, in the small village of Kunde, close to the monastery of Thyangboche in Khumbu. He was the eldest of three sons. The family was considered poor even by the conditions of this spare, windswept region, and so his parents sent six-year-old Tharkay to live with an aunt across the Tibetan border. The boy had a wonderful few years with his beloved aunt, but when he turned twelve, his father brought him back home to work for the family. Ang Tharkay tended goats and cows, spending the whole day on the mountain slopes alongside rushing torrents and deep ravines. He watched Thyangboche Monastery being built and watched traders carry loads of wool across the high passes into Tibet. Ang Tharkay also encountered young men returning from expeditions, and was hypnotized by their tales of adventure. Finally, in May 1932, at the age of twenty-five, he ran away to Darjeeling.

Ang Yangje was born in Namche Bazaar and spent her youth in Khumbu. Although she'd encountered Ang Tharkay in Kunde, they had not become acquainted; coincidentally, she arrived in Darjeeling a week after he did. The two fell in love and were married shortly thereafter.

Ang Tharkay's expedition life over the next few decades was peerless, not only because of the number of formidable peaks he went to but because of the value he brought to each expedition. In 1933, he went on his first significant expedition, with Hugh Ruttledge to Everest. Writing about the bitter cold and extreme wind conditions at Camp V, Ruttledge noted that every one of the eight porters was frostbitten. As Ruttledge wrote in *Attack on Everest*, "Only one, the great-hearted little Ang Tarke, ever went high again." In 1934, Tharkay accompanied Eric Shipton and Bill Tilman on the fabled Nanda Devi exploration (in the Northern Indian state of Uttarakhand). During the expedition, the Sherpa formed a lasting bond of friendship with the two Britishers.

In *Upon That Mountain*, from the anthology *The Six Mountain-Travel Books*, Shipton writes of Ang Tharkay:

> He was small even for a Sherpa, but very well built. We soon learned to value his rare qualities which made him outstandingly the best of all the Sherpas I have known. He had a shrewd judgement both of men and of situations, and was absolutely steady in any crisis. He was a most lovable person, modest, unselfish and completely sincere, with an infectious gaiety of spirit. He has been with me on all my subsequent journeys to the Himalaya, and to him I owe a large measure of their success and much of my enjoyment.

The 1934 exploration was to be historic. The men found a way through the steep and narrow Rishi Ganga Gorge into the Nanda Devi Sanctuary, and discovered a way to climb the mountain. Several expeditions, from as early as 1883, had tried to find a way into the basin but failed, until Shipton and Tilman with their small band of Sherpas discovered the route that opened the beautiful area for other adventurers.

The team went back to continue their exploration post-monsoon that year, and when Tharkay returned to Darjeeling, he learned of the horrifying tragedy that had befallen his fellow Sherpas on Nanga Parbat. In his autobiography, *Sherpa: The Memoir of Ang Tharkay*, he wrote, "I would have been on the German expedition with my friends if Mr. Shipton had not taken us to Nandadevi." The explorations of 1934 paved the way for the first successful climb to Nanda Devi's summit in 1936 by Tilman and Noel Odell.

In these early years while Ang Tharkay was consolidating his life as a mountaineer, Ang Yangje and he had five children. The oldest was a girl called Ongmu. Tenzing was the next, followed by Sonam, Lhakpa, and Dawa. We learned that after Ongmu there was another daughter. "I have no memory," said Tenzing Tharkay. "She passed away when I was small." Tenzing Tharkay recalled that Tenzing Norgay and his father had a good relationship when he was young. When Ang Tharkay named his son Tenzing, Tenzing Norgay affectionately called the little boy "Ming Daw," which means "one of the same name." He also gifted the Tharkays a puppy that he brought back from Tibet—a little black Lhasa apso called Ghariya Ghazan.

In 1939, at age thirty-one, Ang Tharkay was one of the first Sherpas to receive the coveted Tiger Badge—official recognition of his stature as a porter. He bore his Himalayan Club identity—HC no. 19—proudly. For the next few years, however, the horrors of World War II brought life in the mountains to a standstill. Times were tough for all the Sherpas during the war years and after. They scratched out a living wherever they could, some going back to farming and a few joining the British Army. An enterprising Ang Tharkay began to advertise as an agent, providing ponies, cooks, and porters for treks and explorations.

In 1950, as countries began slowly getting back on their feet and as people wanted to put visions of death and fascism behind them, Maurice Herzog came to the Himalaya with his French team to attempt Annapurna. Ang Tharkay was the sardar. His dearest friends Aila, Ang Dawa, Ang Tsering, Dawa Thondup, Sarki, Phu Tharkay, and Ajeeba were part of the team. In

Ang Tharkay's Advertisement in *The Himalayan Journal* in 1946

The following notice is published at the request of Angtharkay. (For the many who desire to make the most of a short time in Sikkim his services as Sirdar may be called invaluable):

Travellers wishing me to make arrangements for them for transport and/or servants for touring in Sikkim or Tibet are requested to supply the following information:

Particulars.

(i) Route proposed, or area to be visited.

(ii) Itinerary and starting-point.

(iii) Whether using Dak Bungalows or tents.

(iv) Total weight of kit and transport requirements, i.e., riding ponies, mules or coolies.

(v) Number of party, including personal servants if any.

(vi) Whether cook, tiffin coolie or sweeper required.

Rates. Travellers are advised that the rates will be as follows:

(i) Riding pony Rs. 10 per day.

(ii) Transport mules Rs. 6 per day.

(iii) Cook Rs. 5 per day.

(iv) Coolie Rs. 3 per day.

(v) Sweeper Rs. 3 to Rs. 3-4 per day.

These rates are subject to fluctuations, which will be notified in advance. Half rates will be charged for transport returning unladen. There will be a 25 per cent, extra charge for days spent above the snow-line.

Passes. Travellers are advised to apply at least one month in advance for Dak Bungalow passes from the Deputy Commissioner, Darjeeling. It will also be necessary to obtain from the Political Officer in Sikkim, Gangtok, Sikkim frontier passes for each member of the party, and, if visiting Tibet, special permits to enter Tibet. These should also be applied for from one to two months in advance of the starting date. If it is intended to leave the "beaten track" (Dak Bungalow routes), or cross the frontier into Tibet, the Political Officer will require a medical certificate in the form to be obtained from him.

Food. Very few supplies are available in Sikkim or Tibet and practically none at all off the beaten track. It is, therefore, advisable to supplement tinned and other ordinary stores with a supply of fresh vegetables, eggs, butter, flour and a few chickens, which will be arranged for from Darjeeling or Gangtok if required, at the current market rates. The above-quoted rates for coolies, ponies, &c. are inclusive of food along the Dak Bungalow routes, but extra food for them will be required for portions of the journey beyond the beaten track plus the additional transport involved. The extra food will be arranged by me, if desired, at the current market rates.

Correspondence. During my absence, correspondence addressed to me in Darjeeling will be dealt with by my wife, Ang Yang Tsen. Telegrams may be addressed to me: Angtharkay, Bhutia Basti, Darjeeling.

Angtharkay Sirdar,
Lama Villa,
Bhutia Basti, Darjeeling.

Ang Tharkay (seated) and Jack Henderson *(Photo by Jill Henderson)*

Ang Tharkay's autobiography when he talks about the walk in, the landscape, and finally the summit that rendered the Frenchmen frostbitten and led to a stupendous retreat from the mountain, it is a story simply told. Tharkay was offered a go at the summit by Herzog, who, as he wrote in *Annapurna*, said, "You are the Sirdar and the most experienced of all the Sherpas. I should be very glad if you will come with us?" Ang Tharkay replied, "Thank you very much, Bara Sahib, but my feet are beginning to freeze . . . and I prefer to go down to Camp IV."

   Annapurna was the first 8,000er to be climbed, but the team paid dearly for this accomplishment. Tharkay headed a group of outstanding Sherpas who brought the members back barely alive, carrying the severely frostbit-ten climbers on their backs most of the way. His feat earned him the French Legion of Honor, making him the first and perhaps only Sherpa to receive the award.

The success of Annapurna ended with Ang Tharkay being invited to Paris, where he was feted and entertained by the expedition members and their families. They showed him the city, including a memorable visit to the Folies Bergère. Dorjee Lhatoo, who met some of the climbers years later, said that he was told that those who were present spent the entire performance watching Ang Tharkay's astonishment and delight. Indeed, Tharkay wrote in his autobiography, "When I later described certain scenes in the show to my Sherpa countrymen, they could do nothing but laugh incredulously as if these were fairy tales or stories that I had invented. Bangdel explained to me that Paris is a city of pleasure and the Folies Bergère is its Temple. I too was intoxicated by the seductive spectacle." Tharkay's connection to France would later become stronger when his younger son, Dawa, married a Frenchwoman and went to live in that country.

In 2016, a journalist, Saprina Panday, interviewed Ang Tharkay's grandson, Renaud, who shared a lovely story with her. As a child, he would travel with his father from France to visit his grandfather in Nepal. Once, he chanced upon a copy of *Tintin in Tibet*, and it suddenly dawned on him that the Sherpa in Hergé's book was his grandfather! He was even called Tharkey and wore the same hat!

Panday wrote in her article that Hergé, the pen name of the Belgian creator of the series, did not have any pictures of Sherpas. It was only after Annapurna, when Ang Tharkay was received in France, that Tharkey, the loyal Sherpa who helps Tintin as he searches for his Chinese friend, came to life. *Tintin in Tibet* went on to become one of Hergé's biggest successes, with many calling it his most profound story of friendship and love.

IN 1951, THARKAY WAS ON his fifth expedition to Everest when he met his old friend Eric Shipton, twelve years after their last encounter. Wrote Shipton of the meeting, "He had cut off the handsome pigtail and his clothes were distressingly smart but I was relieved to find the same quiet reticence and the same quiet humor that I remembered so well. There was no sign of dissipation and he looked no older; indeed, he had changed remarkably little in the last twelve years."

Of course, 1953 was the year that changed many things. Everest was climbed, and the brilliant Tenzing Norgay became an overnight celebrity. The HMI was set up to impart the craft of mountaineering, and its first instructors were sent to the Swiss Alps for specialized training under the tutelage of Arnold Glatthard. Ang Tharkay was one of this select group. Although senior to Tenzing Norgay, he accepted his role of head instructor, while Tenzing was made director of field training—Tharkay's boss. Things between the two soon soured. As Lhatoo reminisced about a visit to Kathmandu many years later:

> Every evening at the table Tenzing Tharkay's mom would tell me about her days in HMI. She would laugh as she spoke, but there was frustration, anger, disapproval, and sadness on how they were evicted [from the HMI]. There were personality clashes between Ang Tharkay and Tenzing Norgay. Tenzing used crude ways to show contempt for Tharkay. [Tharkay] wanted to leave rather than remain there and fight a losing battle. [She'd say,] "We left the HMI with my four kids." Whatever money Tharkay had was dwindling, and there was no income.

Ang Tharkay HC No. 19: Expedition List

- Kangchenjunga (Paul Bauer), 1931
- Everest: (Hugh Ruttledge) 1933; (Eric Shipton/Tenzing Norgay's first expedition) 1935; (Hugh Ruttledge) 1936; (Bill Tilman) 1938; (Eric Shipton) 1951; (with Indian team) 1962
- Nanda Devi (Eric Shipton/Bill Tilman; he was first made sardar), 1934
- Garhwal (Gordon Osmanston), 1936
- Shaksgam, Karakoram (Eric Shipton), 1937
- Karakoram (Eric Shipton), 1939
- Chomiomo and Pauhunri (T. H. Tilly and Wilfrid Noyce), 1945
- Kangchenjau, 1949
- Annapurna (Maurice Herzog), 1950
- Cho Oyu (Eric Shipton), 1952
- Nun (Claude Kogan and others), 1953
- Dhaulagiri (André Roch), 1953
- Kamet (Major Nandu Jayal), 1955
- Makalu (William Siri), 1954
- Annapurna Sanctuary, 1975
- Dhaulagiri, 1978

[Ang Yangje] was a dynamic woman—the Chogyal [of Sikkim], Palden Thondup Namgyal, had studied in Darjeeling and was known to the family, so she managed to get an audience with him. Comfortable from all those years of prostrating before the gods, she went down on her knees, face down: "My husband, Ang Tharkay, is out of a job; I have four children and I put my fate at your feet."

The Chogyal was moved by her plight and promised to help. He got Ang Tharkay a licence to be a road contractor, and he was given the task of building the Teesta Malli–Yoksum road. He used to set [up] a camp with a tarpaulin—they would cook and live there on the roadside. Yangje was looking after her husband, cooking for him, staying with him in the shack. They would see the HMI courses pass by. "We were on the roadside. Living like beggars. The instructors would pass by with their mountain gear. They thought we were finished. Tenzing Norgay would pass grinning"—she would say all this, laughing.

Tenzing Tharkay told us, "Tenzing [Norgay] totally changed after he became rich and famous. He did not get along with friends, family, relatives. My father thought it would be better if he worked somewhere else. He left the job and worked in Sikkim and then came to Nepal." Tenzing Tharkay's younger brother Dawa too had memories. He said that his father had wanted the children to study at Saint Joseph's school in Darjeeling. But as the Catholic private school was very expensive, he petitioned Prime Minister Jawaharlal Nehru to increase his salary at the HMI. Dawa recalled that the principal, Nandu Jayal, a good friend, came over one night for dinner. "Jayal told my father that Tenzing Norgay had opposed the idea. That's the reason why my father left HMI around 1957," said Dawa.

"And how did your mother cope?" we asked Tenzing Tharkay. This is when the floodgates opened and vague memories of his father gave way to clear recollections of his mother. "My mother was an amazing woman," said Tenzing Tharkay. "She would say, 'I am not afraid of anything except bad people.' She told us, 'If I stay at home, you cannot go to school. I will have a helper to cook and I will earn.'"

That brings us back to where this chapter began, after Tharkay had started his second career, as a road contractor. His son Dawa was a young boy at the time. He told us that while their parents were away, life in Darjeeling was very difficult for the children. For instance, an ice cream that cost two *annas* was a luxury. His brother Tenzing, ten years older, was in charge of the house and was very strict. "We could do nothing without his permission. If we wanted to go and see a film, he would never give us the money. We would sell copper, glass, or anything we could find [to raise money for treats]," recalled Dawa.

While life was not easy for any of the climbing Sherpas, those determined to set their children on the road to a better life had to make extremely tough decisions. Men like Tharkay, Gombu, and even Lhatoo later on worked in season and out, climbing and toiling in factories or in shops or on roads to put together a few extra rupees for a good education. Many of them lost out on precious time with their families, becoming strangers in their own homes. In Ang Tharkay's family, with Yangje also away most of the time, it must have been doubly hard on the children, the parents' absence taking an emotional and psychological toll. The climbing life was not just a fairytale of wonderful people and heroic deeds; it included poverty, neglect, and tremendous hardship that, later on, when the money came, translated into excess and dysfunctional lives.

After he launched his road-contracting business, Ang Tharkay realized he did not have a head for figures or enough experience to prepare estimates for labor and materials, so he took on a partner. When the payments came in, this man, predictably, ran away with the money. There were workers to be paid and rations to be bought. Ang Tharkay became indebted to the local shopkeeper. At this low point of their lives, the old shopkeeper took a liking to the hard-working couple. Dawa told us that the shopkeeper advised his father to keep on working. He said, "You will make a lot of money and you will pay us back." Gradually, their fortunes did improve. In five years, Ang Tharkay made enough money to build a small house in the town of Jorethang on the banks of the Rangit River. Dawa had memories of happy holidays spent there, and their mother took a few days' break from roadwork as often as she could to visit her children in Darjeeling. Lhatoo recalled:

> Mrs. Tharkay was known among Sherpas as the woman who rescued Sherpa girls from Calcutta brothels. They used to call her Bijlee ["Lightning"]. In those days, one-third of the porters were young Sherpa and Tibetan girls who used to carry for daily wages up to the basecamp. From these a few would be selected to gather firewood. The others would have to return. They made money for going up to basecamp, and for the

return they would get half pay. That was not enough for their upkeep, and they would have to wait months for the next job.

There used to be talks of these girls being trafficked in Calcutta. Traffickers were Tibetans and maybe Sherpas. Ang Tharkay's wife could not stand that; others could not either. But she did something. She had relatives who were businessmen in Kalimpong and Calcutta. She bought a police uniform, [and] spent some time looking for them with help from Nepali policemen in Calcutta [whom] she paid. She went disguised as a man to the brothels. She rescued them and brought them back.

Tenzing Tharkay recalled his mother's efforts as well, saying, "The girls were brought to Darjeeling, handcuffed. They stayed in my house and then they were sent to Nepal." After that success, Yangje went on to help other women fight for their inheritance and land. "She always wanted to help women who were underprivileged," recalled Tenzing.

Around 1962, a British gentleman whom Dawa remembered only as Mr. Weather invited Ang Tharkay and Yangje to Nepal. The company he was working for was building roads, and he offered them employment. The move was profitable for the whole family, and by 1966, Ang Tharkay acquired a sizeable tract of farmland not far from Kathmandu. He grew vegetables and tended livestock while Yangje and the children lived in a beautiful house next to the American Embassy in the heart of the city. They founded a travel agency called Nepal Trekking.

Ang Tharkay thought he had hung up his boots, but he was destined to go to Everest one more time.

In 2014, Captain Kohli, who had been a member of the 1962 Indian Everest expedition, told us, "I was appointed the Deputy Leader, and the very first thing I did was decide I must get Ang Tharkay. At that stage he was not ready to go. 'I am getting old, and I don't think I should be going to Everest again,' he said. But I was able to persuade him. When I came back to Delhi, within a few days John Dias was selected as the leader, and he too was very happy to know that Ang Tharkay would be our Sherpa sardar. Tenzing [Norgay] and I had a much longer association, and it doesn't look nice to say it, but I think as a human being Ang Tharkay was a step further than Tenzing. His face was like a rock; his strength was so much and he was so easygoing and self-sacrificing. But the main thing was that he looked upon his Sherpas like a father figure. Everybody loved him. And when he said, 'Let's go!' he would lead from the front. He was a good leader, and as a sardar he was a gem. Technically also, he was strong. If I were to name one Sherpa who was most loveable, it was Ang Tharkay."

Back in Kathmandu, Yangje came into her own. She was ever restless and feisty, and Tenzing told us that she would travel alone to Sikkim, Darjeeling, and Kolkata. She made friends everywhere and would bring home people that she met on her journeys or even at bus stops.

When the Hendersons left India, the two women stayed in touch, and Mrs. Henderson came to visit Yangje in Kathmandu. Doubling up with laughter, Tenzing told us that on one of those days, the two women squatted side-by-side in the garden to pee. His mother, ever unconventional and irreverent, had convinced Jill Henderson that it was absolutely a fun thing to do!

Ang Tharkay took part in two final expeditions. In 1975, he took a party to the Annapurna Sanctuary, and in 1978, at the age of seventy, he was named sardar of the French expedition to Dhaulagiri. Nonetheless, despite all his time in the mountains, Ang Tharkay, recalled Dawa, "never talked to us about the mountains. We just overheard when he talked to others." Dorjee Lhatoo spoke with deep respect: "He was a Sherpa leader. He was a good friend, good company, good organizer, good cook."

Ang Tharkay succumbed to cancer on July 27, 1981, at the age of seventy-four. In an obituary published in volume 39 of *The Himalayan Journal*, Trevor Braham wrote:

> Ang Tharkay accompanied me on two of my journeys in Sikkim over 30 years ago. It was his enthusiasm and ability that provided the main driving force. And I learnt much about human relationships by watching the way in which he treated his men, and witnessing their respect and affection for him. He was a man of the highest integrity.

After his death, Ang Tharkay's farm lay neglected. Then a landslide claimed the family farm—everything, entire forests and fields, disappeared. The family donated whatever was left to a gompa. The fertile farmland was reduced to exposed rocks.

Ten years later, Ang Yangje died after a fall in her home. With the couple gone, not one, but two unforgettable people were taken from this world.

The flamboyant Pasang Dawa Lama with his family *(Malati Jhaveri Collection)*

CHAPTER 7

Porter, Tantric, Rogue: Pasang Dawa Lama

In the late 1940s or early 1950s, when Dorjee Lhatoo would have been nine or ten, the road between Chowrasta and Toong Soong was sparsely populated. Beyond the last house where children were forbidden to go was an isolated Sherpa cemetery surrounded by forest—the kind of deep, dark woods that conjure a fear of ghosts. Lhatoo and his friends had snuck into the cemetery to spy with macabre fascination on the ceremonies being conducted there. Lhatoo recalled:

> We were looking from the top, at the funeral pyre burning and the things going on down there. Pasang Dawa Lama was leading a funeral ceremony. He was wearing a white outfit. Conventional lamas have red or liver-colored clothing. But Pasang Dawa Lama was part of the sect of the Nyingma religion that practices Lamaism mixed with Tantra. He was in white, but it was not white any longer; it was the color of clay. He had a thigh-bone instrument, the bugle, and his *damar*, and he was dancing around the pyre. A climbing Sherpa called Ang Karma had died. I remember another expedition porter was there. He brought [out] a drill . . . and the body was laid bare, with a big tummy. The porter poked this drill into the stomach and there was a water fountain—crystal-clear water, and it went on and on and then slowly became yellow and then became red. He had died as he could not pass urine, so it had collected in the body.

The sight must have been traumatic for the young boys. Lhatoo's friend Chong Rinzing fell into a ditch with an epileptic fit, and all the boys screamed. To Lhatoo, the incident remains a vivid memory more than sixty years later.

Death is an important event in Tibetan Buddhism, and when a Sherpa dies, the rituals to assist his passing and reincarnation are complex. It is a critical period for balancing karma and deciding rebirth, part of the ongoing cycle of life and death. (Buddhists believe that when someone dies, they will be born again as something else. What they are reborn as depends on their actions in their previous life [karma].) The lamas who perform the ceremonies are highly trained and venerated. Training to become a lama begins at a very early age, and even today many Sherpa families send one son to a monastery. At the end of their education, these lamas, like priests in other religions, conduct prayers and perform rituals and ceremonies. In Pasang Dawa Lama's case, he carried his training even further through rigorous periods of ritual and seclusion to become a Tantric lama—a lama who combines ritual prayers with magic and incantations.

PASANG DAWA WAS BORN IN 1911 in a small village near Namche Bazaar in Khumbu. He came to Darjeeling as a strong and ambitious young man and soon got jobs carrying loads for expeditions, rapidly distinguishing himself. He was with a German team led by Paul Bauer on Kangchenjunga (8,586 meters) in 1929. Four climbers including Pasang Dawa reached a height of 7,190 meters before bad weather turned them back. They were climbing without supplemental oxygen, and Sherpas Pasang Dawa and Ila Kitar were carrying loads of eighty pounds each!

In 1937, British climber Freddie Spencer Chapman obtained permission to climb Chomolhari (7,326 meters), a mountain no one had attempted before. Pasang Dawa, one of three Sherpas on the climb, became the first Sherpa documented to have achieved a summit.

Later the same year, he accompanied John Hunt and Conrad Reginald Cooke to examine the Zemu Glacier at the base of Kangchenjunga, and in 1938, Pasang was part of the team led by James Waller to climb Masherbrum (7,821 meters) in the Karakoram. In 1939 on K2 (8,611 meters), Pasang Dawa reached 8,371 meters—the highest altitude climbed by any Sherpa up to that time.

The German-American Fritz Weissner led the team that attempted K2 that summer. Nine of the most reputed Sherpas of the day were enlisted from Darjeeling, though only eight ultimately joined the expedition: Pasang Dawa Lama, Pasang Kikuli, Phinsoo Sherpa, Pasang Kitar, Tse Tendrup, Dawa, Tsering, and Sonam Sherpa. Unfortunately, the name of the ninth porter is not mentioned. He appears to have fallen ill early and not climbed at all. By this time, Pasang Dawa had finished his training as a Tantric lama, and it is the first time in expedition records that the religious title is attached to his name in print. This expedition reiterated three facts that had been recognized after the disastrous Nanga Parbat expeditions of the previous years: how unprepared many Western climbers were for the scale of and conditions in the Himalaya and Karakoram; the importance of communication; and the astonishing heroism and initiative displayed by the now-famous Darjeeling porters.

ON JULY 19, 1939, PASANG Dawa Lama and Fritz Weissner were poised to make a summit push on K2. Just 200 meters below the summit, the usually eager Pasang Dawa insisted they return to summit camp, as darkness was descending. Two days later, they made another attempt but had to call that off as well because of poor planning and preparation. Meanwhile, unknown to them, tragedy was unfolding elsewhere on the mountain. Six Sherpas had been left rudderless, without any orders, at different camps. Four expedition members had dropped out early and were waiting at basecamp. A fifth, Dudley Wolfe, was isolated without food or water at Camp VIII—no one lower down knew where he was.

In the absence of communication or directives, the Sherpas organized themselves and began to search for Pasang Dawa, Weissner, and Wolfe, but thinking the men had perished, they stopped just short of Camp VIII. Two Sherpas—Ila Kitar and Phinsoo—descended to Camp VI while the rest returned to basecamp. On July 24, Pasang Dawa and Weissner made their way down, having helped the weakened Wolfe move to Camp VII, from where he could descend no farther. Hearing their tale, Sherpas Pasang Kikuli and Tse Tsering rushed up from basecamp to Camp VI at 7,132 meters in one day (Kikuli hoped that the two Sherpas waiting there to bring Wolfe down could help). When they reached the climber on July 29, he was in a bad state.

They made him tea and pitched his tent again, but couldn't get him to move. Kikuli and Tse Tsering were tired, it was late, and they had no provisions. They determined to return the next day and carry Wolfe down, or at least obtain a chit saying that they had done their best.

On July 31, Kikuli, Kitar, and Phinsoo set out to rescue Wolfe once more. They disappeared into the snow—never to be seen again. This tale was brought down by Tse Tsering, who waited at Camp VI for his companions until he was forced to return. Four men perished on the mountain that day: three heroic Sherpas and the unfortunate Wolfe. If Pasang Dawa Lama had not stopped Weissner from attempting the summit on July 19, there would very likely have been two more deaths.

Kenneth Mason, a British explorer, geographer, and surveyor of the Himalaya, was the first editor of *The Himalayan Journal*, a position he held from 1929 to 1940. In his article "Himalayan Accidents in 1939" in volume 12 of *The Himalayan Journal*, Mason wrote:

> What is there to excuse the catastrophe on K2? Almost every rule of prudent climbing appears to have been broken, and only good luck and the occurrence of fine weather prevented a far worse disaster . . .
>
> . . . Through sickness and strain half the original strength of a small and mobile party was ineffective; several of the rest were tired. Of the three remaining climbers, one cracked on the 13th and one on the 17th. The morale of the porters remained intact to the end, as is evidenced by the superhuman efforts they made to avert the disaster. Had there been one climber capable of reaching Wolfe and of forcing him to descend on the 28th, that disaster would still have been prevented; but every climber was beaten.
>
> These may seem harsh words; but the sooner climbers forget their little Alps and Rockies when they are climbing the great Himalayan summits the sooner they will meet with success.

For his achievements on the mountains, Pasang Dawa Lama, Himalayan Club porter no. 139, was one of the first recipients of the Tiger Badge awarded in late October 1939. K2 would not be summited until fifteen years later by an Italian expedition.

Early in 1940, Pasang Dawa Lama accompanied John and Joy Hunt and Conrad and Margaret Cooke as they attempted the small peak of Pandim

(6,691 meters). In 1944, Pasang Dawa Lama, along with his brother, Ang Nima, accompanied a three-member British team to attempt Nanda Ghunti.

When expeditions started again in earnest after World War II, the Nepalese government gave permission to a Swiss expedition led by René Dittert. In 1949, the team spent three months exploring northeastern Nepal, climbing several small peaks. Pasang Dawa Lama led the eighteen porters who accompanied them.

BACK IN DARJEELING, PASANG DAWA strengthened his Tantric powers. In the Sherpa cemetery there was a small bamboo shed where lamas could do their penance or meditation. Dorjee Lhatoo remembered another experience, in which Pasang Dawa Lama had finished such a period of retreat:

> Pasang Dawa Lama had finished forty days there (someone would bring him food or water), doing whatever the Tantrics do in seclusion. Now he was coming out, and this journey had to be done ceremoniously. At Toong Soong, the Sherpas and Sherpanis laid out chang and *khapse* [a traditional biscuit made during festivals] on small, decorated tables along the road. Pasang Dawa Lama came dancing to the beat of his instruments all the way, and he had drunk chang and eaten the people's offerings. We too were watching from the railings. This was a big accomplishment on his part. He was a learned lama; not only did he know Lamaism, but he did all these special things to qualify him as a Tantric lama. So, he was of his time, someone to be reckoned a somebody.

The Western climbers also recognized Pasang Dawa as someone to be reckoned with—not because of his religious stature, but because of his strength and power as a porter and sardar.

Norman Hardie, the New Zealander who made the first ascent of Kangchenjunga in 1955, told us that there were two Pasang Dawas in those days. One of them had been with Tilman on the 1950 Annapurna expedition. When the young geologist Bill Packard fell ill with polio, that Pasang Dawa nursed him tenderly, escorting him to Mumbai, where he got on a boat to England. The news of his dedication reached New Zealand. In 1951, when Earle Riddiford was preparing an expedition to the Garhwal Himalaya in the state of Uttarakhand, he wrote asking Jill Henderson to employ four Sherpas and send them to Ranikhet, a nearby hill station, insisting that Packard's man Pasang Dawa be included. But the man who appeared was instead Pasang Dawa Lama. However, he was a great success and made the first ascent of Mukut Parbat (7,242 meters) with Riddiford and Edmund Cotter.

As Pasang's abilities on the mountains and his skill as a lama grew, so too did his arrogance and natural bullying behavior in Darjeeling. He strode around like a colossus. Lhatoo told us, "In Darjeeling town, he wore a long baku like the King of Sikkim and the skull cap that the kings and the Chinese wear. He looked a grand person. He looked good. And he looked big." But he also had a vile temper. Children fled from his sight because he kicked anything that came in his way.

One day, Lhatoo, Chong Rinzing, and other friends were playing on the road that looked down on the municipal garden. Flanking the road were three chang shops, one of which belonged to Pasang's wife. She had children from an earlier marriage who were also playing on the street when someone shouted, "Au Lama is coming!" All the boys hid. The lama came down the road chanting *"Mani padme, mani padme"* (commonly translated as "The jewel is in the lotus," a mantra chanted to bring enlightenment). Meanwhile, a man who had come to drink chang was leaning over the railings looking at the garden below. Said Lhatoo, "Pasang crept up behind him, grabbed him by the legs, and threw him over the railing. Just like that. For no reason at all. He was that kind of man." On another occasion, he threw a Tibetan lama into a sewer, kicking him viciously.

Lhatoo admits that he had a grudge against the man. After a particularly nasty encounter when Pasang Dawa Lama chased after him with a stick, he swore, "When I grow up, I am going to bash him." But their paths would not cross again for a very long time.

PASANG WAS ALSO SAID TO have had a voracious sexual appetite. There is an old Sherpa custom: if a man has slept with one hundred women, he celebrates his virility by tearing off his clothes, running naked through the village, and plunging into a cold river. Pasang Dawa Lama is believed to be the only Sherpa to have observed the custom.

Older Sherpas told us that Pasang was officially married between three and five times. He had many other unofficial wives and children in Khumbu, Pharak, and Darjeeling. Lhatoo recalled, "The ones who lived close to us were also like the father—bullies! You see, kids were terrified by them because if you touch these kids, their father and mother would all come in a gang. So it was taboo to mess with these kids." The image of Sherpas in the media has always been of easygoing, faithful workhorses. "But there were rogue Sherpas," continued Lhatoo. "They preyed on women, when they went to Tibet mainly. Tenzing Norgay would tell us lots of stories." Lured by the promise of Darjeeling in return for sexual favors, Tibetan girls would accompany these men up to the Indo-Nepalese border. Once at the border, the poor women would be abandoned with some food and just enough money to return to their homes. Perhaps it is appropriate that the most repeated story about Pasang Dawa Lama contains all the elements that characterized him: a mountain, his ego, and a woman.

IN THE SUMMER OF 1954, Pasang Dawa Lama completed a long and arduous climb with the first Argentinian expedition to Dhaulagiri (8,167 meters). After reaching a height of 8,050 meters, they had to turn back. Francisco Ibáñez, the leader of the expedition, got frostbite at the summit camp. He was evacuated to a hospital in Kathmandu, where he died two days later.

Within a couple of months of this tragedy, Pasang was back doing what he enjoyed immensely—striding through open country, enjoying the company of sahabs and keeping porters in check. This time, it was to Cho Oyu, with an Austrian party led by Herbert Tichy along with Helmut Heuberger and Sepp Joechler. Pasang was the sardar leading a team of seven experienced porters. At 8,201 meters, Cho Oyu is the sixth-highest peak in the world, and lies about thirty kilometers west of Everest. The post-monsoon expedition set out from Kathmandu in September.

On Cho Oyu, the Austrian team established their basecamp near Nangpa La at 5,486 meters and Camp I at 5,791 meters. Camp II was established at 6,156 meters. A steep snow-covered ridge led upward from this point. In 1952, Eric Shipton's party had reconnoitered the northwest face and estimated that it would take two weeks to find a break in the defenses of the wall. Tichy, in an account of the 1954 expedition—"Cho Oyu, 26750 Feet," volume 19 of *The Himalayan Journal*—wrote that as they reached this point, he was tired and looking forward to a hot drink. "But Pasang was so eager, like a dog on a fresh scent, that he wanted to lose no minute in getting on. While I was still panting from our long strenuous ascent, he fetched ropes, ice and rock pitons, draped them round himself and Ajiba and looked questioningly at me. I could have waited and postponed the search for a route until the morrow which would have been the easy, reasonable way out, but I silently roped up and knew that I was really doing the right thing."

Pasang led with confidence instilled by experience. At one point he called out, "No way through," then going around the ice wall, he disappeared and called, "Follow!" Remarkably, a route had opened up; climbing out onto a flat shelf, the three men saw an easy slope leading up to the summit. While the Sherpas fixed ropes, Tichy returned to camp and was greeted by the excitement of the other porters.

A storm kept the climbers in their tents all the next day, but the day after dawned cloudless. Tichy set off with five porters, and at 7,010 meters they pitched camp. Tichy spent the night there with Pasang, Ajeeba, and Ang Nima, and sent the other two porters back. "Tomorrow, without a doubt, we will reach the summit," said Pasang, beaming.

During the night, the climbers awoke to a raging storm. The tent was flapping about like a loose sail, a tempest that only intensified as day broke. Tichy and Pasang came out to see how the other two men were faring, only to find themselves unable to stand upright. As Ajeeba and Ang Nima crawled out of their flattened tent, the wind suddenly tried to lift it off the ground. Tichy threw himself onto it; as his hands sank deep into the snow, he realized he'd lost his mittens. In the few minutes it took to find them, his hands became frostbitten.

In a panic and leaving everything behind, the men hurried down to Camp II, where other expedition members waited. As Tichy wrote, "Pasang and the others wanted to leave for the next Camp down so as to give us more room. I could not give him my hand in farewell, and when he saw that he bent down and kissed my cheek. Apart from the torment of the pain and misfortune, I experienced a new feeling during the days that followed: the wordless friendliness and comradeship that united us and never let us feel alone." *He bent down and kissed my cheek!* What a far cry from the Pasang of Darjeeling—the bully feared and loathed by Dorjee Lhatoo and so many others who had heard of him or knew him in their youth.

A council of war was conducted and it was decided that Pasang with two or three Sherpas would descend to nearby villages to collect provisions while the rest waited at Camp I, allowing Tichy time to heal. They prepared for another attempt, while waiting for provisions to arrive, but then they received a bombshell: A Swiss expedition had appeared, eager to have a go at the mountain. They decided to allow the Austrians one attempt. With no alternative, the team had to go on. Tichy recounted from his article in *THJ*:

> While we were finishing preparations for the trip to Camp IV we thought we could see two figures on the ridge below us. Our longings had become fact—it was Pasang with the stores. We would wait half an hour together, then we would go on to Camp IV, and the following day push on to the summit. Pasang's was an incredible feat—in the course of three days he went from Marlung, 13,000 feet, over the Nangpa La, and up to the summit of Cho Oyu. He had heard of our meeting with the Swiss Expedition and had declared passionately, "If the Swiss reach the summit before us I will cut my throat." We were convinced that these were no idle words, and were spurred on by his fanaticism.

THROUGHOUT THE CLIMB, PASANG DAWA led while Tichy and Joechler followed. Not only was this the first ascent of Cho Oyu, but it was also accomplished without supplemental oxygen. The climb rewrote Himalayan mountaineering techniques, as it showed the possibility of an alpine-style assault on an 8,000er. However, there is also another side to this story: While fetching supplies in the quest to beat the Swiss to the summit, Pasang fell in love with a young lady at a village near basecamp and asked for her hand in marriage. Her father refused, as Pasang was twenty years older and already had one wife. They struck a deal—if Pasang became the first man to climb Cho Oyu, he could marry the daughter. If he failed, he would leave the girl alone and pay her father a handsome sum of money.

When the 1954 team returned to Namche, it is said that the celebrations turned into a two-week wedding festival. Pasang is said to have cheered again and again, "A very high mountain!" Rumor goes that following every Himalayan success after that, he chose a new bride for himself.

Pasang Dawa Lama continued climbing. He was sardar for the 1956 Swiss expedition to Everest and Lhotse, which culminated in the first successful ascent of Lhotse and the second and third ascents of Everest.

Pasang had developed a special bond with the Tyrolean climbers, and he was to them what Tenzing was to the British or Ang Tharkay to the French. In 1959, they appointed him sardar once more for an Austrian expedition to Dhaulagiri, but a storm at 7,800 meters forced them to turn back. In September of the same year, Pasang was sardar for an Indian expedition to Neelkanth and Chowkhamba, two challenging peaks in the Garhwal Himalaya. By this time, he was a well-respected climber; the expedition report shows just how much the team depended on his advice and experience to make their mountaineering decisions.

In 1965, though Pasang Dawa Lama was well into his fifties, Captain Kohli chose him to be part of a highly sensitive mission to Nanda Devi. As it was a military expedition, Kohli recruited Pasang as a junior officer in the Indo-Tibetan Border Police. It would turn out to be Pasang's last expedition.

Dorjee Lhatoo shared a serendipitous story about the rogue Sherpa of Darjeeling:

> Many years later, I happened to be in a bank queue with my Aunt Lhakpa Diki. We stood in line to draw money. In front, there was a man in a suit and a felt hat; next to him was a Tibetan woman in a baku—they were a bit shorter than me. I saw his face; it looked familiar, but then there are so many people in Darjeeling, you know, and old men often look familiar.
>
> My aunt said, "Is this Lama Dawa?"
>
> *It was Pasang Dawa Lama! What old age does to a man!* He was a giant when I was a little boy, and we used to be scared of him. He was rough; he was a dangerous man, even to the kids. He would kick anybody like a rogue horse. And here this man was much smaller than me, old, stooping, and standing in line in the bank.
>
> So my *uru* [aunt] said, "Au Pasang Dawa Lama!"
>
> "Hrrr," he grunted.
>
> Same old man, same old arrogance; but now, to see [his] size, I could handle ten of those! You know this is what you read in history: every tyrant has a day of fall. So he looked like that. And then after a few months I heard in the community, Pasang Dawa Lama had died.
>
> *He was the famous Pasang Dawa Lama!* Ethnic Sherpa. An amazing character. He was a lama; he was a famous climber and he was a famous *dada*—[in Hindi, an "older brother" but also "bully"] in Darjeeling, and, yes, he was a ladies' man, to put it nicely.

To these faces of Pasang Dawa, perhaps we can add one final facet. In a letter he wrote to Herbert Tichy in 1979, Pasang Dawa included this poem:

The more good in it is
that everything
is not permanent.
It changes and
so change
is a must in life.
I will not be wrong
if I say that
Change itself
is life.

Life had indeed been good to Pasang Dawa Lama.

TOP: Ang Tsering's family: Standing is his nephew Nima Tsering, son of his brother, Ajeeba. Sitting from left to right are his daughters: Daki Sherpa, Pema Diki, and Phur Diki. Kneeling in front is Lhakpa Chamji. *(The Sherpa Project)*; BOTTOM: Ang Tsering in front of his house *(Ang Tsering Collection)*

CHAPTER 8

Family Man: Ang Tsering

We walked along Dr. Zakir Hussain Road, the main entry point into Toong Soong, several times as we collected Sherpa oral histories. During our first visit, Dorjee Lhatoo led us past the gompa, pointing out the homes of various Sherpas who lived there. There was one in particular that we returned to year after year—the house of Ang Tsering Sherpa. On the home's broad white-washed terrace lined with potted geraniums, the family's Indian spitzes often lay soaking up the warm sun. We had seen pictures of Ang Tsering sitting here whittling; even now, years after his death, his presence was everywhere.

By the time Ang Tsering passed away in 2002, mere months shy of his hundredth birthday, he had amassed medals and citations from all over the world; they now formed part of a precious legacy, safeguarded by his daughters. On our visits, one daughter always climbed onto the sofa to bring down her father's awards. The medals were mounted on blue velvet and always highly polished; meanwhile, photo albums, files, fading newspaper clippings, and certificates were ever close at hand. Pema Diki, Phur Diki, and Lhakpa Chamji greeted guests with loud laughter, comic Hindi film dialogues, and lashings of hot tea; when they talked about their father, however, they lowered their voices and became reverential. They interrupted each other frequently to make sure that even the tiniest detail did not get overlooked. Often, during our visits, we'd be joined by their brother Tharchen, who lives next door, and their cousin Nima Tsering, son of Ang Tsering's younger brother Ajeeba.

Many people have actively sought out this place, for Ang Tsering is a legend. Awarded a Tiger Badge for his role in the 1952 Everest expedition at age forty-eight, he continued climbing well into his sixties.

Ang Tsering is almost always smiling in photos, his crinkly eyes and creased brown-paper skin indicating a life in the sun, hearty kindness scribbled everywhere. Over the years, we visited this refuge several times to piece together the story of this remarkable climbing Sherpa, who stood atop his first summit at the age of fifty-six in 1960.

Tharchen told us, "The people of Khumbu led a hard life of agriculture. The men of Solu started doing business, got into politics; they started following Hindu rituals as well. Those who had settled higher had potato farms [or] yaks or grew rice and retained their Buddhist character. My father was one of five brothers, growing potatoes, until maybe 1919 or 1922. He thought, 'If this is what we are going to do, we will be finished.' He saw men from places like Darjeeling dressed up like the world dresses—wearing mountaineering clothes. They told him about their life and business in Darjeeling. Father decided to walk here with his brother." The sisters add, "He had ten rupees [about twelve cents] when he left home. He was looking for people from his village, but found nobody. He stayed in gompa *dharamshalas* [free religious boarding houses] along the way."

Ang Tsering was one of many young people who arrived in the Darjeeling of the 1920s, a tranquil, beautiful place to get work, start your family, and lead a better life. His career as a climbing Sherpa began when he was selected for the 1924 Everest expedition at twenty years old. He would continue climbing for the next fifty years.

We asked Phur Diki about Everest 1924. She said Babuji [father] went. But he met an important lama at the Rongbuk Monastery, who advised him against climbing. He said that defiling the holy mountain would make the gods angry and bring calamity on the expedition. The lama advised, "The sahabs will want to go up, but tell them not to." Phur Diki recalled, "Babuji knew he could not convince the sahabs, but he did not go up." Ang Tsering watched as Mallory and Irvine climbed toward the summit, then clouds suddenly rolled across the mountain and the climbers disappeared from view. "An avalanche swept them away as they were about to reach the top," Phur Diki told us with drama and gusto, acting out roles and recreating dialogue with flair.

When journalist Ed Douglas asked how much he had earned per day on the 1924 expedition, Ang Tsering replied, "Twelve annas, that's three-quarters of a rupee." (This would have been a daily wage; in 1924, a rupee could buy 15 kilograms, about 33 pounds, of rice.) Ang Tsering continued, "I made ten rupees a week as a woodcutter."

"So why did you go to Everest for less money?" Douglas asked him. After a wheezy chuckle, he responded: "Because the work was easier."

After Everest, Ang Tsering was selected for three attempts on Kangchen-junga with German teams led in turn by Paul Bauer in 1929 and 1931, and by G. O. Dyhrenfurth in 1930. None of them succeeded, but Ang Tsering made a mark as one of the strongest, most dependable porters of the time.

Ang Tsering was also a member of the 1933 Everest expedition. Despite adverse weather, the team established Camp VI at 8,351 meters. Hugh Rut-tledge, the expedition leader, wrote that they reached 600 feet higher than the previous Everest expedition of 1924 and went on to mention the porters, including Ang Tsering, who had "behaved superlatively."

The sisters knew little about their father's expeditions, except for a shaky account of the infamous German attempt on Nanga Parbat in 1934, during which four Germans (Alfred Drexel, Ulrich Weiland, Willo Welzenbach, and Willi Merkl) and six Sherpas (Gaylay, Dakshi, Nima Dorje II, Nima Tashi, Nima Norbu, and Phinjo Norbu) lost their lives. After this expedition, Ang Tsering shot to fame at age thirty as a mountaineer, not merely because of his skills but because he was able to survive in harsh conditions, famously finding his way down the mountain while living on ice for nine days.

His daughters Phur Diki and the older Pema Diki retold the story they'd heard from their father, though they were uncertain about names, profes-sions, heights, and other facts. Pema Diki stood behind Phur Diki while the latter talked, muttering loud stage whispers, her lips barely moving as if she was cueing the performance.

In 1934, Babuji went to Nanga Parbat—we have only heard the story—we are not sure. It was a German expedition. There was Merkl—and the Sherpas, Gaylay and Dakshi. I don't remember the others. Babuji, Gaylay, and others were sent up by the leaders. The weather turned bad. They had taken food, but it ran out while they waited for the weather to clear. They had reached Camp VIII. What to do? Babuji thought, "We can't go up, can't go down . . . " Seven days passed. Merkl was very sick and weak—he asked Babuji to get help. Gaylay stayed with Merkl, who died that night. On the way down, Babuji became snow-blind. He could not see, and there was nothing to eat. He finally came down eating ice.

So many died—he saw bodies hanging on the ropes . . . Finally he could see the basecamp. "Hai hai"—he tried to call, but no sound came out. The people could not see or hear, but he could see them moving around. He went farther down. A man who was carrying food from one tent to another finally noticed him. They thought they were seeing a ghost . . . then someone helped bring him down.

"Where is Merkl?" they asked. [Ang Tsering responded,] "They are coming down slowly. There is no food; send some people." They sent five people up. Babuji was brought to basecamp and then admitted to hospital. His feet were frostbitten, and they put leeches on them to stop the gangrene. He lost some toes. *"Nau din dekhi home hiun khayo"* he said—"For nine days, I ate only ice."

Dorjee Lhatoo told us that, after recovering from his ordeal, Ang Tsering married Pasang Diki, the widow of his friend Nima Dorje II, who had perished on Nanga Parbat in 1934, and he adopted their young son, Dawa Temba. Ang Tsering and Pasang Diki went on to have a large family of their own, including the sisters we met at the Toong Soong home. But these weren't the only children, as the most remarkable stories we heard about Ang Tsering involved his ability to take under his wing, no matter how penurious his own circumstances, the children of other Sherpas who needed looking after. Lhatoo told us he would say, "Forget it. These are all my children."

Ang Tsering also took in his fellow climber Kitar and his family. Kitar had a daughter and a son. His daughter was Dawa Thondup's first wife, while Kitar's son, Jabeng, was a hunchback. When Kitar died of dysentery on the 1936 British Nanda Devi expedition—the first group to summit the peak—Jabeng became part of Ang Tsering's family too. A bright and scholarly boy, he unfortunately died of a heart attack in his final year of school. "Children in those days were looked after when their father died on the mountains. They were looked after by Gyalzen Sardar and by Ang Tsering," said Dorjee Lhatoo. When Lhatoo's family first arrived in Darjeeling, Lhatoo's mother contacted her cousins Ajeeba and Ang Tsering and a few others. "That is how we happened to stay below Ajeeba's house," he added.

Ang Tsering and Pasang Diki began their life together in 1935. His amputated toes did not heal well after Nanga Parbat in 1934, so he started working treks and getting local porter work—jobs that involved less risk. Joan Townend of The Himalayan Club bought him a horse so he could take tourists around Darjeeling, and over the years he came to own several horses.

Phur Diki said, "Mother also came from Nepal. She was a young nun. We don't know how they met, but it was here in Toong Soong, I think. Babuji loved his wife a lot. Called her 'my Lachchmi'"—a reference to Lakshmi or Laxmi, the Hindu goddess of good fortune—"He would bring goodies from the bazaar and pamper her."

According to Tharchen, Pasang Diki and Ang Tsering's children were Dawa Temba (Pasang Diki's son from her earlier marriage to Nima Dorje II), Daki Sherpa, Norbu Tshering, Tharchen, Chiten Doma, Pema Diki, Phur Diki, and Lakhpa Chamji. Daki Sherpa, the oldest sister, recalls that the couple had twelve children altogether.

The list of Himalayan porters drawn up by Ludwig Krenek noted Ang Tsering's Himalayan Club number as 36. He was known as Ang Tsering I to distinguish him from two other porters of the same name. His birth date was listed erroneously as 1910—a common mistake, as few Sherpas in that period knew when they were born, reckoning dates based on natural events or festivals. Sometimes the wrong birth year was put on record to allow for longer periods of employment. Ang Tsering's expeditions until 1950 were recorded as Mount Everest in 1924, 1933, and 1936; Kangchenjunga in 1930; Kamet in 1931; Nanga Parbat in 1934; and the Lahaul region in 1939. The porter list identifies him as such: "German Order of the Red Cross (Nanga Parbat, '34). Works as sirdar on treks below snow line."

The frostbite Ang Tsering experienced on Nanga Parbat never healed fully, but he started expedition work again after close to two decades. He went as Sherpa sardar to Kamet in early 1952, and climbed eagerly but only up to 7,437 meters. In his Himalayan Club porter book, Major General Williams, the leader on Kamet, wrote, "He was nervous about frostbite and this height would appear to be his limit now." That autumn, Ang Tsering was part of the Swiss expedition to Everest, and in 1953, he accompanied an expedition to Dhaulagiri.

In January 1954, at Jill Henderson's tea party in Darjeeling, twenty-two Sherpas including Ang Tsering were presented Coronation Medals from Her Majesty the Queen of England. "Mount Everest Expedition" was specially inscribed on these medals. At the same function, Tiger Badges were awarded to eight Sherpas including Ang Tsering for exceptional services during the 1952 and 1953 seasons. Recognition for his services on several expeditions had come at last, almost two decades after he had received the Red Cross Medal, endorsed by Adolf Hitler.

But this strong Sherpa had not yet finished his tryst with the Himalaya—he continued climbing for at least another ten years. He was part of the *Daily Mail* Snowman expedition, which set out to discover the existence of the Yeti in 1954. The team had no confirmed sightings, but one morning Ang Tsering discovered a footprint that was believed to have been made by the Yeti and received 100 rupees ($1.21) as a bonus.

M. S. Kohli devotes a chapter of *Sherpas: The Himalayan Legends* to Ang Tsering, with whom he first climbed in 1959. Kohli was leading an Indian Navy expedition to Nanda Kot (6,861 meters), and on the advice of Tenzing Norgay, he recruited both Ang Tsering and his son Dawa Temba. Ang Tsering performed exceedingly well, turning back only about 240 meters below the summit, as his feet would allow him to go no further. Kohli and K. P. Sharma reached the top, and when they descended, wrote Kohli, "Ang Tsering was the first one to rush and embrace me. He was full of joy. Almost 44 years have passed but I still recall Ang Tsering's noble face and his hard work on the expedition."

In 1960, Brigadier Gyan Singh, the principal of the HMI, led the first Indian Everest expedition with twelve other climbers. Some 700 porters were recruited, several of which were Darjeeling Sherpas, including Ang Tsering. Heavy winds and the approaching monsoons beat back two attempts on the summit.

On the way home afterward, Ang Tsering went to Khumbu to bring his ailing mother to Darjeeling, where she could be cared for. Upon reaching her village, he discovered that she had just passed away. He stayed for a month to perform the necessary rituals. Phur Diki told us, "Then he met Dawa Thondup, who had to cut short an expedition, as his wife had died. He asked Babuji to take his place, and so his return to Darjeeling was delayed even further." Besides, Ang Tsering had spent all his earnings on the funeral; he needed to earn money before he returned to his beloved wife.

Unknown to Ang Tsering, a tragic drama was unfolding back home. His youngest daughter, Lakhpa Chamji, had suffered a serious fall from the second story of their building. Pasang Diki had also become seriously ill. The older siblings did not tell their mother that the baby was in a coma in the hospital. "We would say, 'You are not well. You cannot handle Choti. You cannot carry her.'" Pasang Diki died without knowing of her little one's condition.

Ang Tsering learned of his wife's death while he was still on the expedition. After the expedition ended, he went to her family home in Namche Bazaar and gave her brother money to perform the necessary rituals.

For the second time that year, he had spent all his money, and needed more. Dawa Temba looked after the children like a mother. "Choti was released from hospital, but she was permanently damaged in the fall. She has epilepsy and is mentally challenged," said Phur Diki, adding, "She is our life. We must take care of her."

This tragic end to his last expedition had an epilogue, perhaps equally as painful as losing the love of his life. The usually cheerful Phur Diki broke down several times while telling this story: Ang Tsering had taken Dawa Thondup's place in the 1960 Everest expedition as the kitchen-in-charge. A hungry porter came to Ang Tsering outside regulation mess hours asking for food, and he was fed. Brigadier Gyan Singh, the principal of the HMI and leader of the expedition, heard of the transgression and accused Ang Tsering of theft.

Upon returning to Darjeeling, Ang Tsering went to collect his salary from the HMI. He asked for a little extra, as he had spent all his money on his wife's last rites and his youngest daughter was still in the hospital. When Brigadier Singh heard of his arrival, he is alleged to have said (according to Phur Diki, quoting in English), "I shoot him!" Ang Tsering was very angry. According to Phur Diki, he replied, "If you are ready to bring up my children, then I am ready for you to shoot me." Both men were agitated. When the brigadier learned what Ang Tsering had been through, he apologized. However, Ang Tsering's pride had been deeply hurt by the accusation.

In October of the same year, Ang Tsering joined the expedition to Nanda Ghunti organized by the *Anandabazar Patrika* newspaper. It is said that he stood atop a summit for the first time in his life at the age of fifty-six.

What we gathered from our long interviews with his family and friends was that Ang Tsering was not an ambitious mountaineer; he climbed simply to earn an income. Deeply superstitious and religious, he continued to believe that mountaintops were sacred and not to be stepped upon. He became famous for the 1934 Nanga Parbat expedition, but of all the Sherpas we got to know, what stood out was his larger-than-life heart and his dedication to family.

On a stormy night in June 2001, Dawa Temba had a massive heart attack and died. Ang Tsering's heart broke once again, and he survived his beloved oldest son, Dawa Temba, by just eleven months.

Ang Tsering's was one of those families that did not get rich by climbing mountains. As Dorjee Lhatoo put it, "This generation did not get an education. All Sherpas understood that educating children was important for better opportunities. Carrying loads up and down the mountain for other people was out of compulsion. It was never a pleasure, but they toiled cheerfully—that was the quality that made them wonderful porters.

"You have met the simplest ones. Some haven't come up much—Ang Tsering's children have remained humble, uneducated. Perhaps Ang Tsering did not have the resources to do something about it. He was an old-timer; he left it to God."

To feed his large family between expeditions, Ang Tsering started giving pony rides to people in Chowrasta and cultivating potatoes. He taught the children farming. Phur Diki said, "Babuji was left with so many young children to look after but he never married again—he loved only my mother. He would drink with his friends and come home, calling out to his wife Lachchmi to give him food. He would check if we were asleep. If our blankets had slipped, he would cover us up. Pema and I did not marry, as our father and our younger sister needed to be looked after."

One relationship that kept Ang Tsering humble was that with Tenzing Norgay. Tenzing's first wife, Dawa Phuti, belonged to Ang Tsering's clan. When she fell in love with Tenzing, he was a poor Bhutia boy with few prospects. Ang Tsering initially opposed the union, a fact that Tenzing did not forget.

Then, when Tenzing married his second wife, Ang Lhamu, who helped to raise his children from his first marriage, Ang Tsering worried about how she would treat her stepchildren. Later, in a bid at reconciliation, Ang Tsering's family started referring to Tenzing as their son-in-law, but the damage had already been done. During the early days in Darjeeling they had climbed together, but Tenzing was of another, more ambitious breed. When the HMI was set up, Tharchen informed us, "Tenzing told my father if you want a job, come to HMI. My father, a man of self-respect, could not beg his son-in-law for a job. He decided that he did not need HMI to earn a living. When he went on the Nanda Ghunti expedition, Tenzing raised an objection, as this expedition was not mounted from HMI. This is the little I know of the story."

There were other incidents too. In 1973, Darjeeling hosted an International Mountaineers Meet. A galaxy of Himalayan climbers from all over the world descended on the town to relive memories and reconnect with old friends. Paul Bauer was there, wanting to see Ang Tsering, his climbing buddy on Kangchenjunga in 1929 and 1931. Lhatoo said, "But Ang Tsering was not invited because Tenzing Norgay did not want him. The only Sherpas invited were the HMI instructors." While Ang Tsering waited on the steps of the venue, Lhatoo told Bauer's son that Ang Tsering was waiting to pay his respects. "[Bauer] was so surprised!" recalled Lhatoo. "They had been told that 'the Sherpas that went with you on those expeditions are all dead. All those who are alive are here.'" When Bauer finally came outside, the two men had an emotional reunion.

Another incident included a run-in over Ang Tsering's horse, which Tenzing had rented to carry loads on a trek. When the horse died, Ang Tsering asked for compensation, but Tenzing refused to pay. It is possible that the fortunes of the Ang Tsering family would have been better had the relationship between the two men been different. However, the family says that there was some sort of rapprochement between the men toward the end of Tenzing's life. If not friendly, they were at least polite to each other.

Ang Tsering outlived his contemporaries—all his friends, with whom he shared the rope, the drink, and often, the same home. Ang Tsering died on May 22, 2002. He was ninety-eight.

Ed Douglas wrote in "The Face of Everest" for *The Guardian*:

> Ang Tsering was born in Nepal in 1904 in the remote village of Thame close to the border with Tibet. One of five brothers, he tended the family yak herd, but left the Everest region in October 1920, looking for work in Darjeeling. Through a combination of chance and courage, he ended up being one of the best-known Sherpas of the pre-war period, going to Everest with the British in 1924 and 1933 and to the huge peak of Nanga Parbat, now in Pakistan, with a German team in 1934. As he turns the pages of his photo album, revealing team photographs from the 1920s and 1930s, his hand brushes each page and he utters one word in Nepali: "*Chaina.*" They are gone.

For more than seventy years, Ang Tsering was a mountain man earning accolades and medals, yet he lived a simple, difficult life. If there is one man whose presence is invoked on a daily basis, it is Ang Tsering. His daughters like to say, "We know who to turn to when life gets tough in some way. It is our father who guides us in our dreams each time we are heavy-hearted about something. At times we make mistakes. Then, when we sleep, he appears in our dreams and directs us—it feels like an answer to a prayer."

Men like Ang Tsering: *chaina*—they are gone.

Ani Lhakpa Diki at age 101 *(The Sherpa Project)*

CHAPTER 9

Those Magnificent Men and Women

Chowrasta (literally, "four roads") is an intersection in Darjeeling where many roads—four main ones and several pedestrian alleyways—converge. On this flat promenade, the town square, tourists and locals come to lounge in the sun, sit on one of the many benches along the periphery, and take in the wonderful views of the mountains and valleys all around.

Encircling this space are stores like Habeeb Malik & Sons, where we spent hours shopping for turquoise necklaces and Buddha statuettes; Nathmulls tea store, where customers can sit in a glass-enclosed sun room and taste some of Darjeeling's best teas; and Oxford bookshop, with a collection of books on the Himalaya impossible to find anywhere else. The lovely green Chalet Hotel complex features a restaurant and wine store. In the middle of it all are pony rides and popcorn sellers, a fountain recently renovated but almost never in use, and a space called Hawa Mahal for public performances and political rallies.

Starting at the beautiful old Bellevue Hotel, Nehru Road runs from Chowrasta past Kashmiri shops selling shawls and leather, past Glenary's bakery and the famous Das Studio, all the way to the Planters' Club, which houses a hospital and the club itself. Decades ago, sahabs would appear on the veranda (aka "the quarterdeck") to recruit Sherpas for expeditions.

Behind the public performance space on Chowrasta is Mall Road. It goes all the way around Observatory Hill, a scenic walk lined with deodars and uncluttered by stalls. The Raj Bhavan—the Governor's Bungalow—lies at the end of this stretch. From here you can loop back toward Chowrasta past a huge concert hall called Bhanu Bhawan. It is named after the Nepali poet Bhanubhakta Acharya, whose golden statue looms, larger than life, over Chowrasta. Speaking of statues, there is a small but graceful bust of Sherpa Nawang Gombu on this road as well.

Other, smaller lanes lead off from Chowrasta, one of which goes down to Bhutia basti and the oldest monastery in Darjeeling. Another is little more than a footpath lined with vendors of sweaters and hats, knickknacks and crockery mainly from China. This is one of the circuitous pathways that finally leads down to the main taxi stand and the old market.

Fascinating as all these roads are, the one that became most familiar to us during our research was Dr. Zakir Hussain Road, behind the defunct fountain and at the other end of Chowrasta from Hawa Mahal. We walked down this road for several years, to get to upper and lower Toong Soong, the settlement of the older Sherpas, and finally Alubari basti, where most of the newer Sherpas live.

The following are stories of the remarkable people we met in Chowrasta, in the lanes of Toong Soong, down in the old market, and along the steep paths that make up old Darjeeling.

Ani Lhakpa Diki: Missing Pieces

On a perfect April day in Chowrasta, we met what may have been the most gorgeous woman in all of Darjeeling. She sat comfortably on one of the benches, her skin glowing, posture erect, translucent eyes brimming with curiosity. She wore a colorful scarf on her head and a blue blouse over her baku. Local leader and our friend Phurtemba (the champion of Sherpa causes, whom we met on the occasion of the first anniversary of Nawang Gombu's death) pointed her out to us. From the wine store across the square, we picked up a bottle of Honeybee Premium Brandy and then sat down on either side of her.

At the age of 101, Ani Lhakpa Diki, Dorjee Lhatoo's aunt, wife of Tiger Lobsang Sherpa, mother of two sons—of whom one is alive—walked to Chowrasta every afternoon, a steep two kilometers uphill, to meet friends, eat momos, and watch the world.

We met Lhakpa Diki a bit late in her life, but according to Jonathan Neale in *Tigers of the Snow*, she was born in Paré, near Thame in Solu Khumbu, in 1912. She ran away with her friends to Darjeeling probably when she was twenty-four. She found work as a porter on treks and expeditions, carrying loads of up to thirty kilos. In the early 1940s, she fell in love with and married Lobsang, a fellow porter and rickshaw puller. They had a good marriage and finally saved enough to buy two horses to take people around Darjeeling.

Lobsang was on the 1924 Everest expedition and sardar on the 1938 expedition. In The Himalayan Club records, he was listed as Lobsang II, with the club number 144. "He wasn't a Sherpa actually," Lhatoo told us. "He was a Khampa. My aunt was his second wife." He was among the first porters to receive the Tiger Badge, and there is a beautiful sketch of Lobsang by Bip Pares in her 1940 book, *Himalayan Honeymoon*.

As we chatted with her, we soon realized that many stories in Lhakpa Diki's head had become mixed up like a jumbled jigsaw puzzle. "What was your husband's name?" we asked.

"Ang Phurba. He climbed, he became a major . . ."

"She is talking about her son," explained Phurtemba.

"My husband, my son. Everyone's gone."

Lobsang died in 1945 on a reconnaissance expedition to Kangchenjunga. Two sahabs, another porter, and Lobsang had reached Green Lake, on the Zemu Glacier at the base of the Kangchenjunga massif, when the other porter took ill. They left him in a cave with some food and went on. Lobsang and the two sahabs never returned. Ani Lhakpa Diki didn't remember the year, only that she waited and waited. Finally, the agent who hired Lobsang came and gave her 3,000 rupees ($36), either as compensation or as payment owed to Lobsang—she did not know.

The Sherpanis: Carrying Their Own Weight

Back in the early days of Himalayan mountaineering, women were often employed to carry loads to basecamps. Most were recruited from villages along the way, and they hauled loads as heavy as those carried by any man. Expedition accounts report women with babies on their backs carrying double loads even up to Camp I on the great peaks, and then returning to ask for more work. Money was not easy to come by in villages that depended on subsistence farming, so when there was a chance to earn, women were eager to. The Darjeeling Sherpanis like Ani Lhakpa Diki were employed to carry bags of coin on the expeditions, to settle the wages of all the low-altitude porters.

Her older son, Ang Phurba, was three and his brother, Ang Norbu, was nine months old. Once the money ran out, she put the headstrap back on. Leaving her baby in a basket near the horse stables in the care of his three-year-old brother, she carried loads all day for the planters who came into town. Those were the hardest days of her life. She continued as a local porter but insisted on seeing her sons through school. Finally, eleven years later, she hung up her headstrap when Ang Phurba began to earn. He eventually joined the military, retiring as a major in the Gurkha regiment of the British Army. Ang Norbu, the younger son, finished his education, got a job, married, and continued to live in Darjeeling, looking after his mother.

In the mild Darjeeling sunshine, Ani Lhakpa Diki was off on another trail of memories: "My sisters and brothers are there. They have yaks. We drink the milk. We sell the yak babies ... I was twenty years [old] when I left Solu Khumbu to see Darjeeling, and I did not go back. I sit here all afternoon. I do not have teeth but I eat everything. My children make all the food, even meat, soft for me. I make my bed, clean my room myself."

We asked her the secret of her soft, beautiful skin. "Exercise, soft meat, and a tot of brandy is the best diet," she told us.

Then we gave her the bottle of Honey Bee. "What is this? Brandy? Thank you, thank you. Before going to bed I will have a little," she said. Phurtemba offered to deliver the bottle home, but she hugged it close and refused to part with it.

Ani Lakhpa Diki passed away in 2013 after a brief illness. Even at 102 she charmed the nurses at the hospital, regaling them with her stories and jumbled memories.

Ang Tsering Phenzi: The Forgotten Coin Box

It was the day after the puja at Nawang Gombu's home. We climbed the steps of a stilted wooden building to meet Chong Rinzing, Dorjee Lhatoo's childhood friend. Chong Rinzing and his brother, Ang Nima, were the sons of Ang Tsering Phenzi "Pansy," one of the most prominent Sherpas in the early years of climbing.

Pema Yangste, who answered the door, was Ang Nima's widow. Her son, Lhakpa Nuru, lived next door with his family, while Chong Rinzing lived downstairs with his wife and children. She would send for him, she said. Meanwhile, she told us that she knew nothing about her father-in-law or his expeditions. She remembered a vague reference to a box stuffed with "useless papers" that may have belonged to Phenzi. Her son would know, but he was away.

Just then, Chong Rinzing arrived. As he told us, "My father's name was Ang Tsering, but as there was already another Ang Tsering, my father came to be known as Ang Tsering Phenzi. It comes from 'fancy,' and was given to him by the Japanese. His brothers were Aila and Ang Dawa who went with Tenzing to Everest. Ang Nima and I were born and grew up in Toong Soong. I am seventy-six years old now [in 2012]."

Coin boxes carried on early expeditions (*The Sherpa Project*)

The Himalayan Journal porter list recorded Phenzi as having been born in 1907; his club number was 51. He was on Everest in 1936 and in 1937, and on a surveying season in Garhwal later that year. In 1938 and 1939, he was in Sikkim with a Swiss team that made the first ascent of Tent Peak (Kirat Chuli: 7,365 meters), and in 1949, he was on the Swiss Himalaya expedition to Nepal.

"Pansy," as the Westerners called him, was part of the all-star team of Sherpas led by Ang Tharkay on the historic expedition to Annapurna in 1950, under Maurice Herzog. At the end of the expedition, Pansy along with another Sherpa, Sarki, accompanied Herzog all the way to Kathmandu. On reaching the city both Sherpas had only dreamed of, wrote Herzog in *Annapurna*, "He (Sarki) had earned this reward a hundred times over and so indeed had Pansy, a Himalayan veteran whose devotion and quiet good nature made him a most lovable character."

The note running alongside his accomplishments in the porter list states, "Rather old now but still going strong. Tiger's badge." This is all we could learn of Phenzi's career through *The Himalayan Journal*, and so we hoped Chong Rinzing could tell us more.

He continued, "When my father and mother came from Solu Khumbu, we lived in Toong Soong in a rented house. It was owned by Aji [Uncle] Rinzing—Pem Pem's father-in-law. He was a very rich man. Our neighbors were the old Sherpas. We lived below Gyalzen Sardar. My mother and father broke stones for making houses and earned three annas a day. Then, on expeditions, [my father] would earn three to four rupees a day."

In 1950, Pansy bought a piece of land in Phulbari, close to Toong Soong in Darjeeling, and the family moved there. Rinzing was placed in a monastery when he was a child but he did not like it, so he ran away and returned home. He worked with his mother and sisters at home and on the farm, and did not go back to school. At age nineteen, he joined the police.

"The Sherpa is a small man," said Chong Rinzing. "He does as he is told, sits when asked to sit, goes when asked to go." Taking that as a sign to make our exit, we left, with promises to come visit again. Pema Yangtse's mention of a box of "useless papers" had intrigued us. What if it did indeed contain Phenzi's papers? It would be nice to fill the huge gaps in his career. So, after several days, when Pema's son, Lhakpa Nuru, was back in town, we sent word that we would like to visit again.

Lhakpa Nuru's wife was extremely house-proud, and their small space next door to Pema Yangste's home was neat and orderly. According to her, the "box" we'd come to look at was an eyesore filled with useless, crumbling documents; she'd wanted to throw it away for a long time but Lhakpa Nuru had resisted, so it was relegated to the loft. When we entered, however, we saw not one, but two boxes sitting in the corner—mute spectators to a hundred years of history.

They were old coin boxes, made of metal and painted a dull navy blue, measuring about two feet long by twelve inches wide, still sturdy with their locks intact. Boxes such as these would have been filled with bags of coin and carried by Sherpanis to basecamps.

We lifted them carefully and took them over the lintel into the open to photograph them in better light, then brought them back inside. We opened the lid of the first one. The box was stuffed with scraps of paper with children's drawings, Lhakpa Nuru's report cards, and pieces of unfinished craft work. Perhaps it was a treasure trove for a small boy, but not what we'd come to see.

At first glance the second box seemed to contain more of the same, but then near the bottom we spied a picture frame, and then another, and then a pair of old books.

It was far more than we'd hoped for: Ang Tsering Phenzi's porter book, letters from leaders of various expeditions, a framed certificate from Hugh Ruttledge, and a framed photo of Phenzi with his medals.

The certificate from the 1936 Mount Everest expedition recorded Phenzi's daily wages and rations, days of employment, and his next of kin for compensation in case of death or injury. At the very bottom under "FINAL REPORT," Ruttledge had written, "Chief Messboy but was desperately keen to go high. Very hardworking and always cheerful, often in very difficult circumstances. Extremely strong and kept his efficiency even at Camp III. Would recommend him for any expedition."

At the top in writing now barely visible were the words "Rs 20/= Bonus for . . ." and then the rest was lost.

The porter book contained pages and pages of testimonials, including one from the Swiss Everest expedition of 1952 and the Japanese Himalayan reconnaissance expedition of the same year. Phenzi went to Manaslu the next year with the Japanese and was with Edmund Hillary in July 1954 on the New Zealand expedition to Barun Valley.

A particularly heartwarming testimonial written by Joyce Dunsheath and Hilda Reid, dated July 3, 1956, ended with, "Above all, his wisdom, arising out of his experience on so many expeditions, was invaluable to an all-women's party climbing for the first time in the Himalayas."

In the blank spaces between testimonials were phone numbers, accounts, and long lists of porters and rations—and even someone's attempt to practice English. It appears that after he retired, Pansy continued using his porter book, providing a valuable historical record for future generations.

The most rewarding page, however, revealed a small fact sandwiched between two testimonials. It simply stated, "Tiger Badge issued on 19-3-45." The badge itself was mounted within a frame as absolute proof. We photographed as many of the documents as we could and congratulated Lhakpa Nuru for having kept them safe. There were more, he said, but some Europeans came and took them away. We were horrified. This treasure belongs to the Sherpa community, not to souvenir hunters.

Two years later, we met with Chong Rinzing again, in his home. He was bundled up and in bed looking far weaker than before. He had to be propped up to talk to us. Some months later, Dorjee Lhatoo informed us that he had passed away.

The coin box is still in Lakhpa Nuru's loft. We have no idea how many other forgotten boxes lie in the neglected corners of Sherpa homes. We hope that someone someday takes the initiative to gather them and safeguard this legacy of archival material. Otherwise, these hidden troves of historical treasure will fall prey to greedy collectors, spring-cleaning youngsters, or hungry mites and silverfish—none of whom respect the riches they contain.

Khamsang Wangdi: The Butterfly Catcher

At 8,200 meters, Cho Oyu is the sixth-highest mountain in the world. On October 19, 1954, Herbert Tichy, Sepp Joechler, and Pasang Dawa Lama made its heroic first ascent. They had only one chance at the top, for hot on their heels was a Swiss team with Raymond Lambert and Claude Kogan.

In the event, the Swiss did not make their summit, but Kogan set a new world record for highest elevation yet attained by a woman: 7,803 meters. On their team was a Sherpa, less flamboyant than Pasang Dawa Lama but just as passionate, and intent on making his quiet mark upon the climbing world. This was Khamsang Wangdi's first expedition. Five years after his climbing debut, he was a sardar himself.

Born in 1932, Wangdi worked his way up from kitchen boy, and then carried loads to lower camps. Like Ang Tharkay, he too became a favorite of French climbers. Wangdi was with Jean Franco on the first ascent of Makalu in 1955 and on Trisul in 1956.

In 1959, Wangdi, then twenty-seven, was sardar on Cho Oyu with Kogan once more. She was leading an international women's expedition, attempting the third ascent of the peak. In the 1959 film *Cho Oyu All Women's International Expedition*, a carefree Wangdi is seen chasing butterflies in one frame and getting his tooth extracted in another. The group reached basecamp (5,593 meters) on September 14; despite the unsettled weather following the monsoon, they would go on to establish three higher camps in the next two weeks.

On October 1, Kogan, Claudine van der Straten-Ponthoz, and Sherpa Ang Norbu established Camp IV (7,102 meters). The weather turned bad, there was an avalanche, and the party perished in the snow. The next day, Wangdi and Sherpa Chewang were sent to find out what had happened to the climbers, but they ended up being caught in another avalanche a little above Camp III. After a two-hour struggle, Wangdi freed himself but could not rescue his companion. It was a tragic end to what had begun as a happy expedition.

In 1962, Wangdi was with Lionel Terray on Jannu (aka Kumbhakarna; 7,710 meters). He made the summit and was awarded the Tiger Badge. Soli Mehta, editor of *The Himalayan Journal,* later wrote, "In all my meetings with Wangdi he was the same quiet, gentle self, looking rather frail, but ter-

ribly wiry and tenacious in purpose. He was more intellectual
than other Sherpas and his independent spirit burned fiercely
inside him."

Around the same time,
Wangdi joined the HMI as an
instructor. Harish Kapadia, who
trained under him, said that his
intelligence and talent stood out.
Kapadia recalled, "Tenzing and
Gombu had natural instinct, but
Wangdi was a simply brilliant
Sherpa. As my rope instructor in
October 1964, he taught so well,
encouraging a lot of discussion."

During this period, Wangdi
visited the Bombay Climbers
Club several times to teach rock
climbing. One of his friends, Dr.
Srikar Amladi, told us, "He was
a quiet man. He neither sang nor

Khamsang Wangdi (center) at Manali Guide
School *(Photo by Dr. Srikar Amladi)*

danced like the other Sherpas around the campfire, but he was an excellent
climber. Once, he had not brought his climbing boots for the course. He was
in Hawaii chappals [flip-flops]! The fact that he could wear practically any
footwear and take on the toughest climb was an eye-opener."

Wangdi didn't last long at the HMI. Some say he left because he was
overlooked for the post of senior instructor, others, because his desire to
marry Tenzing's daughter Nima was thwarted. Dorjee Lhatoo, a few years
his junior, heard rumors that Wangdi was upset at being excluded from the
1965 Indian expedition to Everest. "But the fact is," Lhatoo says, "by this
time, he was ready to branch out on his own."

Wangdi had an idea that was far ahead of its time. In 1966, he resigned
from the HMI and, recruiting twelve Sherpas from Darjeeling, established
the Sherpa Guide School at Vashista, four kilometers from the town of
Manali, in the Indian state of Himachal Pradesh. It was a forerunner to the
present-day trekking agencies. The school supplied equipment, Sherpas,

food, and logistics to expeditions and also conducted courses. Kapadia told us, "Wangdi purchased his equipment in Kathmandu. It was on one of these trips that he met Doma, who fell for his charms. The young couple eloped to Manali, where they soon had a son."

Wangdi's Sherpas were the backbone of several expeditions in the mountain districts of Kullu and Lahaul, close to his guide school in Manali.

In October 1967, the Mumbai-based Climbers Club organized an expedition to Mukar Beh (6,069 meters), a beautiful unclimbed peak near Manali. Leading the team was Geoffrey Hill, an Australian mountaineer, while Wangdi provided Sherpas and equipment from his guide school.

Unfortunately, the expedition was plagued by bad weather. On October 24, Hill and two other climbers faced unstable snow conditions—labeled "horrible" in Hill's diary. Sometime during the next night, an avalanche killed them. Their bodies were retrieved twelve days later after the weather cleared. Xerxes Boga, a Bombay climber, and Wangdi brought down the bodies, along with Hill's diary describing the situation.

The repercussions of the accident for Wangdi were far-reaching. Just a few years before he established his school in Manali, the Western Himalayan Mountaineering Institute (WHMI)— known today as the Atal Bihari Vajpayee Institute of Mountaineering and Allied Sports (ABVIMAS)—had started courses in skiing and mountaineering. Its principal, Harnam Singh, allegedly resented Wangdi for the competition his nearby Sherpa Guide School posed. When the accident on Mukar Beh happened, Singh refused to help with the rescue efforts and instead used the opportunity to malign Wangdi, stating that his tents, equipment, and staff support were of poor quality, leading to these deaths, accusations that led to a government inquiry.

All written reports praised Wangdi's efforts in the rescue attempt, but the sustained smear campaign had its desired effect, and Wangdi's business sank. In "Obituary, Ajeeba and Wangdi" (*The Himalayan Journal*, 1975), Soli Mehta wrote, "I shall never forget the tremendous part he played in the operations that followed the fatal snow slide that enveloped Suresh Kumar, Geoffrey Hill, and Pemba on an October night in 1967—a part that not only received no thanks but an additional burden of financial loss and mudslinging attacks on his reputation and no small bullying from bureaucracy that should have been better informed."

Lhatoo visited Wangdi during this low period. He told us that "Wangdi's was a typical Sherpa reaction to stress. He began drinking and deteriorated.

Even on the regular four-kilometer walk from Vashista to [the] Manali bazaar, he would have to stop ten times to rest. At the Mission Hospital of Manali, Dr. Peter Steel, a well-known climber himself, warned Wangdi, 'If you don't stop drinking and smoking, you will die of multiple cirrhosis or tuberculosis.' His words came true: the brilliant Sherpa died in 1975 at age forty-three."

Wangdi's wife, Doma, had to sell the school and equipment to pay the Sherpas. We have been told that she returned to Nepal and married a Tibetan, but the marriage didn't last. Forced to return to Darjeeling, she became a porter at the HMI, where she met and married a fellow Sherpa. It is not clear what happened to the son she had with Wangdi.

Thus ends the saga of one more unsung Sherpa hero. Luck ever eluded Khamsang Wangdi, just like the butterflies he chased all those years ago on the way to Cho Oyu as a carefree young man.

Dawa Thondup and Lhamu Yuten: A Bittersweet Life Together

Dawa (aka Da) Thondup was one of the survivors of the 1934 Nanga Parbat expedition. He was also part of the group of twelve who, along with Tenzing Norgay, ran away from Khumbu to Darjeeling in 1932.

In his book *Tenzing: Hero of Everest*, Ed Douglas wrote, "Included in that little band of adventurers was Dawa Thondup, who filled Tenzing's head with ideas about how they would both get jobs on the expedition to Everest the following year. Their lives would become interwoven over the years on various expeditions the length of the Himalaya. In the list of porters held by The Himalayan Club in Darjeeling Tenzing would hold the number 48; Dawa Thondup 49. But Dawa Thondup, older by seven years, would be the first to find work."

We met Dawa Thondup's widow, Lhamu Yuten, in late 2013. Eighty-seven years old, she lived in a tiny room just above the main bazaar in Darjeeling. Her daughter Lhakpa Doma and son-in-law lived with her. One wall of the room was taken up by an altar. A huge bed covered the rest of the space, leaving no place to set up a tripod. The kitchen was in an adjacent room, even tinier than the main one. No natural light entered.

Lhakpa Doma recounted, "We live on rent. I have grown old in this house. Even when Da Thondup was alive, we lived here, this same house.

"Tenzing Sherpa and Dawa used to work in the Himal. He met my parents in Khumbu, and they got me married and we came to Darjeeling. He was

Lhamu Yuten in her one-room home
(The Sherpa Project)

fifty years old, and I was twenty. At the beginning we stayed in Toong Soong as Ang Tharkay's tenants. Since the children were born, I have been staying here. I have three daughters. All of them are married. My oldest daughter and her husband look after me. The other daughters are in Nepal.

"My husband went to Everest and to Dhaulagiri. He set up the tents, he made the sahab's beds, and cooked. He was a good man. He got lots of medals. My brother-in-law's children are abroad; they took [my husband's] documents and certificates and medals to show around. They did not pay for anything."

Dawa gets special mention in the 1951 porter list: "Though rather old [he was forty-three], he is still really excellent. He reached the summit of Abi Gamin in 1950. Order of the Red Cross." An asterisk by his name indicated that he was one of the best men available. Only eight porters out of one hundred and seventy-five were given this mark.

Dawa Thondup was a young porter on Everest in 1933 and one of the heroic Sherpas who came down from the Silver Saddle on Nanga Parbat in the storm that spelled tragedy for Willi Merkl's 1934 expedition. He was one of two Sherpas who accompanied John Hunt's Peak 36 (later Saltoro Kangri) expedition to the Karakoram in 1935, and joined him on two expeditions and several treks in the Sikkim Himalaya. Da Thondup made the summit of Abi Gamin in 1950 and was also on the Annapurna expedition that same year. He was on the Swiss Everest expedition in 1952, and at the age of forty-eight, he was by far the oldest member of the 1953 Everest expedition (Hunt had specially asked that Dawa Thondup be included in the Sherpa team). The doctor who checked his health before he was selected said he should not go beyond 20,000 feet (6,096 meters). However, once on the mountain, he carried loads as easily as younger, stronger Sherpas. Dawa Thondup not only reached the

South Col without any ill effects, but he proved himself an obvious choice for subsequent ferries, all without supplemental oxygen.

After the 1955 international expedition to Everest, leader Norman Dyhrenfurth wrote, "He appears to be ageless since he can still keep up with the fastest and the strongest of the younger Sherpas."

While Da Thondup was climbing, Lhamu Yuten washed dishes in people's houses and raised their three daughters. She was only thirty-five years old when her husband died a long, drawn-out, painful death from stomach ulcers.

Lhamu Yuten recounted, "He was not employed by HMI. There was no pension. We got nothing! I went to The Himalayan Club, too. They gave me nothing. Tenzing Sherpa forgot us." One kindly local gentleman gave the children gumboots and raincoats to wear to school—"That's all the help I got," said Lhamu Yuten. "I have known sadness all my life. Da Thondup was married earlier, but I did not know. He had a temper. He used to drink a lot. They woke up in the morning and drank in the mountains and here." Daughter Lakhpa Doma said her mother never told her anything about her father. Lhamu Yuten said with a laugh, "What words can come from my heart? What I desired, I did not get."

By any standard, Dawa Thondup had a formidable climbing record. He received medals, recommendations, and citations, but his family never managed to move out of the one-room tenement to which he took his bride so many years ago.

Tenzing Norgay with all his awards *(Dorjee Lhatoo Collection)*

CHAPTER 10

Bedrock: Tenzing Norgay

Hamro Tenzing Sherpa le chadyo himal chuchura
Jamker bajyo kheychadi jhamker nachyo mujura
(Our Tenzing Sherpa has climbed to the top of the Himalaya
Play the band and dance)
—Dharmaraj Thapa

Ghang-la, the house that the people of India built for Tenzing Norgay when he returned as a hero after "conquering" Everest, is three stories high and sits on the eastern slopes of Darjeeling, away from Toong Soong and the HMI. Extensions to the original building have been added over the years. There is a back garden and a front enclosure for dogs—if you so much as touch the imposing gate, a couple of ferocious hounds growl. An upward slope leads to Tenzing Norgay's private museum on the left and the house on the right, where Tenzing's son Jamling and his family live.

In the late 1950s and 1960s, when Tenzing was at the peak of his career, the house was full of people. James Ramsay Ullman, author of Tenzing's first autobiography, *Man of Everest: The Autobiography of Tenzing*, wrote that at any given hour, you could be sure that tea was being served. Among those in the house were its kindly mistress Ang Lhamu, daughters PemPem and Nima, nieces Doma and Ang Nimi, constant visitors, Sherpas living and working there, and as many as forty Lhasa apsos. The handsome, ever-ready-to-tell-a-story Tenzing towered over this world, grinning broadly beneath a mop of glossy, combed-back hair. After Everest, Tenzing's life had become one of basking in demigod glory and meeting tourists, media, and stars.

But sometimes a cloud would descend over Tenzing's face. Usually the cause was a Sherpa, claiming to be his cousin, brother-in-law, uncle, wife's niece's husband, or just a clansman, demanding a favor or job like it was his birthright. Tenzing did his best to help, but his position became a millstone. He became a slave to his greatness.

The darkest cloud descended upon his visage when the politics of the Everest climb took over, when questions to which he had no answers cropped up: *Who stepped on the summit first? Why did Hillary get knighted while you only received the George Medal? How come Hillary became ambassador and high commissioner, but you did not get an international position? Why is the world sending aid to Nepal and not India? What are you doing for Darjeeling Sherpas? Are you Bhutia? Are you Sherpa? Are you Indian?*

The cacophony of questions beleaguered this simple man for three decades after he stood atop the tallest mountain on Earth. He became a bitter shadow of who he'd been when it all began.

Tenzing laid bare his experiences in two books, written at different stages in his life. His honesty, passion, and disappointments came alive on their pages, as they did in the large number of articles and other books written about him. It is hard to find men who are not afraid to be perceived and judged, so straightforward and passionate, comfortable in their skin. Tenzing began as such a man. But these qualities were cruelly peeled away, layer by layer, until the lonely, drunk, and bitter core was laid bare. We tried to understand Tenzing by talking to a few people who were close to him.

The Kinzom Years: Tenzing's Childhood

As Ed Douglas wrote in *Tenzing: Hero of Everest*, Tenzing's mother, Kinzom, was a "tough but kindly woman, devoted to her faith." She was married to Mingma Ghangla, a yak herder of repute, and the two lived in various areas in and around Tibet's Kharta Valley, above which towered the massif of Chomolungma ("Goddess Mother of the World," Mount Everest) and its accompanying peaks and turrets. She bore fourteen children over twenty to twenty-five years; Namgyal Wangdi was the eleventh, presumably born sometime in late May 1914. Eight of the couple's children died in infancy or childhood. Apparently, Kinzom was on a pilgrimage to Tse Chu (4,419 meters) in the Kama Valley in Tibet when she gave birth to Wangdi.

Kinzom and Mingma took young Wangdi to see the Tibetan Buddhist master Ngawang Tenzin Norbu, the Tenth Dzatrul Rinpoche, one of the greatest religious leaders of the time. He declared the child a reincarnation of a rich man and rechristened him, giving him his own first name, as was common practice: Tenzing ("supporter of religions") and Norgay ("wealthy").

When he was still very young, Tenzing's parents sent him to a monastery. However, discipline was harsh there, and the boy ran back home to the Kharta Valley after a monk struck him on the head.

The Kharta is fertile, one part of it comprising a huge pastureland called Ghang-la, an ideal summering grounds for large herds of yaks. The area is exquisite, with turquoise lakes and glossy glacial sweeps feeding the rivers; the name of a sacred monastery in the valley translates as "perfectly pure god's palace."

Mingma's family was bound to a powerful landlord, and they had some land and a house within the landlord's property. But for most of the year, the family tended yaks. Mingma became famous for his healthy and expanding herd, and so his family lived a hard but satisfying life, moving with the pastures and the seasons.

While driving in the Tibetan or Ladakhi highlands, you may notice rings of stone. This is where the herders pitch their yak-hide tents every season. Nowadays, you can see solar panels, cooking-gas canisters, motorcycles, and even cars surrounding these tents, but back in the early 1900s, they were simple constructions just ten feet wide, with a fireplace in the center and an altar on one side. There was a barrel for fermenting yak milk and a press for making *churpi*, or yak cheese. Tea had salt and yak butter, with tsampa (maize or barley flour) mixed in it for meals. Yak dung served as fuel, and there would be meat for the family only when a yak died. It seemed an idyllic pastoral life, but the edges were sharp because there is much to be done in these high regions' brief summers. Winters are harsh—animals tended to get excitable so sometimes a little blood was drained to "pacify" them, which was in turn added to tsampa, making it delicious and nutritious.

During the winters, the family inhabited their permanent house: a flat, fortress-like structure where they lived on the upper floor above the animals. They didn't have much, but there was always food on the table. This was the world inhabited by Dokmo Kinzom (a *dokmo* is a female yak herder) and Drokpa Mingma (a *drokpa* is a male yak herder) and their children—older sons, Kesang and Chingdu; older daughters, Kipa and Thakchey; youngest son, Tenzing; and youngest daughter, Sonam Doma.

At some point, probably during the 1920s, a mysterious disease overtook the herd, killing all the yaks. It must have been devastating. Mingma's family returned to their meager property as servants, enslaved to the landlord. Kinzom became a laborer and a load carrier, doing anything to keep her children fed. Curious to see the world, Tenzing ran away to Kathmandu for the first time at age thirteen. Homesickness brought him back in two weeks. Kinzom first embraced him for returning and then thrashed him for running away.

By now, it was the late 1920s or early 1930s. The world was changing rapidly. One reconnaissance and two expeditions to Everest had already been mounted, India was fighting fervently for independence, and Nepal wanted freedom from its monarchy. China was making inroads into Tibet. But Mingma was still indebted and Kinzom continued to work as a laborer.

During this time, Kinzom's favorite son, Tenzing, carrying bags of salt over the pass into Khumbu, got a flavor of the expeditions that were traveling to Everest. He learned that he would have to travel to Darjeeling in order to join them. In 1932, the handsome young man caught news of an expedition going to Everest the following year. At age eighteen, Tenzing had honey-colored eyes; a broad, open smile; long jet-black hair; and a naturally lithe body. At 5'8", he stood unusually tall for a Sherpa. He could already see himself reflected in the yearning eyes of Sherpa girls.

The Dawa Phuti Years: Tenzing's Youth

Dawa Phuti, a beautiful Sherpani from the village of Thame in Khumbu, fell in love with Tenzing Norgay. He had nothing to offer but ambition, which she recognized. The couple eloped to Darjeeling, as many youngsters did in those days. They arrived at their destination with stars in their eyes but luck initially eluded them. Tenzing was not chosen for the 1933 Everest expedition. Being Khampa or Bhutia made him an "outsider," and the established climbing Sherpas treated him as such.

In January 1934, a tremendous earthquake struck Nepal. Its effects were felt far and wide, and Tenzing's family home was destroyed, as was the Thyangboche Monastery. Hearing about the disaster and fearing the worst, Tenzing rushed to check on his parents. They were safe, and Kinzom was overjoyed at seeing her son again. This time he did not get thrashed. He helped them rebuild their home. His parents wanted him to stay, but Tenzing couldn't go back to the life of a salt carrier, so he returned to Darjeeling and Dawa Phuti. They settled down in Toong Soong basti, in a room rented from Ang Tharkay.

In 1934, the community mourned the loss of their men on the tragic Nanga Parbat expedition, while Ang Tsering, Dawa Phuti's cousin, returned a hero for coming down the mountain alive. In early 1935, Dawa Phuti married Tenzing, although her relatives (including Ang Tsering and his brother Ajeeba) did not exactly approve of their new son-in-law. In fact, her father is said to have disinherited her, instead willing his wealth to her sister's husband. But Dawa Phuti was happy and in love—and true to her name, which means "the wife who brings children," she was soon pregnant.

That year, Eric Shipton began recruiting for the 1935 reconnaissance of Everest. Tenzing had no HC book or recommendation, knew no English, and did not have any experience, but Shipton was known to be unconventional. Out of one hundred applicants, fifteen were chosen—nineteen-year-old Tenzing Norgay/Norkay/Bhutia was among them. He now had a chit book and a promised salary of twelve annas a day—three-quarters of a rupee, or less than one cent in modern dollars—so he bid his wife goodbye and marched north. He got noticed and ticked all the boxes that Sherpas had come to be known for: "cheerful lad," "willing to work hard," "strong climber" (Tenzing had never climbed before but began to learn by watching), "grinning face in the tent door bringing bed tea." His father came to spend time with him at basecamp, which was a bonus for young Tenzing.

Upon Tenzing's return to Darjeeling, Dawa Phuti had their first baby—a boy they named Nima Dorje. During the few years leading up to World War II, Tenzing honed his climbing skills, and, just as importantly, his social skills. He warmed up not only to the sahabs but to his fellow Sherpas, with whom he created lifelong bonds. Dawa Phuti was still his first love but now she was not the only one. Tenzing had also become addicted to adventure—staying home became harder and harder.

In these years, he met John Martyn and Jack Gibson, teachers at the Doon School, an elite, all-boys boarding school in Uttarakhand. Tenzing accompanied them to the massif of Bandarpunch in the Garhwal, which they summitted on their fourth and final trip. These were happy times for Tenzing. Dawa Phuti was pregnant again, but all Tenzing dreamed about was going back to Everest. In 1938, he went on the last of the pre-war

Everest expeditions, led by Bill Tilman. It was a smaller one compared to 1936, and while they did not get very far, it afforded Tenzing another chance to show his strength and initiative at high altitudes. All the porters who carried to Camp VI at 8,300 meters—including Tenzing—were awarded Tiger Badges.

That same year, Tenzing and Dawa Phuti had their second child, a daughter they named Pemba and called "PemPem." There were no upcoming expeditions to Everest, so in 1939, Tenzing went along with the well-known explorer couple Miles and Beryl Smeeton to climb Tirich Mir, the highest peak in the Hindu Kush. Again, Tenzing, then twenty-five, left an impression. "Tall, open faced, charming, friendly, uncomplicated, loyal" were adjectives Miles used in his memoir, *A Taste of the Hills.* "He was a thoroughbred. He was more than that; a hill peasant, a carrier of burdens, but we felt he had been touched by some divine spirit which made him different from ordinary men."

In the war years, getting work was hard, so when Tenzing was offered a job as an orderly in the Chitral Scouts—an Indian military regiment, now based in Pakistan—he took it. The stunning Hindu Kush range encompasses the Chitral district, which is counted among the highest regions in the world and packs in more than forty peaks standing 6,100 meters or higher. Chitral seemed like a wonderful place for Tenzing to settle, offering fruit of all kinds; trout in the river; sheep and goats for meat, milk, and curd; and fields of wheat. December 1939, however, brought bad news from Darjeeling: four-year-old Nima Dorje had died of dysentery. Tenzing returned home heartbroken. Then, in 1940, Dawa Phuti gave birth to their second daughter, whom they named Nima after their late son.

PemPem told us, "He was a wonderful father, very responsible, very loving; he worked really hard for his daughters. After my sister was born, Daddy took us to Chitral, where he had a job in some regiment. We trekked from Darjeeling to Chitral, but my mother could not adjust and remained in poor health until she died in 1944. My father found it hard to look after us, as we were very young. In 1945, he moved back to Darjeeling so we could get an education and be with our own people. He needed somebody to take care of us. So he married my mother's cousin Ang Lhamu. My mother's relatives were uncertain about how a stepmother would treat the children, but she never made us feel that she was a stepmother. She was a wonderful lady. In fact, I did not even know that she was not my birth mother. Many years later when somebody told me, I asked her. 'Who told you?' she asked. She was so mad."

The Ang Lhamu Years: Tenzing's Glory Days

At age thirty-one, Tenzing was back in Darjeeling. Seven years had passed since he'd last gone to Everest, and probably six years since he'd last attempted a mountain. As Ed Douglas wrote in *Tenzing: Hero of Everest*, "The interruption in his climbing career was now longer than the career itself."

Ang Lhamu was a matronly figure, four years older than Tenzing, widowed, and without children. She worked as a nanny and servant in various British homes, even having traveled to England as one. It appears that she and Tenzing were good friends, but not lovers. Theirs was a stable family characterized by friendship and peace. Tenzing did odd jobs and bought horses to race at the Lebong Race Course. He took tourists around Darjeeling and up Tiger Hill, from where they could see Everest in the distance. PemPem reminisced, "Down in Lebong is the old race track—it is still there. My mother, father, and I were fond of [horseback] riding. My father had five or six beautiful horses. We would get up at 2 a.m. and go to Lebong and ride. Then we would gallop to the Calcutta road and Jorbangla [a village outside Darjeeling]."

Another trip with the Doon School teachers to Bandarpunch in 1946 was followed by an expedition to Everest the next year with a strange and complex loner from Canada, Earl Denman. Denman came to Darjeeling with a dream and very little money. Although he did not have a permit to climb Everest, he convinced Karma Paul that he was not crazy like the ill-fated Maurice Wilson, who'd attempted the peak solo in 1934. Karma rightly thought Tenzing would be the man to go with Denman. Tenzing admitted that anyone else would have refused to go along with Denman's hare-brained plan, but for him, the call of Everest was too compelling. They camped four times, and returned after reaching the slopes below the North Col. At Rongbuk, Tenzing had a special meeting with his sister Lhamu Kipa, who was married to a monk named Nawang Gyaltzen.

The same year—1947—a Swiss expedition to Kedarnath with André Roch and others was a turning point. Sardar Wangdi Norbu's accident on the expedition led to Tenzing becoming the sardar. With the Swiss, he experienced a sense of camaraderie and equality for the first time. They laughed a lot, shared food and labor, and even reached the summit of Kedarnath together, hugging and shouting with excitement. That evening they drank a glass of wine together to celebrate.

Tenzing was finally becoming the man he would be when he achieved the unimaginable in 1953. It was not just that he was at the right place at the right time. These experiences leading up to Everest were cementing his resolve; he was working steadily to achieve his goal, long before he actually did.

In many ways, that year—1947—was a landmark year for Tenzing. He truly broke free, just as India rid herself of her British occupiers. He was in his tent in Garhwal when Prime Minister Nehru made his famous midnight speech: "A moment comes, which comes but rarely in history, when we step out from the old to the new, when an age ends, and when the soul of a nation, long suppressed, finds utterance." Tenzing's soul found utterance on the expedition to Kedarnath, but he crashed back to reality with a thud. He spent all his earnings trying to get home in the chaos and nightmare that followed the post-independence partition of India and Pakistan.

Once he returned to Darjeeling, he was out of work for the rest of the year. The Sherpa world fell into a pall of gloom because their sahabs, their *zhindaks* (patrons), had left. *What would happen to them now?*

And then Italian explorer Giuseppe Tucci took Tenzing to Tibet. This was his eighth trip as part of a thorough study of the country. As they traveled through Chumbi Valley, it is said that Tenzing got an education about his land and people. His meeting with the Dalai Lama on that expedition created a lasting impression. Another hallmark of Tenzing's happiest and simplest days in the mountains, this trip would also be his last carefree expedition, as a new order was quickly replacing the old.

Dorjee Lhatoo shared this wonderful memory of meeting Tenzing in his home village of Yatung in the Chumbi Valley of Tibet. "I had first seen Tenzing Norgay when he came to Yatung and to my house. I was a small boy. Among the Tibetans also, you can make out an outstanding, good-looking fellow. He was that. Long hair; his hair would come into his eyes, and he would shake it off . . . he had a polka-dot scarf around his neck. . . . [When] we came down from Tibet as refugees and lived in the same *mohalla* [a synonym for *basti*—settlement], we were neighbors, and that's when he was ready anytime for a drink and a dance . . . happy!"

In 1950, a French expedition led by Maurice Herzog climbed Annapurna, and the race for the 8,000ers began in earnest. Sherpas and sardars like Ang

Tharkay, Pasang Dawa Lama, and the much younger Tenzing Norgay began to vie with each other for plum expeditions. Ang Lhamu stoically continued working as an ayah (maid) and as a receptionist for a local dentist. She took tourists around Darjeeling on the family's horses. She devoted most of her time, though, to being a wonderful mother to the young girls who were growing up rapidly in a one-room tenement in Toong Soong.

In 1950, Tenzing got an unusual job: exploring Pakistan's Karakoram. With him were Ajeeba and Phu Tharkay of Annapurna fame, as well as Ang Temba, who would be an instructor at the HMI. They were prevented from proceeding much farther than the city of Gilgit, as their permits got cancelled. Nonetheless, their employers Jim Thornley, Dick Marsh, and Bill Crace decided to sneak an attempt on Nanga Parbat. The crazy plan ended in tragedy when Thornley and Crace disappeared on the mountain. Tenzing was now at the make-or-break age of thirty-six.

In 1951, he was chosen for the first attempt on the Nanda Devi traverse. Hoping this expedition might write his history, Tenzing begged the French sahabs to allow him to accompany them to the top, but they refused. Roger Duplat and Gilbert Vignes disappeared on the ridge somewhere below the main summit, and Tenzing and Louis Dubost summitted Nanda Devi East to look for the missing climbers, but Duplat and Vignes were gone.

Rounding out the series of tragedies that would have broken lesser men, Tenzing was part of an expedition to Kangchenjunga's north side with Swiss climber George Frey. On a small acclimatization peak, Koktang, Frey slipped past Tenzing, who tried unsuccessfully to catch him. Tenzing slipped as well, but managed to arrest his own fall while Frey plummeted to his death.

The early 1950s were a time of change. Tenzing had become a leader who influenced men and cultivated non-climbing friends like Ravi Mitra. The British, Germans, and French were joined by the Swiss who, in the race to climb the 8,000ers, threatened to upset the applecart with their egalitarian attitude toward the Sherpas and their generous provisions of food and equipment. Now the Sherpas wanted better equipment, a better diet, and an equal shot at the summit. In the summer of 1952, Tenzing went to Everest with the Swiss, attempting the deadly Khumbu Icefall on the south side. In the course of this expedition, he and Raymond Lambert developed an immediate and lifelong friendship.

Kinzom, now eighty, and her daughter Lhamu Kipa crossed the Nangpa La to Thame, just to meet Tenzing. It had been at least twenty years since she'd

Happy days—Tenzing with his niece
Doma *(Dorjee Lhatoo Collection)*

laid eyes on her youngest son. Tenzing's younger sister, Sonam Doma, and niece Phu Lhamu accompanied the expedition as porters, along with several other women from Khumbu.

This expedition has been documented widely as a precursor to the following year's success. Just 198 meters below the South Summit, at the limits of their strength, with malfunctioning oxygen equipment, Tenzing and Lambert wordlessly decided to turn around. They had so wanted to step on the summit together, a desire left unfilled but remembered by both friends forever.

In fact, the Swiss had another go at the mountain that same year, post monsoon. But they were late by just a few weeks, and the winter winds blew too strongly. Lambert, Tenzing, and others made it to the South Col, but were forced back by extremely cold weather.

And then came the invitation to travel to Everest with the British again—in 1953.

Dorjee Lhatoo's wife, Doma, told us, "My mummy, Lhamu Kipa, was Tenzing's older sister. When the Everest team went in '53, my brother, Gombu, went with them. Tenzing told my mother that on his return, he would take me and send me to school in Darjeeling. I was fourteen years old . . . I was so happy to go with him."

That expedition achieved the most celebrated summit in the history of mountaineering, and the team returned to Kathmandu to a heroic welcome. Doma was with her uncle and described the triumphant return: "There were so many people! *Arrey baap re* [Oh my God]!

"Hillary and Tenzing were walking together and I was in the middle, holding both their hands. We came down the road for the welcome. There were so many people that I could not hold on. My uncle told me, 'Don't let go of my hand. Hold it tight!' No matter how tight I held on, we were being pulled apart. I disappeared. . . . I lost my uncle. Topgay [Tenzing's older brother's son] and Phu Lhamu [the daughter of Tenzing's oldest brother] and I were together. I did not like Kathmandu. So many people, cars, trucks . . . How much I cried! I had never seen a car before! 'Let's go, let's return back to our home; we will not stay here,' I cried. 'No, no, you are going to Darjeeling, don't cry,' said Topgay. Then my uncle came early the next morning saying, 'Where are my girls?' He came to take us to the [Hotel Royal]. That was the only good hotel where the Europeans could go and stay; it had big open grounds. The king and ministers were all there.

"My uncle told us to go with Topgay to Darjeeling, as he was going to London. Topgay brought Phu Lhamu and me. Phu Lhamu had been to Darjeeling a number of times so she had an idea. I was innocent, thirteen or fourteen years old, and had not gone out of my village ever; they were in their twenties. Topgay was a high-altitude Sherpa, and Phu Lhamu was a porter on those expeditions."

Dorjee Lhatoo says that Doma's village home had two stories: goats and cows lived on the ground level, while the family lived upstairs. When she saw Tenzing's ground-floor home in Toong Soong, with the landlords living upstairs, her reaction was priceless. She said, "Topgay daju, there are people in the house!" She told us in her endearing English, "I shocked! When I saw my uncle's room, I said, 'That's all?' What a small room! A kitchen on one side, two beds, and a few utensils! We had heard that he had a lot of work, that he was doing so well, and this [was his] house?"

Little did Doma know of the significance of what she had witnessed in Kathmandu. On May 29, 1953, Edmund Hillary and Tenzing Norgay became the first humans to stand atop Mount Everest. Upon his return to Everest Basecamp, Hillary would issue the now-famous quip "Well, we knocked the bastard off." That they did. But neither man could have imagined the global euphoria that followed. Was it because four nations—Nepal, India, England, and Tibet—were involved? Or because there were celebrations on England's streets as the young queen, Elizabeth II, was being crowned, and this was the nation's best gift to itself? Or was it because of a young, ambitious India, in search of its own heroes after decades of servility? Or then, maybe it was a newly open Nepal, just realizing the pot of gold at its doorstep. For Tibet, was it perhaps a question of Tenzing's identity as a Bhutia? For Tenzing

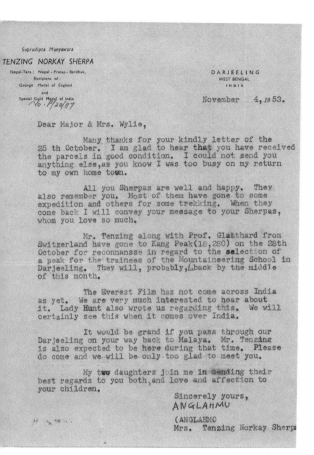

Letter written by Ang Lahmu on behalf of her husband Tenzing Norgay *(The Sherpa Project)*

Norgay, it was the beginning of a life that no one could have imagined.

Jan Morris wrote in *Coronation Everest,* "Tenzing, hat pushed back on his head, his face permanently wreathed and crinkled with smiles, laughed and nodded as he ate his omelette, while the worshipping Sherpas at the door gazed at him like apostates before the Pope. Indeed, he was a fine sight, sitting there in his moment of triumph, before the jackals of fame closed upon him."

Tenzing's friend Ravi Mitra and the poet and folk singer Dharmaraj Thapa were at Glenary's in Darjeeling when they learned of the remarkable victory. Mitra immediately sent word to Ang Lhamu and arranged for her to travel to Nepal to meet Tenzing. He also began to map Tenzing's trajectory even before the hero returned to Darjeeling. Thapa wrote the song "Hamro Tenzing Sherpa Le," which was put to music and recorded in Kolkata; it became a huge hit, only adding to Tenzing's legend. Finally, Tenzing caught the fancy of India's first prime minister, Jawaharlal Nehru, a man who had it in him to make "mountains move." Within a few hours of meeting each other, they developed a mutual fondness, and Nehru, while encouraging Tenzing to travel to England for the celebration, famously opened his wardrobe of *bund galas* and *sherwanis*—both a type of traditional Indian suit—for Tenzing to select and carry. This gesture touched Tenzing deeply. The next effort was to "make a thousand Tenzings," and for this Nehru built the HMI. Nehru was astute in his handling of Tenzing, as he wanted this hero to claim an Indian identity, yet Nehru's efforts remained paternal, not patronizing. A crowd-funding effort by *Anandabazar Patrika,* the Kolkata-based newspaper, gathered more than enough money to build Tenzing a palatial house in Darjeeling: Ghang-la.

And so it came to be that a non-Sherpa, non-Nepali, Khampa Bhutia became the name that put every Nepali and Indian Sherpa on the global map. Tenzing "wrote" his autobiography, *Man of Everest;* traveled to different parts of the world; found joy in teaching; and got embroiled in the politics of being "owned" by the government of India. In short, he took on the trappings of fame.

Tenzing was well on track for the next phase of his life. PemPem reminisced:

> After Everest, he was extremely busy . . . But my mother was a great lady, and she supported him. He was offered a lot of facilities in Nepal. But all he wanted was a good education for us. He had not seen the door of a school, but he knew its importance. We learnt academics, and life skills such as sewing, knitting, cooking, and gardening. Every week, although he was busy, Daddy would come to see how we were progressing in the convent [Catholic schools in India are colloquially referred to as 'convents']. When he returned, it was another world, a very different life. Meeting different people, talking to them—it was sudden exposure. We had led a very simple life until then. This was also an education, an experience.
>
> Within five to six years, the HMI had students coming from all over India. My father worked hard along with the principal and dedicated people to produce good Indian mountaineers. Not only that, there were students from Nepal and Australia, England, etc. The achievements of Indian mountaineers show my father did his duty well. After he passed away, it was handed over to the new generation, and I don't know what they are doing. My father never left his people. Even in the HMI office, if any vacancy came up, he would put [in] a Sherpa as office staff. During my father's time, until 1986, there were plenty of Sherpas working at the HMI.

In 1955, Tenzing founded the Sherpa Climbers' Association, which helped expeditions hire Sherpas and negotiated better wages than The Himalayan Club. It also helped families financially in times of need.

PemPem once asked her father why he took the name Sherpa when he was a Bhutia. "He said when he got his first job, it was as a Sherpa. He would say, 'I live in India, in Darjeeling; I love this place.' My father married a Sherpani, and when he climbed Everest, he called himself a Sherpa. Before Everest, Sherpas were known as load carriers. My father always objected: 'Coolies are local people who carry loads from the ground to the basecamp and return. We don't return; we carry loads higher and higher.'"

Tenzing was touching forty when he stood atop Everest. Ang Lhamu and he were feted in different parts of the world. They made an unlikely pair. Tenzing was lithe and almost ageless; Ang Lhamu was matronly—she loved the good life, and it showed. She was hardly willing to give it up to become a memsahab! It is said that when Tenzing first went to London, Ang Lhamu carried with her some Tibetan crafts and jewelery popular with Westerners. As soon as she got a chance, she laid these out on the pavement to sell as was done back home!

The Daku Years: Tenzing's Decline

A decade flew by filled with the headiness of fame, family, and work. The good life was getting to Tenzing in different ways. At age fifty, he could hardly resist beautiful young Sherpa girls fawning over him, vying with each other to please. He began to enjoy coteries, developing strong likes and dislikes of people around him.

Dorjee Lhatoo, who was close to him, observed, "Once he became the famous Everest hero, then we would see him with that permanent artificial smile. But behind that, he was an angry man. And he had to find a victim. He had to vent his anger . . . [he was an] amiable, likeable person but when he was angry, it was no point being around . . . But when he told stories, of old Sherpas and expedition times, he was an amazing storyteller. He would speak in Nepali and Sherpa [and] Tibetan, and then in between he would use some Urdu words. The kind of language Pandit Nehru spoke."

The intoxication that comes with power began its slow but steady corrosion. Now the need of the hour was a trophy on his arm. In those days, the HMI employed sixty to seventy load-carrying girls on its courses. Among these women was Daku—the most attractive and most sought after. She fit the bill just right. Tenzing was smitten by this bubbly, bright soul, who was younger than PemPem. They married, and Daku quickly learned how to be a famous man's wife. It has sometimes been said that Ang Lhamu encouraged him to take a second wife because he did not have a son. From what we gathered, she did not have a choice. As one Sherpa we spoke with recalled, "When Tenzing married Daku, Ang Lhamu was very sad. She carried her sadness in her. She had no one to tell because she was very loyal to Tenzing and she didn't want to spoil anything for him."

Dorjee Lhatoo told us, "I worked with him for twenty-four years, going to the mountains together. He would come home, and Doma would make coffee for him. Uncle and niece would have a chat about other members of the family and so on. Daku was pregnant when she came in to take her place as the mistress of Ghang-la. In the years to come, they had three sons—Norbu, Jamling, and Dhamey—and a daughter, Diki. Norbu was initially looked after by Ang Lhamu as Tenzing and Daku traveled the world." In 1964, Ang Lhamu developed lung cancer. PemPem and Nima nursed their mother, while friends who had drifted away, like the Lamberts and Ravi Mitra, returned to visit. Ang Lhamu, his rock, and Pandit Nehru, his friend and mentor, died the same year. Tenzing would realize the depth of these losses only later.

For now, the HMI was not generating enough income for his growing family. He traveled more, endorsed travel agencies, and posed for photographs to earn money—there was some interest in his achievements again. He also hiked and trekked with his young family when he could. Gradually, he began to become obsolete at the HMI.

Dorjee Lhatoo spoke emotionally about this embittered man: "He was happy to be in the mountains. And he felt that he was removed against his wish from HMI." Lhatoo recounted Tenzing telling him, "'Panditji [Prime Minister Nehru] told me: "Tenzing, this is a job for life. Don't think about leaving the country. India is a good country. It is going to be great, and you would be a part of it." And look what they have done to me. Now I am jobless.'" Lhatoo continued, "He told this story to lots of people, and it must have gone to the ears of some well-meaning, powerful people in Delhi so then he was made the advisor of mountaineering, on nominal pay. But he was already hurt, and he said, 'What is this *advisor*? What does it mean?' As Director of Training, he had power. But *advisor* was some kind of honorary thing.

"About that time, a very famous travel company, Lindblad [Expeditions], contacted Tenzing. They not only organized travel in the Himalaya, but also cruises in the Arctic, Antarctic, and so on. When Tenzing was asked how much he got in his job—in those days, Tenzing's salary was 1,400 rupees a month [approximately $17]—Mr. Lindblad said, 'You can get Rs 1,400 for shaking an American hand! How many hands can you shake?' He joined Lindblad's tours as a celebrity. He and his wife were invited for cruises with American millionaires, and he got the idea of what money is. Then he became a travel-company owner."

Age is cruel; it catches up with you. Tenzing was tiring. As the years separated him from his 1953 achievement, he did not command as much importance in the public's imagination. His wife Daku looked after the household, led a hectic social life, and ran the family trekking business with unmatched zest. It's no surprise that when we met Jamling and later spoke with Norbu, they paid regular homage and respect to Tenzing without saying anything extraordinary or soulful—emotions of the sort Dorjee and Doma Lhatoo, PemPem, Tenzing Lhotay, and other early friends of Tenzing's expressed. *Tenzing after Everest*, his second autobiography with Malcolm Barnes, was a litany of the injustices Tenzing felt he faced. That the energetic Daku had begun to avoid him probably had more to do with his persona than hers.

In early May 1986, PemPem visited her father as she did every Tuesday afternoon, on her way home from work. At the time, Norbu, Jamling, and Diki were in American universities; Dhamey was in school, and Nima was in Singapore. Tenzing had made *aloo parathas* for lunch, and they chatted. PemPem said that they talked about Daku.

PemPem recalled, "Daddy told me, 'I should have listened to you at that time. [Daku] has no time for me.' I responded, 'It is too late—I told you in the '60s.' Towards the end, I was the only one. 'Stop drinking,' I would say. 'Don't end your life like this, just because of a woman.' But what to do, he married a very young woman. That afternoon, I said, 'I am your oldest daughter. Daddy, I know you—before Everest, after Everest. If I don't look after you, if I don't see your problems, who will?' Two days before he passed away, I was there to do all his personal work, his correspondence." That very day, Daku also returned from Kathmandu after having been away for two months.

Over the next couple of days, Tenzing continued his routine of walking and visiting friends in Darjeeling, wearing a large-brimmed hat and dark glasses to cover his puffy eyes and face. He had coffee with his niece Doma and Dorjee Lhatoo, met his friends at the HMI, and had tea with Gombu. Everyone believed that although he was unwell, he would get better. Tenzing had a sunny, strong personality. He was certain he would be able to convince Daku to be with him now that she was here. His death two days later came as a huge shock to everyone. His friend Tenzing Lhotay said, "When Tenzing died, no one was with him. He had no illness, no worries. That evening he was fine and he went to bed, but he slept and didn't wake up."

Durga Das, another friend who owns a photo studio in Darjeeling, told us, "It was sad the way he died. He didn't die a happy man. He had family problems, pressures. He couldn't understand the way people treated him—on one hand, praise him; and on another, push him around. He never knew where he stood. He was lonely. When he had problems with Sherpas, he would tell me."

After Tenzing passed, Daku is said to have become almost an ascetic. She died not too many years later while traveling through the jungles of Northeast India.

Of course, Tenzing's funeral was that of a hero. Daku was present, and his children arrived, as did Sir Edmund Hillary and several dignitaries. His body was taken to the HMI in a long procession and kept in state for the hundreds who wanted to pay their last respects. He was cremated on a hillock above the institute that had been built for him.

On May 29, 2013, exactly sixty years after Tenzing stood atop Everest, Phurtemba Sherpa spoke to crowds who had gathered at the HMI to celebrate the occasion. "This Himalayan Mountaineering Institute was made because of Mr. Tenzing Sherpa. All the people who are working at the HMI today, all the families that are growing up here today, all the people sitting here today, are here because of Mr. Tenzing Sherpa," he said.

Tenzing Norgay is the bedrock upon which the universal recognition of the Sherpas was built. He was indeed the first among equals.

"To create a thousand Tenzings!" The Himalayan Mountaineering Institute opened with great fanfare and excitement. Celebrating the event is Prime Minister Jawaharlal Nehru (center foreground in light-colored jacket); his daughter, Indira Gandhi; and the chief minister of West Bengal, Bidhan Chandra Roy; along with newly appointed staff members and well-wishers. *(Himalayan Mountaineering Institute Collection)*

CHAPTER 11

The Gang's All Here: The Himalayan Mountaineering Institute

New Delhi

15 November, 1954.

My dear Chief Minister,

Immediately on my return from China, I went to Darjeeling to inaugurate the Institute of Himalayan Mountaineering. This may appear to some as specialist work in which only a limited number of persons are likely to take interest. I consider it as having a larger significance. It seemed to me a symbol of our new India full of energy and aspiration and daring. Standing almost under the shadow of Kanchenjunga, I felt exhilarated and I sensed this new youthful spirit of our country. The Institute is not merely to instruct in high-class mountaineering, but also to train, I hope, large numbers of people in the smaller feats which produce initiative, endurance, and character, and not to mention good health. Also, it is to encourage winter sports. I hope, therefore, that all States in India will take interest in it and help it, more particularly those States which might be called the Himalayan States and which touch this mighty range of mountains which has been our friend and sentinel for ages past.

—Pandit Jawaharlal Nehru

First Prime Minister of India

In a nondescript building in the old district of Bhowanipore, Kolkata, we climbed narrow steps to a near-empty apartment and met Amitava Sain. His grandfather Manindranath Sain had been the first designer and curator of the HMI museum. His father, Brojendranath Sain, had taken over this role upon Manindranath's retirement. Amitava lived nearby, but this was the flat where he had stored his father's and grandfather's paintings and various memorabilia. Influential figures in Darjeeling, the Sains were highly regarded artists whose paintings of the surrounding mountains still grace the walls of the institute.

Amitava told us, "The chief minister of West Bengal, and my grandfather's good friend, Dr. Bidhan Chandra Roy, used to frequently visit our house. Once the dust had settled following the successful Everest expedition, he said we must do something for the youth of the country; we should start an institute so that this sport of mountaineering percolates to our youth as well."

The two men took their idea to Jawaharlal Nehru, who welcomed it enthusiastically, for this idea fit in perfectly with Nehru's vision. After the momentous first summitting of Everest in May 1953, Jawaharlal Nehru saw Tenzing Norgay as representative of a newly independent India bursting with youthful energy, ready to scale peaks literally as well as metaphorically. With the hope of firmly establishing Tenzing as a son of India, Nehru agreed to give the Sherpas of Darjeeling an institute that would create "a thousand Tenzings."

The government of India appointed Arnold Glatthard, a famous alpinist and founder of the Swiss mountaineering school Bergsteigerschule Rosenlaui, as a consultant and Tenzing Norgay as director of field training. Tenzing, Glatthard, and Major Nandu Jayal, the proposed principal of the HMI, searched for suitable field classrooms and settled on the peaks of Kabru and Rathong. The HMI basecamp was established at Kabru Saddle, near Dzongri in Sikkim, hiking distance from Darjeeling.

Along with Jayal and Tenzing, a group of ace Sherpas was selected to be the first instructors and trained in Rosenlaui, Switzerland, under Glatthard. They were Ang Tharkay, Nawang Gombu, Nawang Topgay, Ang Temba, and the brothers Gyalzen "Mikchen" ("the big-eyed") and Da Namgyal. They had all climbed with some of the biggest names in Western mountaineering and had porter books and Himalayan Club numbers. Their names cropped up in expedition accounts, and although unknown to the world at large, within climbing circles they were already legends.

Ang Tharkay, sardar on the 1950 French expedition to Annapurna—the first 8,000er to be climbed—was known as the "little man with the big heart" long before Tenzing made the word *Sherpa* famous. Nawang Gombu, while at the HMI, would go on to become the first man to climb Mount Everest two times, and Gyalzen Mikchen had been with Ruttledge on Everest in 1936 and later with Shipton, Tilman, Odell, and the Swiss and Japanese. Gyalzen's younger brother Da Namgyal was John Hunt's personal Sherpa and had carried oxygen tanks beyond the South Col for Hillary and Tenzing's summit push. Topgay and Ang Temba were on the Everest teams of 1952 and 1953, and in 1952, little Ang Temba, the shortest of the Sherpas, proved his mettle by climbing up to the South Col three times, bringing 25-kilogram loads on every ferry.

On the crisp, clear morning of November 4, 1954, with the white slopes of Kangchenjunga glistening in the sun, Nehru, his daughter, Indira Gandhi, and other dignitaries were welcomed by the governor of Bengal and Tenzing and his daughters at a pavilion tastefully decorated by artists from Shanti Niketan, a town identified by its university in West Bengal, famous for attracting some of the most creative minds in the country. Sherpa monks chanted hymns, and then Nehru addressed the gathering. He hoped that "the generation which was growing up in the new India of today would raise the country's prestige as high as the Himalaya." He added that "the institute had been built in honor of Tenzing and his brave band of Sherpas." Laying the foundation stone, Nehru said the work ahead would be hard because "mountaineering patience was needed to build a new India." The guests watched a thrilling rock climbing demo that included Tenzing's nieces Sonam Doma and Phu Lhamu in checked shirts and blue breeches. They scrambled up the steep rock face and rappelled down gracefully.

Thus began the HMI. The silhouette of a climber scaling a mountain with the words "May (You) Climb from Peak to Peak" is the first graphic on the institute wall and greets visitors who enter today.

Soon after the HMI, the government opened more mountaineering institutes; in 1959, the Indian Mountaineering Federation (IMF) was established to promote expeditions and otherwise act as godfather to mountaineers and mountaineering clubs. The HMI was no longer the sole teacher of the craft of climbing, though it was still acknowledged as the best. A certificate from the institute became a trainee's prized possession, recognized all over the world. The first presidents of its governing board were all prime ministers of the country. Today, the government of India and the government of West Bengal jointly run the institute. Its executive council is headed by the defense minister as its president and the chief minister of West Bengal as its vice president.

In the early, heady days of the HMI, every instructor was larger than life. They were all imbued with a passion for the task set to them and eager to pass on everything they had to offer. The HMI gave them a dignity—the great dignity of being teachers—that life thus far had not offered, and they flowered. Also, with the charismatic Tenzing Norgay heading the training, mountaineers from all over the world were drawn to visit, thus giving the early batches of students an international perspective on climbing and the mountains.

Tenzing accompanied most of the courses with his Lhasa apsos in tow, and took a keen interest in the training programs. As a teacher, he was inspiring. He started at the age of forty and continued as field director for twenty-three years. His work absorbed him enough that he gave up serious peak climbing. It almost seems like he lost his appetite for it, but that was all to HMI's gain. Despite all the trouble that had come from overnight fame, Sherpa Tenzing Norgay did his best to prove to his mentor Nehru that the latter's trust had been well placed.

While the Sherpas and Bhutias did the field training, the post of HMI principal has always been held by an army officer. One reason was that Tenzing and the early Sherpas were illiterate. Another reason was that the institute has always been politically important in a strategically sensitive geographical area. However, there was mutual respect and friendliness. Nandu Jayal and some of the other early principals looked to their Sherpa instructors for guidance and trusted their abilities.

In *Alpine Journal* in 1994, Harish Kapadia captured the mood of those days: "We sat around a roaring campfire. Raymond Lambert was visiting Sikkim as a special guest of Tenzing Norgay, and we, the students of the Basic training course of the Himalayan Mountaineering Institute, were entertaining the guests in exchange for superb Scotch whisky. The Indian pre-Everest expedition was also there. Students and Sherpas mingled with leading mountaineers of India, taking in the ambience of food and fun. As the fire turned to embers, the night passed into memory; but the bonds of friendship forged on that evening back in 1964 have lasted me a lifetime."

Dr. Lala Telang was in the twenty-third Basic course in 1959. He told us, "The aura (of Tenzing) was there, and everybody was in great awe of him. I remember that on my Basic course, ice axes [badges awarded upon course completion] were given by Edmund Hillary, so the institute was still effervescing at that time."

While a first-year medical student in 1964, Rekha Shroff participated in the HMI women's course. She says that her instructors were "open, contented, no complaints about not having something. That touched you as much as the way they took care of you. We called them 'daju,' as they all showed a sense of such responsibility—even someone as young as Ang Kami [a dynamic young Sherpa who went on to climb Everest with the Indian team in 1965]. They were incredibly patient, though they could properly shout if you didn't do as they said! In May 1968, I did the Advanced mountaineering course. With them, you walked in the hills in a way you never [had] before on holiday trips.

"Sherpas don't just live in nature but *with* nature. Besides being kind to the natural world, they were tremendously intelligent and informed about it. And they were ready to communicate their knowledge to city people who were willing to listen—how to tell when it was going to rain, know what fruit or berry was right to eat, spot junipers and their uses, identify and respect every single shrub and tree along any route. Someone like Nima Tashi knew all 108 varieties of Sikkim Himalaya orchids and taught us to observe them. It was never just about walking on this trail or seeing that peak and valley. Learning from them was what attracted me to go again and again."

Many students echoed this comment—what made the HMI special was its teachers, proud Sherpas who instilled in their students a love of the mountains that extended far beyond climbing them.

Nawang Gombu with John F. Kennedy after the first American ascent of Mount Everest in 1963 *(Dorjee Lhatoo Collection)*

CHAPTER 12

Heart of Gold: Nawang Gombu

The Kangshung Face forms the eastern wall of Everest and Lhotse. Its glacier in the Tibet Autonomous Region is one of Everest's three main glaciers, while the border between Nepal and Tibet runs across certain summits in this area. Yak herders have roamed these lands for centuries and farmed in fertile valleys fed by its glacial waters. Life here is harsh, and the men and women become weathered accordingly. Today, this region is a trekking thoroughfare, leading to the Khangshung Face and to Everest's north-side basecamp.

It was through this area that early expeditions such as the 1921 Everest reconnaissance led by Charles Howard-Bury would have passed. In those days, the governor of a region was known as Dzongpen (*dzong* means "fortress," so "keeper of the fortress"), and his band of tax collectors were Penlops or Pembas who were rich and powerful in their own right. Poor villagers, with their small, barely fertile plots of land and livestock destroyed by disease, often got into debt traps with these tax collectors, who enslaved them for generations to pay off the unending debt.

Nawang Gyalzen was the youngest son of a wealthy, landowning Pemba, and in the 1930s trained to be a monk at a monastery. On one visit home, he fell in love with Lhamu Kipa, eldest sister of Tenzing Norgay and daughter of yak herders who were indebted to his father. Their romance blossomed surreptitiously. When the young couple decided to elope, they were caught before they could reach the Nepal border, and the lama was sent back to the monastery.

However, Lhamu Kipa was pregnant so the landowner decided to punish her in a creative, particularly cruel manner. He had a hole dug in the ground, into which Lhamu was placed face down so that her belly snugly rested in the hole to keep the baby comfortable while Lhamu was beaten. This was the Tibetan way of thinking—the innocent baby was not harmed, while its mother was thrashed for tempting the rich man's son.

The child that was born in 1935 was called Nawang Gombu. Knowing that there was no hope for the little family under the Pemba's glare, the couple attempted to escape again. This time they succeeded in crossing the border into Khumbu, Nepal, helped by numerous villagers along the way.

As Nawang Gyalzen was already a lama, he found a caretaker job in a remote monastery. The couple had more babies, but the only other one that survived was a baby girl they called Sonam Doma. When he was ten, Gombu was sent off to the Rongbuk Monastery to study. Gombu's granddaughter Kunzes Goba shared a personal tribute to her grandfather called *Popo*. In it, she wrote:

> I remember being only ten years old when I approached him for an interview for a school assignment. While I was more focused on getting the job done as soon as possible, Popo was persistent about telling me more about his childhood, about how he had to climb through the toilet hole to escape the monastery with his friend, about how this friend abandoned him halfway through because of exhaustion, about how at nine years old he already knew what he wanted from life. It fascinated me that he always went back to the same story. Even when he was in his sixties, everything went back to that moment so long ago.
>
> I searched for Rongbuk Monastery on the internet and found out that it was listed as one of the best places to live in as a recluse. I realized that this is where the crux of Popo's character lies. He never wanted to settle. Settling, for Popo, was a sign of danger. It was a sign that a person no longer felt the need to grow.

Talking to the author, Himalayan historian and documentary filmmaker Mick Conefrey, Gombu said, "My father sent me there to study for five years—I stayed for one year, but it was very hard, you know . . . Sometimes if you made a mistake in reading or writing they took out a huge leather stick and hit you fifty, sixty, seventy times. And we only got to eat supper. After one year, I thought, 'How could I go out from here?'"

Gombu and a friend escaped on a bitterly cold moonlit night by slipping into the gaping holes that made up the monastery toilets—surely an unpleasant experience. It took five days for the eleven-year-old, wearing plastic bags for shoes, to cross the frozen 5,791-meter pass of the Nangpa La to get home. Gombu was not sent back, and years passed as he and his sister, Doma, grew up, tending yaks.

One day in 1952, Lhamu Kipa heard that her youngest brother, Tenzing Norgay, now a famous sardar, was on his way to Everest with a Swiss expedition. Tenzing had sent word to his mother and sister to come meet him; he came laden with gifts, and the family embraced after more than twenty years. It was then that Nawang Gombu, only sixteen, met his renowned uncle for the first time.

The following year, Gombu accompanied Tenzing to Everest. He was the youngest member of the expedition, plump but filled with energy, always looking for jobs to perform. Gombu left his mark. That year, the seventeen-year-old twice carried a fifty-pound load to the South Col at 7,925 meters without supplemental oxygen, and after Hillary and Tenzing's landmark ascent, he was awarded the Tiger Badge and the Queen's Coronation Medal.

Nawang Gombu was strong and stocky. He had a baby face and a child's forthrightness. He asked John Hunt during the 1953 Everest expedition, "I am carrying two oxygen cylinders, why are you carrying only one?" and at another time he said to Michael Ward, for whom he was working as a personal Sherpa, "Please slow down—I can't walk as fast as you."

After Everest, Gombu came to Darjeeling with Tenzing. They lived in a rented room, amid other climbing Sherpas. In Tenzing's rooms were his wife, Ang Lhamu; daughters, PemPem and Nima; and Gombu's sister, Doma, who had also been brought to Toong Soong. When Gombu was not busy as a helper with treks and expeditions, he cooked, cleaned, and collected firewood for his aunt Ang Lhamu. Dorjee Lhatoo said, "Near Toong Soong there used to be a big forest. I remember Gombu daju carrying heavy loads of firewood from the forest. How much can be used in the home? The rest he would sell. My mother bought firewood from him. We all started from such humble beginnings. He definitely did."

Today, walking from Chowrasta toward the HMI, you will see an elegant memorial to Nawang Gombu. This man of humble beginnings went on to be the first person to climb Everest twice; he traveled the world and was feted by international leaders.

In 1955, Gombu was twenty years old and already becoming quite successful when he married a young Sherpani called Dawa Phuti (a fairly common name in those days). Climbers recruiting people for expeditions came looking for him, and he took a job as one of the first instructors at the HMI. Apart from everything else, it meant an assured year-round salary instead of seasonal payments. Throughout this period, Gombu was like a sponge, learning from everyone around him. He already knew Tibetan, Sherpa, and Nepali, but now he learned Hindi and endeavored to speak a little English as well.

GOMBU WAS WORKING REALLY HARD. By all accounts, he thoroughly enjoyed both teaching and climbing. While forty-year-old Tenzing was more or less retired from active climbing, Gombu had only just begun. He went on expeditions to Makalu, Saser Kangri, Cho Oyu, and Nanda Devi.

Child of Two Fathers

The Indian Mountaineering Foundation is India's door to the climbing fraternity worldwide. Permissions, logistics, information, and whatever else is needed to climb within the country are available at its headquarters on the road of Benito Juárez Marg in New Delhi. A large group of predominantly male mountaineers, ex-mountaineers, and army folks administer the IMF. Standing out among them is an outspoken woman, Rita Gombu Marwah.

This oldest daughter of Nawang Gombu has long been an outspoken opponent of chauvinistic tendencies in the mountaineering world. As she told us of an event at the Indian Mountaineering Foundation, "The IMF gave Brig. Khullar the [Nain Singh-Kishan Singh] Award for exploration. I got up and said, 'Start with the man with the maximum achievements; don't give this award as part of the old boys' club: "I pat your back, you pat my back, and we reward each other with awards."' I was so angry."

That is Sherpa Rita Gombu for you: efficient, blunt, and an accomplished mountaineer. Selected as a candidate for the 1984 Indian Everest expedition, she was widely regarded as one of the two best women candidates to make it to the top. Ultimately, an unlikely contender, Bachendri Pal, became the first woman to stand on the summit. Rita remembered, "[Gombu] had expectations, and when he heard that I had missed the summit—Ongmu told me recently—he threw a transistor or something. He would have been happier if I had climbed [to the top]." Nevertheless, Rita was feted as the first Indian woman to reach the peak's South Summit.

When Nawang Gombu's first wife, Dawa Phuti, died in childbirth, the infant—named Rita after a nurse in the maternity ward—was taken to Tenzing's home, where she was brought up by Ang Lhamu and Doma as a daughter of the house. In fact, she had no idea for several years that Ang Lhamu and Tenzing were not her parents. At first, the family wanted Gombu to marry Ang Doma, Dawa Phuti's younger sister, but Ang Doma refused. "I ran away to Calcutta and returned after six months when [Nawang Gombu] had remarried," she told us. That's when Gombu married Sita, a beautiful young Darjeeling Sherpani who came from a family of illustrious climbers. Some years later, they brought Rita home to grow up with her half-siblings Yangdu and Phinjo. Ongmu was born a few years after Rita came home.

As a teenager, Rita decided to take HMI's Adventure, Basic, and Advanced courses for girls. "My father was deputy director but he never played favorites," she said. A visiting woman instructor and big-wall climber inspired her, so she enrolled for a pre-Everest expedition in Sikkim, attempting Kabru Dome and Mana. Rita's affair with the mountains had begun. Even when she took a job at Air India she continued climbing and occasionally teaching at the HMI. In 1993, she was deputy leader of a successful Indo-Nepalese woman's Everest expedition. In 2003, she led an all-women's team up a virgin peak, Argan Kangri (6,789 meters). "Rita has climbing in her blood," Dorjee Lhatoo told us. Apart from her two paternal figures, Gombu and Tenzing, "her mother's father was a climbing Sherpa called Pema Norbu, and her uncle Pasang Phutar 'Jockey' was another well-known climber and instructor at HMI."

Rita is married to Nilamber Marwah, and they have two children, Vrinda and Nikhil. She continues to be actively involved in mountain affairs as part of the IMF. We met her perhaps three times in Darjeeling and in Delhi; she is a confident, tough woman with kind Sherpa eyes and an attractive, uneven-toothed smile. Most of all, she is forthright and fair-minded, with a clear sense of her own being. You cannot help but salute such women.

It was natural that he would be the most crucial member of the 1960 Indian Everest team, given his experience in the Khumbu Icefall in 1953. Along with Sonam Gyatso and Colonel "Bull" Kumar, Gombu was selected by the expedition leader Brigadier Gyan Singh to be on the first summit team. Weather pushed them back and they had to return, defeated by the mountain. In 1963, the Americans decided to attempt Everest; on May 1 that year, Nawang Gombu and Jim Whittaker stood on the summit. Ten years earlier, a tall New Zealander and shorter Sherpa had achieved the feat; now the 6′5″ Whittaker and the 5′6″ Gombu stood there alongside the spirits of those who had summitted before.

India planned its third attempt in 1965. This time they were successful, and Gombu along with A. S. Cheema made it to the top. We were told that Gombu was not keen on climbing Everest again, but when he was promised land on which to build a house, he decided to go. All through his life, Gombu's focus was his family. The HMI salary of a few hundred rupees a month (800 rupees would be about $10) was simply not enough to feed four growing children. So he earned extra money by selling the equipment given to Sherpas during expeditions. He also brought back secondhand equipment from the back lanes of Kathmandu to sell in Darjeeling and he took on extra jobs.

During the 1960s, Nawang Gombu traveled to Mumbai to teach rock climbing. Harish Kapadia, one of his dearest friends, said, "First here were Topgay, Ang Kami, and Nawang Gombu, who was in his peak pre-Everest form. In superb shape and an absolute terror, Gombu was so good that no student could ever manage to do as he did—a bit demoralizing and intimidating. He was a dynamic person who expected the very best and pushed you along roads which were not for beginners. My body was not ready for rock climbing, and I complained initially. But then we became good friends. He called me Kapde ('Cloth'). It's what I did then—[sold] cloth."

Nawang Gombu was the first Sherpa to recognize the importance of an education in English. Darjeeling is full of great schools where the country's elite send their children. Such astronomical fees are unaffordable for most Sherpas, but Gombu was adamant. He climbed mountains so that his children would not have to. His daughter Ongmu told us, "His own cousin Topgay and he were both good climbers. Dad kept telling him, 'Put your kids through an English school.' In those days there was a very strong divide between an English education and a vernacular education."

In 1969, Jim's twin brother, Lou Whittaker, formed Rainier Mountaineering, Inc. (RMI), which both provided a guiding service and taught climbing. Gombu was a natural choice as guest instructor. Although he never did
leave the HMI, he spent every vacation for several years at RMI, teaching
and earning money to put his children through school and college. RMI
guide Dave Hahn's 2011 tribute to Gombu is worth a read. He writes:

> The most famous RMI guide that ever lived was also a profoundly hum-
> ble man in an arena not known for fostering humility.
>
> Nawang Gombu had met the Queen of England on several occasions.
> You can find a picture of him in a 1963 *National Geographic* magazine plac-
> ing a silk scarf of friendship around John F. Kennedy's neck in the Rose Gar-
> den. But if you worked and lived with Gombu around Mount Rainier in the
> 1970s, 1980s or 1990s . . . you probably don't remember him doing a whole
> lot of explaining as to why he was so special. More likely you remember
> him working very hard. And as he got a bit older and less capable on the
> mountain, some may remember that he also worked hard down around the
> guide shop, pushing a broom or helping with rental gear. . . .
>
> Which brings me back to the guide shop and a typical start to a day
> on Mount Rainier in which I'd meet a bunch of new climbing enthusiasts.
> They'd introduce themselves and detail their previous successes, and
> immediately I'd find out about the banks and corporations they headed,
> and I'd hear about their ambitions for high places and their admiration
> for those that had already been to those places. And amidst all the intro-
> ductory chest-thumping (not just theirs . . . my chest got worked as well),
> I'd look over to see Gombu sweeping dust off the rental counter and I'd
> pause to consider that those captains of industry—and I—might not ever
> meet a greater mountain climber than the small, friendly, quiet legend
> who'd just fitted them for boots.

DORJEE LHATOO SAID, "GOMBU DAJU would bring new equipment back from
Switzerland and America, and introduce new climbing techniques and new
ways of using conventional mountaineering equipment." The importance
of what Gombu was doing was inestimable to the growth and development
of the HMI as an institution. Lhatoo continued, "I observed that his uncle

[Tenzing Norgay] was sometimes unjust. But Gombu would submit and not utter a word. The person who had been mean to him would think, 'Have I done the right thing?' Gombu was that kind of person."

After the success of the Americans on Everest, Gombu was awarded the National Geographic Society's prestigious Hubbard Medal, as well as other decorations. To match it, the Indian government gave him the Padma Shri award, and when he climbed with the first Indian expedition, he was given the Padma Bhushan.

Lhatoo continued, "Fame complicated their lives. Tenzing [became] unhappy as his nephew was getting more and more famous. These were simple, happy-go-lucky people, but once all the adulation and fame came, there were flare-ups in their mental and emotional lives. Throughout his life, though, Gombu maintained a deferential and respectful relationship with his uncle."

We had a long conversation with Ongmu, Gombu's youngest daughter, one afternoon in New Delhi. Born in 1971, she came along much after Everest and the early HMI days. By then, Gombu was a man of the world. She told us, "My first memory is my first day of school, and I remember him standing at the top of the hill, [at the Loreto Convent]. All fathers drop their kids [at] school, but later on I realized the relevance. It must have been a big thing for him, because he didn't go to school. To actually have school-going kids and kids who would speak in English, and write letters for him, was a very big thing." We asked her whether she remembered any climbing stories. She told us:

> I think it became just a way of life, right? When you grow up in a house of, say, an actor, the person goes to work and comes back—there is not much noise created around that. I just remember the fact that my dad used to be out climbing. Climbing equipment, sleeping bags, rucksacks—these were natural stuff around us. We used to have foreigners coming over to visit . . . so we sort of knew that what he did was different. And I remember a lot of climbers because I had an autograph book. I used to go around getting signatures.
>
> He wasn't a father who would sit and tell me about the encyclopaedia and the planets and the stars, because that was not him. But it was certain things that he said, ways he behaved, that grounded me in a good way.
>
> He used to come to all the parent-teacher meetings. I look back now and wonder what he sat and discussed with my geography teacher. My mom was a little hard of hearing so she did not come.

My mom and dad were traditional husband and wife. But my mom did a lot of the banking work. She was more educated than my dad. By default she was the one doing his correspondence, keeping all the bills. If there was an electrical failure, my dad would have no clue about what to do. She was the one who changed the fuses. When the house was being built, she made all the payments. My dad was the bread earner, and of course he used to love gardening.

Tenzing brought my dad and Doma ani to Darjeeling with the promise of school. It was sad because he could have easily put them [into] school, and I think somewhere that stuck with my dad. Even when we had house help, he made sure that those people at least knew how to read and write.

He got people into schools and he got them jobs—that literally changed their lives. He was against just giving donations. My mom used to give donations to the monks, and he would say, "It is worthless. What will you do? Build a wall or a golden thing on the top of the monastery?" I met somebody recently who said, "Only I know what your dad did for my family and me."

[My father] wanted me, the last [child], to marry a Sherpa. One Tibetan New Year, he and Tenzing were sitting and talking—this was in the '80s, when Tenzing had retired and my dad was director [of the HMI]. They were laughing at the fact that our entire family is going to become international, and they joked about it; but it is true. It is a completely international family.

Nawang Gombu's entire career was defined by his passion to learn and in turn pass on what he'd learned. His ego lay in making the world around him better; in this regard, he was always in a hurry, but in everything else, he was humble. One of his wishes was that his story be told like those in the mountaineering books that filled his little study at home. This wish came true when Ongmu and her husband published a scrapbook of the newspaper clippings chronicling Gombu's extraordinary life.

The beloved climber fell ill while on a family trip to Kashmir and was diagnosed with pancreatic cancer. In the last few weeks of his life, he was surrounded by his family. Nawang Gombu passed away on April 24, 2011, at the age of seventy-nine. The little big man had climbed his last mountain.

Clockwise from top left: Ajeeba on trek *(Malati Jhaveri)*; Ani Daku at ninety-two, with her daughter in Gangtok *(The Sherpa Project)*; Kami Tsering and Pemba Lhamu *(The Sherpa Project)*; left to right: Ang Temba with Nawang Topgay, Tenzing Norgay, Da Namgyal, and Nawang Gombu *(Himalayan Mountaineering Institute Collection)*

CHAPTER 13

More Tales from Darjeeling

Whether we were tramping up and down the lanes of this small hill station or traveling some distance in rickety Jeeps, headed to a planned meeting or simply had a chance encounter, the stories and segments of history we encountered so often enlightened and enchanted us. Some of those stories are recounted in chapter 9, "Those Magnificent Men and Women." Here are four more tales of the remarkable Sherpas and Sherpanis of Darjeeling.

Ani Daku Sherpa: A Forgotten Porter

Among the many who migrated from Khumbu to Darjeeling during the golden age of Himalayan mountaineering were several young women, one of which was Daku Sherpa. She was born around 1925, and spent her youth herding yaks and trading handmade paper for salt across the Nangpa La. Everyday life was hard. The glamorous moments occurred when cocky young Sherpas returned from Darjeeling in Western jackets and boots. Daku and her friends caught the "Darjeeling Dream" bug. The practice in those days was to run away, so that's what they did. It would have been the early 1940s, and so Daku was likely around eighteen years old when she came to Toong Soong.

Several Sherpas told us that she was one of the last living women porters from the early days. From her first home in Toong Soong, we followed her trail to Sikkim, just north of West Bengal. In the capital Gangtok, we met ninety-year-old Ani Daku in the home of one of her daughters. Tall, broad-shouldered, and attractive, she radiated strength and vitality. Our meeting stood out not because of any great mountaineering achievements by Ani Daku but for the discovery of a life lived well with grace and humor.

Ani Daku still wore the traditional baku. She spent her time, she said, in Gangtok with her two daughters during summer and with her three sons in Siliguri during winter.

She recalled, "In Toong Soong, I lived with many other girls below Tenzing's house. PemPem lives there now. We did coolie work, spun wool, and knitted sweaters. Darjeeling was empty then. There were no buildings— only wooden houses and a few bungalows where the English stayed. And there were tea gardens. If you became a coolie, the English would give good money—Rs 10 [roughly 12 cents]—for carrying one basketful!

"As a porter, I first went to Sandakphu [a 3,636-meter peak on the border with Nepal] and Sikkim with English tourists. Later I crossed mountains in Nepal and went with the Swiss to Everest in 1952. They gave us clothes and a sleeping bag. The salary was two rupees and eight annas [31 cents] a day, and the load would sometimes be as heavy as carrying a man."

We told Ani Daku we'd heard that she carried boxes full of coins to pay porters' salaries. She clarified, however, that they instead used "canvas bags made out of old tents, and very heavy, maybe forty kilograms," adding, "The sacks were too heavy to be carried by one person so we took turns. Ang Peme, Diki, Lhakpa, [other women porters] and I shared one tent. And the food was sufficient, it was tasty—rice and other things." Her daughter added, "She was treated well. She doesn't know what they gave to others, but mother was very active; she did everything very well. So they would ask her to work and give gifts."

Once, said Ani Daku, a sick tourist left at basecamp wanted an omelette, but Daku did not speak English. The tourist made signs to start the stove, then said, "Cock-a-doodle-doo." Ani Daku finally understood, and made the omelette. "He gave me a beautiful new sweater. And he also gave me five rupees!" she recalled. Ani Daku's job was also to make the porters' tea: "I would wear gloves and a feather coat and break ice with an axe. Then I put the ice in big buckets, put wood together, and lit it with kerosene to heat the ice and make water. That was my work," she told us.

Ani Daku married in 1955 at age thirty. Marriage brought with it dreary everyday struggle. Her husband ran a business selling butter, the yak cheese churpi, ghee, and eggs in Darjeeling. They then moved to Sikkim, where for fifteen years they supplied ghee to the king's household. When her husband died, Daku took over running the shop along with raising their children.

Daku never went back to carrying loads, but she missed that life. "It was so much fun to roam around!" she told us. "What's there in staying at one place? You feel better when you travel, don't you? You don't feel bad about carrying loads, if you get to travel!"

Daku remembered returning to Kathmandu with a triumphant team after the conquest of Everest in 1953: "When we arrived at Nepal, there were many people and flowers to celebrate. We rode an elephant. We queued to meet the king. I was given documents after this and a notebook by The Himalayan Club. But it was left at Tenzing Sherpa's house." Hillary gave her a badge and a watch too, but that was more than six decades ago and she has no recollection of where they ended up. Ani Daku recalled, "Hillary was very tall, very fair, and had a long face. Very handsome. And he used to put his arm around my shoulder when I was tired. He loved us."

As evening approached, Daku's daughter told us, "Our mother regrets that she's not educated. She told us not to be like her and worked hard to educate all five of us." We asked whether Ani Daku had a message for the younger Sherpas of Darjeeling. "I pray that they get the best. That people may have no suffering!" she said. We left with the realization that Ani Daku, despite not having gone to school, was far more learned than most.

Ajeeba: A Brother In Arms

The story of the climbers of Darjeeling is often the story of brothers. Two or three siblings would run away from Solu Khumbu, or one would escape and the others would follow. Toong Soong grew in that way. It's also how the newer settlement of Alubari down the hillside from Toong Soong grew.

When two or more brothers were climbing, it often happened that one became better known than his siblings, even though they were all accomplished porters. Such is the case with Ang Tsering I and Ajeeba (or Ajeeva/Ajiba, as he was also called). Ang Tsering deservedly gets a chapter to himself—chapter 8, "Family Man: Ang Tsering." But the story of Ajeeva is no mere footnote to his brother's tale.

On one visit, Dorjee Lhatoo pointed to a building and told us that it was where Ajeeba's son Nima Tsering lived. Minutes later, as we sat talking to the Ang Tsering siblings Pema Diki, Phur Diki, and their brother, Tharchen, their cousin Nima Tsering entered the room. We met him every time we visited the sisters, and he sometimes accompanied Phur Diki as she took us to the homes of Sherpa friends. In between listening to the story of Ang Tsering's life, we also heard that of his brother Ajeeba.

Nima Tsering told us that his father was a young man when he came to Darjeeling. It's where he met and married his first wife, Nima's mother. His first job was probably with the British Army because Nima remembered visiting his father at the army hospital when he fell ill.

Nima Tsering recalled, "We didn't know about expeditions at that time, but [my father] used to say that he was going to climb the Himalaya. He used to get paid well by the British administration. When we were still quite young, my father started working as a sardar. He used to bring the pay and distribute it to the porters. My brother used to sit with my father and help him give out the pay."

Nima Tsering had an older brother called Karma Wangchuk. He became a porter like his father and got jobs on two expeditions before completing his courses at the HMI. On his third expedition, to the 6,791-meter peak of Leo Pargial in 1962, Karma Wangchuk, along with two others, fell to his death in a terrible accident. In the porter book issued to him in 1961, he looks heartbreakingly young in the photo that accompanies his personal details. Karma was in fact only twenty-two when he died. Soli Mehta, longtime editor of *The Himalayan Journal*, remembered meeting Ajeeba soon after and commiserating about his loss. He wrote that the big man accepted his son's death as fate, without bitterness or grudge.

"My mother died when I was born," Nima told us. His eyes welled up as he added, "I don't remember how we grew up. Later, Father married again, but his wife was ill all the time so she could barely look after us. Most of what my father earned went towards taking care of her."

Nima Tsering studied until ninth grade, when Ajeeba sent him to the HMI, where he took the Basic and Advanced climbing courses in 1958 and 1959. Soon after, the institute sent Nima and others to lead a batch of boys from the Dehradun-based Doon School on a trek in the Garhwal. Nima Tsering said, "At that time, the principal gave us a bonus of Rs 5,000 [$61]. We had never seen so much money before! Now we had done all the courses and had experience, but when we returned we were told to be coolies on their expeditions." So, Nima Tsering stopped working with the HMI but would occasionally accompany his father on independent expeditions as a porter. "If there was no work at home, he would take me along. He would treat me like a porter. As his son, he would not give me the smallest bit of the bosses' food," recalled Nima Tsering. "Seeing all that meat, we really wanted to eat it, but he would say, 'Go to your tent and cook your food.' We were given rice and dal. My father was an expert in baking cakes. We did not have an oven at home so he baked on a wood stove. We didn't even have good utensils, but he would manage somehow." Nima later on gave up expedition work altogether and joined the army.

"My father was a good man. People said that he was honest and hard-working. Sherpas lived a good life in those days. When they left on expeditions, family members from the villages would line up with khadas to wish them luck. Later these traditions vanished. After Tenzing climbed Everest in '53, those who got jobs in HMI shifted there. Some went to [the nearby villages of] Rimbik, others to Sonada. Some stayed on in Toong Soong. The Sherpas got dispersed. Before that, all of them were together."

The porter list tells us that Ajeeba was given Himalayan Club number 10. He was with the Everest expeditions of 1933 and 1936, then Siniolchu in 1937 and Gangotri in 1947. He made several trips in between to Sikkim and one to Rakaposhi in 1938. By the time he accompanied Maurice Herzog and the French team to Annapurna in 1950, Ajeeba was highly regarded as a climber, sardar, and cook. In 1951, he was on Everest again on a reconnoitering expedition led by Eric Shipton, when the Khumbu Icefall was identified as a feasible route to climb the mountain from Nepal. He was on the same mountain twice the next year with the summer and autumn Swiss expeditions. He was awarded The Himalayan Club Tiger Badge in 1952. During this period, he was climbing every year: Panchachuli in 1953, Kangchenjunga in 1954, and Cho Oyu that same year with Herbert Tichy and his good friend Pasang Dawa Lama. Ajeeba was on the Dhaulagiri expedition in 1955 and with the Indian Air Force expedition to the Jugal Himal in 1960. He went with the Japanese to Mana Peak in 1961 and to Nilgiri Parbat in 1962. He also worked at the HMI for a short while.

As Soli Mehta wrote in Ajeeba's obituary, "I well remember him accompanying us on our Advance[d] course in November 1963. What a towering personality he was and how unassumingly he wore his honours. He spoke little but did much. Although a sensitive person, he displayed little emotion. His sense of service was always at the highest level and he would do even the most menial jobs (that were his lot during his declining years) with the same spirit as he had done when he was the Sirdar of an expedition."

While expeditions were the mainstay of Ajeeba's career, they were by no means the only climbing trips he went on. Back in Mumbai, we met Malatiben Jhaveri, a freedom fighter, theatre artist, avid trekker, and photography enthusiast. She was already in her nineties, but her eyes shone with lively interest as she turned the pages of an old photo album. She had trekked across the Indian Himalaya throughout the 1960s, all the while accompanied by her favorite Sherpa companion, Ajeeba.

Brief stories do not do adequate justice to these men who have been forgotten by history. We asked Nima Tsering whether he felt proud or sad that his father had been a porter. He paused to frame his answer, then replied, "They did what they had to, to earn a living. Working hard is better than being a thief. With the work they did they could easily feed their families twice a day and that gave them happiness. My father lived life the way he wanted to even though he wasn't educated."

Ajeeba never made much money. Local lore teems with stories of his drunkenness at parties, his temper when aroused, and his scraps with Tenzing. One infamous account tells how a drunken Ajeeba attacked Tenzing with an ice axe after the 1952 Swiss autumn Everest expedition. Fortunately, Tenzing escaped without injury, but grudges were held and the families of Ang Tsering and Ajeeba felt that Tenzing thenceforth made sure that little work came their way.

Ajeeba died in 1975, his later years bitter in a way that still haunts Nima Tsering. "My father had a lot of problems towards the end. Expeditions from here had stopped, and he was getting old. He didn't have money and suffered a lot," he told us. Ajeeba's end seemed to echo many others we'd heard about—fatalistic, given to drink, living for the moment. Although these men were spectacular mountaineers, some of them left their children a legacy they're still struggling to come to terms with.

Ang Temba: One Summit, Several Times Shy

In 1950, Jim Thornley, Dick Marsh, and Bill Crace decided to sneak an attempt on Nanga Parbat. Ang Temba was on the mountain with them when Thornley and Crace disappeared. In 1952, when the Swiss made the autumn attempt on Everest, Ang Temba was there. He carried heavy loads to the South Col thrice without any signs of fatigue. When he and Topgay were climbing with others above Camp V, a mass of ice came tumbling down, narrowly missing Temba, and killing their friend Mingma Dorje. The following spring with John Hunt's expedition to Everest, he fell into a crevasse and was rescued by Wilfrid Noyce. He continued to carry while Tenzing and Hillary made history. Ang Temba received the Tiger Badge and the Queen's Coronation Medal. When the HMI was formed, he was in the first group of brilliant instructors.

In 1955, when Major Nandu Jayal led an expedition to Kamet, Ang Temba was a full member and selected to be part of the summit team. He stood atop the peak—his first summit. He was thirty-five years old. When Captain Kohli went to Saser Kangri, he was there. When Nandu Jayal went to Nanda Devi in 1957, Ang Temba was there, with a team that almost made the summit. In 1962, he joined the Indian Everest expedition as a team member. He had gone to Everest twice as a porter, but now he finally had an opportunity to summit.

Ang Temba was on the second summit team with Kohli and Chandra Prakash Vohra. But the monsoon hit the mountain while they were on South Col and they had to retreat, in pitch-black darkness through blizzard conditions while skirting deep crevasses—an experience that deeply affected the strong and silent Ang Temba. In 1973, he was on an expedition led by D. K. Khullar to the 6,050-meter Kinnaur Kailash. Here too they were thwarted. In a climbing career that spanned somewhere between four and five decades, he stood on a summit only once.

One rainy day in Darjeeling, we met his daughter Lhakpa Doma, who was visiting from Mumbai, where she lived and worked for Air India. We met at the small cottage where her mother, Da Yangzi, lived with her brothers, situated above Mall Road and Glenary's restaurant on the high route toward the TV tower. Lhakpa was looking forward to retirement and their family's shift to Siliguri, where her brothers were building a new house.

Ang Temba was born in 1920 to a family of subsistence farmers. He came to Darjeeling and soon started to work as a porter on expeditions. Da Yangzi was a load carrier from Lukla. The two met on an expedition; on one of those trips, on the way back from Everest, they got married. Dorjee Lhatoo recalled, "Ang Temba came as a young boy in the '40s. Long before independence. They came in groups—it was common in those days—traveling together from adjacent villages. Villagers would come and want to give you a parting gift, so he got from his close relative a nicely done headstrap. In Khumbu, a headstrap was the most important thing—like a bicycle for easy movement. You could tie it around your waist or shoulder, but it was important—to carry water or wood or fodder or supplies. 'This will last you until you come back again,' he was told. It may sound strange today, but it was an amazing gift."

Da Yangzi was the tallest Sherpani in Darjeeling, or so it seems from the photos we saw. Lhatoo said, "[Ang Temba] was one of the shortest Sherpas I have met. She was average height. Five feet, four inches." When they stood together, the difference was marked, but their heights did not prevent them from having a happy married life. Lhakpa recalled Gombu's son, Phinjo, saying, "You know, Lhakpaji, whenever I see your mom and dad, I feel nice because they go everywhere together. My mom and dad never go anywhere together."

Ang Temba and Da Yangzi had four children—two girls and two boys. Lhakpa is the oldest; her younger sister moved to Kathmandu; and the boys—Ang Tsering and Ang Norbu—became instructors at the HMI, like their father. Lhakpa recalled that as kids they would take ropes and climb the local rocks like it was their playground.

The children grew up in the early years of the brand-new institute, the best years to be there. "We were better off than people living in Toong Soong. Everything was taken care of," said Lhakpa Doma. As a father, Ang Temba was strict and disciplined. He was also very religious and valued the impor-tance of an education. He told his children, "Till you finish school and col-lege, if I ever hear you talking about girlfriends and boyfriends, I will chop you and throw you out. You have to study and stand on your own feet. After that I will not interfere in your life." Gombu's daughter Yangdu remembered Lhakpa's father as a terror: "The thrashing she used to get! She would hide inside a sleeping bag. He would get angry because Lhakpaji was very intel-ligent, good at singing and sports. She was also a lovely person so she would get a lot of proposals. He wanted her to concentrate on her education." A brilliant student, Lhakpa got into the prestigious Jawaharlal Nehru Univer-sity in New Delhi and could have become a civil servant, but Tenzing and the eminent mountaineer Captain M. S. Kohli, both close friends of her father, insisted that she try for a glamorous job in the airlines instead.

We met some of Ang Temba's students from the HMI as well as from the Bombay Climbers Club. Dr. Srikar Amladi remembered him as a tough climber of the old generation, saying, "He was with every student at once. He would shout his instructions from above, below, everywhere. I would hover around, camping right with him. Watching him helped a lot with my personal development. Ang Temba would never sing or dance. He was civil, courteous, extremely polite, a thorough gentleman among Sherpas—though they were all gentlemen actually." Khurshid Elavia, a student at the HMI, said, "Ang Temba, in his kind, paternal voice, would say, 'Don't give up; there's only a bit of a walk left now.'"

Lalit Chari and his wife, Malvika, came to know Ang Temba through the Climbers Club and also from the many treks and climbs that they did together in the lower Himalaya. They were close friends of the whole family and became guardians to Lhakpa when she first came to Mumbai. Lalit wrote in his book *Mountain Memories*, "[She] became to all intents and purposes a member of our family. At various times, Lhakpa's mother, brothers, and her younger sister also stayed with us."

Da Yangzi was still alive when we met Lhakpa. As her daughter told us, "She is a down-to-earth person; not educated, but her thinking is much broader than other people. She would not hesitate to do anything for her kids. If something happened at school, she would meet the teachers to tell them what she felt and how kids should be treated. She had to take all the decisions and run the house all alone, as dad was always away."

Although worldwise, the family did not seem particularly awed by Ang Temba's medals, unlike the Ang Tsering home, where his daughters so carefully tended every award and scrap of recognition. When we asked Lhakpa about her father's Tiger Badge and Coronation Medal, she told us, "You know, from childhood we have been seeing these. We never understood their importance. I don't think medals ever were of interest to him. He would bring one home and keep it away."

Ang Temba passed away at eighty-two after a long illness. He finished his prayers and met all the monks and his relatives. He told his wife, said Lhakpa, "'I have no regrets; I have recited all the mantras that I had decided. I am not worried about you because the kids are good—they will take care of you. When I pass away, don't feel sad. I am happy to leave now.' He had a peaceful life and a peaceful death. They say in Buddhism [that] you die the way you live. If you've lived your life well, your death will be like that . . . peaceful."

Kami Tshering and Pemba Lhamu: The Lovebirds

If you walk along any of the roads leading to Chowrasta, you might spot an elderly Sherpa walking purposefully, followed by his bird-like Sherpani wife.

He is also a lama, so you may notice him counting his prayer beads he keeps in a small bag tied to his right wrist. The couple is temperamental, so be prepared either for a warm embrace or to be ignored completely.

Kami Tshering and Pemba Lhamu, both in their seventies, are known to the residents of Toong Soong as "the Lovebirds." For years we spotted them often, and never one without the other. Their routine was to set out after an early lunch, walk around town until tired, and then return home to begin again the next day.

Both were born in Khumbu and came to Darjeeling in 1965, after they married. We met the couple once, inviting them to our friend Tharchen's house for a chat. They brought us tea leaves, milk, sugar, and biscuits—a gesture that moved us deeply. Once we settled in, Kami Tshering talked freely. He said he went to Tenzing Norgay for work. "He never gave me work, always shooed me away. I was unemployed but he did not care," said Kami. "When Tenzing and Gombu gave me work, it was to wash their dirty handkerchiefs; to serve them like a servant."

He continued, "I started going on expeditions in 1965. I carried loads and also cooked. I learnt climbing by myself. I did everything on my own. I summitted Kamet, Satopanth—it's all there in my biodata [résumé]." Indeed his biodata listed him as having been on thirty-four expeditions between 1966 and 1993. He asked us for a hundred-rupee note, and then proceeded to identify the peaks on it: "Kangchenjunga, Kumbhakarna, Kabru, Mana, Koktang." When we asked Pemba Lhamu whether she was sad or worried when her husband went to the mountains, she said, "No, we were happy—we would celebrate and send [the men] away after drinking chang."

When there were no treks, Kami worked as a local porter and on construction sites doing manual labor. They had children. One daughter immigrated to America and started sending money home. The old couple also got a small pension from the government. "Today, if there are clouds, tomorrow will be sunny; today, if there is sorrow, then tomorrow will be happy," the old man started chanting during our sit-down with him. With the money he saved, Kami Tshering built a small house. The Lovebirds live in one half, sharing the chores at home, while their son's family lives in the other half. "I cook chow mein and momos!" Kami said. More than anything else, the couple loved to travel, to destinations like Kathmandu (where one of their daughters lives), Siliguri, and Gangtok.

Two years after our interview with the Lovebirds, we happened to go to lower Toong Soong. It was early evening, and as we passed their house, Pemba Lhamu came to the stoop. We were excited to see her looking just as she had the last time we met. We greeted her enthusiastically, but this time the mercurial Sherpani frowned at us and swatted with her hands as though driving away flies.

Nawang Topgay's medals (*The Sherpa Project*)

CHAPTER 14

The Last Tigers: Nawang Topgay and Sona "King Kong"

The idea of awarding Tiger Badges was first suggested by Joan Townend of The Himalayan Club in 1938. That year, it was decided in a club meeting in Darjeeling that porters who performed exceptionally well at high altitudes could be nominated by their expedition leaders for these badges of excellence. Club members felt that awarding badges would inspire other porters to the high standards set by the Tigers.

The first badges were distributed in 1939, and the following year, *The Himalayan Journal* published this list and note on the recipients:

Dawa Thondup (No. 49)
Tenzing [Tenzing Norgay, known at the time as Tenzing Bhote] (No. 48)
Pasang Dawa Lama Sherpa (No. 139)
Ang Tenzing [Ang Tenzing II, HC No. 3] Lobsang (No. 144)
Dawa Tsering (No. 53)
Kusang Namgir (No. 9)
Ang Tarkay [Ang Tharkay] (No. 19)
Paldan [Palden] (No. 54)
Wangdi Norbu (No. 25)
Lhakpa Tenzing (No. 30)

Renzing (No. 32)

Pasang Kikuli (No. 8), Nima Tsering (No. 129), and Da Tsering would have been promoted, but Pasang Kikuli was killed on K2 during the year and the other two died during the spring of 1939.

At a committee meeting on the 8th September 1939, it was decided to promote Lewa to the higher grade, in view of his past achievements.

Dorjee Lhatoo told us, "When they awarded the first Tiger Badges, the British were careful to ensure that there should be no tension between the Bhutias and the Sherpas. Wisely, half the Tiger Badges went to the Sherpas and half to the Tibetans."

Seven of the first official Tigers were ethnic Sherpas: Dawa Thondup, Pasang Dawa Lama, Ang Tenzing II, Ang Tharkay, Lhakpa Tenzing, Renzing, and Lewa. The other six were Bhutias: Tenzing Norgay, Lobsang (who was a Khampa but counted as a Bhutia), Dawa Tsering, Kusang Namgir (Namgye), Palden, and Wangdi Norbu. (Lobsang's name does not appear in the published list.)

After 1939, Tiger Badges were issued sporadically. Three were awarded in 1940. The next set of badges—twelve, in total—were awarded for the Everest expeditions of 1952 and 1953. Nine more were awarded in 1956 for expeditions of the previous year (five for Kangchenjunga, three for Makalu, and one for Dhaulagiri), four badges were awarded in 1960 (all Everest), five in 1962 (two for Jannu in 1959 and three for Makalu 1962), six in 1964, and finally thirteen in 1965—the last year they were awarded—for porters from the first successful Indian ascent of Everest. A grand total of sixty-five badges were awarded over the course of twenty-six years.

Why were badges awarded only in certain years? After the first two investitures of 1939 and 1940, almost all subsequent badges were linked to specific expeditions. The awards were based on recommendations and dependent on leaders proposing the names of deserving porters. In years when no badges were awarded, expedition leaders presumably made no recommendations, for whatever reason. Those leaders who were diligent enough to do so, however, did their porters a service. Possessing a Tiger Badge meant not only higher pay above certain altitudes but also prestige and honor. With the title came the advertisement that here was a dependable man with a proven record, experienced and skilled. It is little wonder that the Tiger Badge was coveted.

Lewa: The Tiger Who Rejected His Stripes

A much respected and highly sought-after porter and sardar of the late 1920s and 1930s, Lewa was with Paul Bauer on Kangchenjunga in 1929 and with G. O. Dyhrenfurth on the same mountain in 1930. He made the first ascent of Jonsong with a fellow Sherpa called Tsinabo, and despite having frozen feet, he was also on the first ascent of Kamet in 1931 with Shipton, Smythe, and R. L. Holdsworth. So severe was Lewa's frostbite that most of his toes had to be amputated. The indomitable Sherpa was back climbing the very next year on Chomiomo. That was followed by Everest in 1933 and Nanga Parbat in 1934. Fritz Bechtold, one of the climbers on the latter peak, wrote, "As first Sirdar, Lewa was chosen, a man who hitherto had distinguished himself on every expedition by his amazing tenacity and endurance both as mountaineer and as leader."

The final entry on his climbing record shows a series of travels through Tibet and elsewhere with the explorer and botanist Ronald Kaulback from 1935 to 1938. In recognition of his phenomenal career, Lewa was awarded the thirteenth badge when the Tiger was instituted in 1939.

In those early days, Lewa was a familiar sight around Darjeeling. Dorjee Lhatoo remembered seeing him and his friends as a child. Walking to Chowrasta from Toong Soong, the men would be holding on to each other for support after one bowl too many of *tomba* (a millet-based alcoholic drink fermented by tribes in Nepal, Sikkim, and Darjeeling). Lhatoo told us this story about Lewa's badge:

Lewa in 1933 *(Frank Smythe Collection)*

"You see, Lewa went to Mr. Kydd, who was the local recruiting agent. He was well known as someone who employed Sherpas to go on expeditions and treks. Mr. Kydd said to him, 'Lewa, you are too old. Give a chance to the younger people.' Lewa asked, 'So, how do we make a living?' 'That's not my problem,' said Mr. Kydd. Apart from Lewa, there were a couple of other people who were also not being employed. They had brought their badges, and they said, 'Then why have you given us this?' They were ignored by Kydd. Then Lewa is reported to have thrown his badge down the hill! Once he

185

did that, the others did it too—they all threw their badges, and then clapped their hands and went home."

Without expedition work, Lewa found a job as a watchman looking after a series of shops in Siliguri, which was just developing. He lived alone, sending what money he could home to his wife and school-going children in Darjeeling. One day in 1948, he didn't show up for work and people assumed he had gone home. No one looked for him. Later on, when there was a stink coming from his room, they discovered the dead Lewa. Ang Tsering told Dorjee Lhatoo that they went down and brought Lewa's body to Darjeeling to cremate, smelling to high heaven. Lewa was only forty-six years old.

ON JANUARY 6, 2000, THE Himalayan Club held a tribute for the last three living recipients of its Tiger Badge—Ang Tsering (Tiger 1952), Nawang Gombu (Tiger 1953), and Nawang Topgay (Tiger 1953). The program, held at the Himalayan Mountaineering Institute, was attended by many climbing Sherpas of Darjeeling. The following year, an even grander felicitation was organized for the three in Mumbai.

Ang Tsering passed away in 2002 and Nawang Gombu in 2011. When we first started our visits to Darjeeling in 2012, we were told that Nawang Topgay was the only Tiger left.

Nawang Topgay

Like Nawang Gombu, Nawang Topgay was Tenzing Norgay's nephew—the son of Tenzing's older brother, Chingdu. Topgay migrated to Darjeeling in search of work when he was a lad of fourteen. He was taken under Tenzing's care and lived with him until he found a place of his own.

The young man got his first big chance as a porter on Everest when his uncle recruited him for the post-monsoon 1952 Swiss Everest expedition. In *Sherpas: The Himalayan Legends*, Captain Kohli wrote that Nawang Topgay took naturally to carrying loads, cutting steps, and fixing ropes. Chosen to carry loads to the South Col, he withstood the thin, cold air better than some of the more experienced porters. In fact, he is known to have said that the loads felt heavier on the long walk from Kathmandu; as he climbed higher, they felt lighter.

Later, he set off for Camp IX with a load, but at 8,230 meters the weather deteriorated and they had to turn back. On the way down, there was a violent storm and Mingma Dorje, his partner on the rope, was struck by a block of ice and died. "We were tied together," Topgay said in an interview. "Mingma looked up to see where it was coming from, and he was hit in the face that instant. The same person I shared a tent with was no more."

The accident shook young Topgay, but he was ready to go again in 1953 when Tenzing chose him a second time for the British Everest expedition. He was around twenty-one now and had an expedition under his belt, while his seventeen-year-old cousin, Nawang Gombu, was just getting his first taste of climbing. Topgay did two carries to the South Col without supplemental oxygen. Then, on May 29, 1953, when Tenzing made history, Topgay was jubilant to have helped put his uncle on the summit.

After Everest, both cousins received the Tiger Badge and the Queen Elizabeth Coronation medal. They were chosen as part of a select team of Sherpas to receive specialized training in Switzerland, and the team returned to become the first instructors at the newly opened Himalayan Mountaineering Institute. From there, however, the two cousins went off on entirely different trajectories.

"Topgay doesn't live in Toong Soong," we were told back in 2012. We followed directions to the corrugated-roof shack, down an adjoining hill, where Topgay lived with his younger son, Da Norbu; his daughter-in-law, Nima; and two school-going grandsons. The small and neat outer room was occupied mainly by a bed and the family altar. Along the walls were framed mountaineering commendations, family photographs, and religious wall hangings. An enormous golden-yellow teddy bear beamed at us from a glass-fronted cabinet. Nima went to see if her father-in-law was awake and then called us to follow. Topgay lay on a narrow cot in a dark cubbyhole barely big enough to admit us. He was bedridden from a fall he'd taken the previous year. His right hand had broken in the accident and, having failed to heal properly, lay awkwardly and uselessly on his chest. Nima smoothed his pillow and explained who we were. "Namaste, Namaste!" he repeated several times, but little else that he said was coherent.

We asked Dorjee Lhatoo about Topgay. "To cut a long story short," said Lhatoo, "in 1960 when the first Indian Everest expedition took place, three HMI instructors were selected to be on the team: Da Namgyal, Ang Temba, and Gombu. Topgay was expecting to be there too. It was the first Indian expedition to Mount Everest. Topgay in those days was strong, but according to the old-timers he was short-tempered and he drank. When he was intoxicated, he was a bit irresponsible; he picked fights. So, whatever may have been his disqualifications, he was not chosen and he felt his uncle didn't help him.

"And there was an incident at Rishi on the way back from the basecamp, after an HMI course. In those days a course lasted forty-two days, and the whole area was wilderness. After a long exposure at high altitude, when they came down, Sikkim was the land of chang—free-flowing and cheap. Invariably the instructors would be drunk, and the students were also encouraged to try this local drink. On the house, the HMI used to provide one bottle of tomba each.

"One day, Topgay and another instructor, Pasang Phutar, came to the camp shouting. Tenzing was sleeping in the tent, and his back was bulging out of the tent flap. With his mountain boots on, Topgay gave him a kick! Tenzing, later on, made a joke out of it. He laughed and told us that he was having a pleasant dream and he thought a boulder had come from the mountain and he was ducking when it hit him. When he realized what had happened, the two fellows were tied up and taken away by the police."

Lhatoo continued, "Pasang Phutar was a clever fellow. The British reported that he was a trade unionist, a rabble rouser. I don't know how true that is, but he was a dashing fellow. He went to Nepal, became a famous sardar with many Japanese expeditions, and he did very well for himself.

"But Topgay was rendered hapless after this incident. He was used to living in a certain style at the HMI. Removed from his quarters, he had to find a rented place in Toong Soong. That was a small one-room home with his wife and three children, and one more on its way. He didn't know any other occupation but load-bearing and going to the mountains."

Topgay struggled to make ends meet, carrying loads on expeditions when he could get the work. Chanchal Mitra, a veteran Kolkata mountaineer, reminisced, "Topgay's feet were frostbitten during the ascent of Nilgiri Parbat in the Garhwal Himalaya during October 1962. That was my first expedition, and I still remember the basic skills in snow and ice craft that he shared. After his toes were amputated, I think Topgay's major breakthrough in the Himalaya was in the Tirsuli expedition in 1965. He kept the icefall route open under inclement weather conditions."

Finally, after a few years, Tenzing either had a change of heart or relented due to family pressure. Topgay was taken back in at the HMI as an assistant to Dorjee Lhatoo, one of the youngest instructors—it was embarrassing for both of them.

Then the Nehru Institute of Mountaineering (NIM) was set up at Uttar-kashi in 1965, and Topgay was sent there as one of the first instructors. Since he was the most senior, he was called "Guruji," a title that stuck to the end. Lhatoo told us, "He was an outstanding instructor for twenty years. He went on several expeditions such as Mrigthuni—reaching the summit despite frostbitten feet and a near-death experience—as well as Shivling, Bandarpunch, and Kedar Dome. He tried to make up for lost opportunities, but the ten crucial years spent in punishment for one misdemeanor could never be recovered. His children grew up in indifferent circumstances, left behind in Darjeeling with their mother."

Phurtemba said to us, "His focus was on how to run the household. The thinking was not 'How do we give the best education to our children?'" This difference became yet another point of divergence in the paths of the two families—the Gombus and the Topgays.

And Topgay's problems were not yet over. In the late 1980s, when the acting principal at NIM wanted new blood on his staff, Topgay was forced to retire early and denied a full pension. Topgay returned to Darjeeling, and it was only later when Colonel Amit Roy, principal at the HMI, intervened that he began receiving his due.

The rift between uncle and nephew never healed completely. Topgay felt that he should have been there in 1960 on the Indian attempt and also when Gombu climbed with the Americans in 1963. Lhatoo put Topgay's feelings this way: "I was older, I was better, I didn't get the chance that I should have got." No matter what else he had climbed, he knew that Everest would have given him recognition. By missing Everest, he felt he'd missed everything.

Everest has always been the yardstick—in those early days, even more so. There was the fame that came with conquering the mountain of course, but also gifts, concessions, land, and opportunities. Topgay's bitterness, though misplaced, was perhaps understandable.

His son Da Norbu was also an instructor at NIM. When we met in April 2012, he too had retired, and the family was managing on two meager pensions. "Children should not go in this line," he told us. "It is unhappy work."

We asked him, "What is the reason for the difference between the families of Gombu, Lhatoo, and Topgay?" Said Da Norbu, "Their children got scholarships for study. They spoke to people. They made money from climbing. They were asked, 'Is there anything we can do for you?' and they replied, 'Help my children.' This was the difference. The one who doesn't have contacts, doesn't have. Who does one approach?"

Da Norbu's reference was almost certainly to Everest. But that was the only trace of bitterness we heard from him. A little later, he brightened up and added, "We are leaving this house and building our own house in Toong Soong but lower down."

A fortnight later, the family did shift to a new apartment built on top of Nima's father's house in lower Toong Soong. Her father, Nima Tenzing, had been a climbing instructor at the Sashastra Seema Bal (SSB) mountain training school in Gwaldam, Uttarakhand. (The SSB is a border-security force deployed on India's borders with Nepal and Bhutan.) Nima Tenzing had kindly invited his son-in-law, Da Norbu, to build on top of his property.

The plight of Topgay disturbed many people. When Dorjee Lhatoo took American journalist Jenny Dubin of *Outside* magazine to meet him, she was apparently horrified. "What can I do for you?" she asked. "Nothing," replied Topgay.

"He had his pride," Lhatoo told us. "Poor but proud. Then The Himalayan Club offered some financial assistance to cover Topgay's medical expenses. It was Rs 5,000 [$61] once in a while. However, members of the extended family said that this was embarrassing; it showed Topgay in a poor light. Then, I believe, the raising of money for Topgay's welfare stopped."

After our visit, The Himalayan Club resumed the financial assistance, but Topgay was to live only a few months more.

Our last interview with Topgay took place in the family's new apartment, in lower Toong Soong. The bright, airy room where Topgay lay was a far cry from the shanty they had called home some months earlier. Next to Topgay's bed was a window with a view of the valley below. Nima climbed onto the bed and lifted him into a sitting position, propping his head and shoulders against the pillows. He complained, "*Dukha, dukha, dukha,*" and whimpered. That was our last meeting with Topgay. On November 2, 2012, the eighty-two-year-old Guruji passed away peacefully while watching TV with his grandson. The funeral was simple and dignified. A square, white, crate-like coffin was topped with a wreath of marigolds. Within lay Topgay Sherpa's body, curled in the traditional fetal pose so he could exit the world the way he'd entered it.

Sona "King Kong"

One evening in our lodgings in late 2012, with a clear view of Kangchenjunga through a side window, we took up the question of the Tiger Badges once more. We looked at all the lists, comparing a comprehensive list published in 1967 with the list published each year that the badges were awarded, and made two discoveries. The first was that Topgay's name is not in the collected list of 1967 or even in the list of 1954 when the badges for Everest 1953 were awarded. He *was* given the medal—we had seen it and photographed it along with his Coronation Medal. He was publicly feted and celebrated as a Tiger. Someone had obviously slipped up. It's a good thing Topgay never knew of this omission when he was alive. It would have been the final bitter pill to swallow.

The second discovery came as a result of looking at the badges awarded on July 30, 1965, for the first successful Indian Everest expedition. The names of the awardees were as follows:

Dawa Norbu (Darjeeling)	HC no. 322
Tashi (Darjeeling)	HC no. 236
Karma (Darjeeling)	HC no. 326
Sona (Darjeeling)	HC no. 357
Kalden (Gangtok)	HC no. 309
Tenzing Nendra (Khumjung)	HC no. 362
Nawang Hilla (Khumjung)	HC no. 363
Pasang Tendi (Khumjung)	HC no. 364
Mingma Tshering (Phorche)	HC no. 365
Tenzing Gyatso (Phorche)	HC no. 366
Pemba Tharke (Phorche)	HC no. 367
Nima Tenzing (Pangboche)	HC no. 368
Dawa Tenzing (Namche)	HC no. 369

Eight of the Tigers were from Khumbu, and their Himalayan Club numbers are in serial order: from Tenzing Nendra, no. 362, to Dawa Tenzing, no. 369. The only explanation is that the numbers were given so that the badges could be awarded. And as no more badges were ever awarded, we now had a figure for the total number of Sherpas and Bhutias on The Himalayan Club rolls: 369.

What was really exciting was that the first four names were of Darjeeling Sherpas. Karma was listed as having died in 1967, but that still left Dawa Norbu, Tashi, and Sona. Who were these men, and might any of them still be alive?

Dawa Norbu and Tashi, we learned, had died, but Sona (aka Sona "King Kong") was alive and residing in Toong Soong. We were informed casually by Phurtemba, "He's a Walungpa, not a Sherpa. You can meet him at my house tomorrow morning."

The next morning, we met Phurtemba at the Toong Soong gompa and walked the short distance to his tiny, two-room house. It was a bright, crisp day, and the tantalizing smell of fresh momos wafted in the chilly air. In a miniscule area outside one building, a large, grey-haired man sat patiently on a little stool while a young woman poured mugs of water over his head and admonished him gently.

We sat in Phurtemba's home, and fifteen minutes later, the gentle giant we had seen being washed by his daughter came ambling shyly into the room. He rubbed his head, sprinkling water droplets everywhere, with perhaps no idea of the historic mantle he carried on his shoulders.

Sona was openly astonished that anyone would want to talk with him or listen to his story. His family had lived in Tibet, he told us. He was born around August 1, 1940, and left home for Nepal when he was very young. Sona said, "I must have been nine or ten years old. Till twelve or thirteen, I washed people's dishes. I did not get anything for it so I came to Darjeeling."

After spending some time working as a porter, he landed a job at the HMI ferrying loads for the courses, which brought some order to his life. Then Tenzing offered him a place in his house. Sona recalled, "We had no fixed jobs, but Tenzing sahab had many little dogs. I looked after them, bathed them, cleaned their area. There were four or five other Sherpas, and many more came to work during the day. Whatever I earned on coolie work I would give to [Tenzing] and say, 'Keep it.' I did not have to spend on anything." It was Tenzing who gave him his nickname "King Kong."

In 1965, Sona went to Everest. He carried three cylinders of oxygen several times up to the last camp. At first, Sona had no recollection of receiving a Tiger Badge. Only when he saw pictures of a badge did he seem to have any stirrings of memory and recall a ceremony. Sona said, "I was given a medal. I thought, 'There is nothing special I have done; how did I get this?' I was really left very surprised and wondering."

After Everest, Sona was inducted into the SSB and chosen to go to Nanda Devi on Kohli's expedition to recover a lost CIA nuclear spy device. After the Nanda Devi expedition, the SSB sent Sona to Gwaldam to teach rock climbing. He stayed there until he retired in 2000. At some point along his journey, he got married and had two daughters, the younger of whom he now lives with.

"Where is your Tiger Badge?" we asked him. He shook his head. When he came to Darjeeling, he abandoned his hut in Gwaldam and everything within it.

Sona was straightforward and guileless. As we talked, his initial befuddlement gave way to enjoyment. His speech, though, was difficult to follow. His rheumy eyes and the constant tremor in his hands betrayed his addiction to the vice to which so many Sherpas fall prey. Sona confessed, "I have nothing to hide from you or anyone—I drink, for sure. I drink because I have no support in life. The drink is some support."

More than once he repeated that he was a nobody and had nothing to offer anyone. After listening for half an hour, Phurtemba could keep quiet no longer. "Excuse me," he interjected. "Mr. Sona is saying that he had nothing— but he had a lot! He was young; he had energy. That is what he had so much of! That's why Tenzing Sherpa took him into the mountains!" Sona looked at Phurtemba with some wonderment, nodded his head, and then said, "Yes, that is right." And both men laughed.

"Is there anything else you'd like to say?" we asked Sona.

He responded, "For me it's like this . . . I want to tell my people that we are all brothers. No one is anyone's servant. Not everyone will agree because all they can do is point to my drinking." Then, with disarming charm, he added, "I hope you are not angry with me."

So, here we are, officially setting the record straight: There were sixty-five Tiger Badges awarded. Pasang Kikuli whose name appears in the first list of awardees, died before he could be honored, and thus he never received the badge. Nawang Topgay should have appeared in the list but does not. We take this opportunity to add Topgay's name to the official list of Tigers and celebrate Nawang Topgay as the last Sherpa Tiger and Sona "King Kong" as the last Tiger of Darjeeling.

Dorjee Lhatoo belaying during an Advanced course at the Himalayan Mountaineering Institute, 1964 *(Dorjee Lhatoo Collection)*

CHAPTER 15

Renaissance Man: Dorjee Lhatoo

Dorjee Lhatoo's home is on Hill Cart Road. A zigzag lane across from his house leads steeply up to the Darjeeling zoo. At road level, there isn't a front door but a gate, and from here the house goes downstairs to the main living quarters. Just within the gate sits Lhatoo's monster—his Enfield Bullet 350 motorcycle. He roars through town wearing jeans, an open-necked shirt, cowboy boots, and a silk cravat, evoking the comparison to Clint Eastwood the hotel owner made on the first day of our visit to Darjeeling in 2012. Lhatoo has built most of this house himself, adding a flatlet upstairs and a prayer room for his wife over the last few years.

We have spent many days seated at the long dining table in the kitchen overlooking the valley, sharing his food, chang, and home-brewed wines. He has told us about people and history; he has translated names and explained genealogies. If Tenzing Norgay was the bedrock upon which the fame of the Sherpas grew and spread, Dorjee Lhatoo is the spine of this book—its primary storyteller, the keeper of memories, and the link that joins the old Sherpas with the new. We wondered just how to present his story, and realized that the only way was to let him talk for himself. So, this is Dorjee Lhatoo, primarily in his own words—as extracted from interviews with us and with Harish Kapadia, to whom we remain indebted for his assistance—and with our own comments added here and there, in brackets. Long story short, as Dorjee Lhatoo would say.

NOWADAYS SHERPAS DON'T WANT TO talk about their forebears. These forebears were not big champions or warriors or heroes; they were porters. Wonderful porters in some ways . . .

It's an almost vertical ascent for the offspring of the simple men coming from the north corners of the world, where there was no electricity, no roads, no schools, no hospitals, nothing. They came from the jungles; I come from there. I saw my first motorcar in Gangtok way back in 1946 and the first electric bulb, the first water pipe there.

Sherpas have evolved in three generations. They have done well for themselves. I would say I'm thankful to this country that gave us this opportunity to achieve. For our kids who have gone abroad, this has definitely been a stepping stone. If we had not come to India, what kind of life would we have had?

Chumbi is a river valley in Tibet. The Amochu flows through it. Probably a thousand years ago, a platform was formed on the side of the river. Here they would have set up a village, and slowly it became a town. Yatung was such a place.

There used to be heavy traffic of mules and muleteers because that was the main trade route for the cities of Tibet like Lhasa, Gyangtse, and Shigatse. All trade from these cities came to the nearest port—Calcutta. So traders came through the Chumbi Valley, crossing the two passes Nathu La and Jhelep La. If you crossed Jhelep La, you came down to Kalimpong— that was British territory; and if you came through Nathu La, you came to Gangtok—that was the Sikkimese kingdom. The choice between these two passes in those days was which one had less snow, which one was comfortably crossable. Either route brought you down to Teesta—the common point—and then to Siliguri and on to Calcutta. There was much trade between India and Tibet in those days—important things for Tibet like their prayer flags. Did you know the prayer flags for the common people were the old *dhotis* of the people of the plains? White saris that women wore were also usable. Agents collected, washed, and nicely folded them, and Tibetan traders bought the bundles for making into prayer flags.

I don't know my exact date of birth. My mother did not read calendars— she was illiterate. She would say, "There was a flood, and you were twenty-one days old." I tried looking on the internet to find that particular flood in the Chumbi Valley. The Amochu was flooded because there was a glacial burst, so this big wall of water came and swept down most of the houses. My father, mother, with three kids went up to higher ground, and from there they could see the houses with hearths still burning, drifting down in the flood like houseboats in Kashmir.

MY GRANDFATHER WAS A YAK HERDER. He is supposed to have been with Younghusband's expedition in 1903–'04, helping transport war material to Lhasa. Soldiers moved with guns and means of fighting. But supplies had to be carried. Thousands of Tibetan, Nepali, and Indian porters were employed. It's amazing. Many Sherpas and Tibetans in Darjeeling talk about their grandfathers and great-grandfathers who were on this expedition as carriers. After the operation, [my grandfather] was waylaid on the way to Solu Khumbu. He lost everything and came back to Yatung; he never returned home. His wife died, and their only son—my father—was looked after by relatives. Finally, my father came to Yatung to look for his father and settled.

My mother's family was from Thame in Nepal. My grandmother, a widow, is supposed to have gone for pilgrimage with her two daughters. They were all very strong women. If you had seen my mother, you would have understood. They went on pilgrimage to Tibet for atonement because her husband is supposed to have sinned. On the way, my mother and grandmother took refuge in my father's home, since he was a Sherpa. My father is supposed to have said, "Leave this one here. I am going to make her my wife so you can't take her back." My grandmother gave her blessings: "Look after her—I will visit to see if you have kept my daughter well. If not, I will kill you." Later my youngest aunt [Ani Lhakpa Diki] came and lived with my mother. She got married there and she came to Darjeeling.

That is how my father and mother happened to settle in Chumbi Valley. Yatung was a rich, fertile place. It is immediately behind the Himalayan range, and it had good climate and rain. We had apples, plums, pine forests. Houses were made of excellent pine wood. People there looked good—because, good food! After crossing Chumbi, you cross the passes and reach [the town of] Phari Thanka and then the bleak, barren, cold, windy, dark Tibetan plateau.

My father was the caretaker of a number of bungalows on the trade route—some of them built by The Himalayan Club. He had the monopoly to supply wood, fresh vegetables, eggs, and chicken to the bungalows; there was profit in that. And there would be porters and horsemen who also needed food. All that would be supplied by my father and mother. The *dak bangla* [government rest house] was always busy. European trekkers came to stay there. Expeditions came through Yatung.

My mother ran a *serai* [inn with a courtyard for animals]. Our house was full of travellers. When the trade routes were open, it was a sight for a little boy! I would count the endless lines of mules led by ruffian Tibetan muleteers. There I happened to see Marwaris [members of a Hindu business community, originally from the state of Rajasthan] fluent in Tibetan on horseback, wearing dhotis, socks up to here, garters to keep the socks up on their thin shins. It was also where I first saw Tenzing Norgay and many other Sherpas who made names for themselves. They would stay in our house. They would dance the marathon Sherpa dance, drink chang the whole day, dance again all night, and the next day they would be gone. We were an affluent family—lots of food, a comfortable house. My mother was very busy, but happy to be busy because she had money coming in.

Yatung was a very important trade depot. We saw the British and Nepali residents being carried on dandis or horseback, and the Bhutanese trade agents and Chinese big shots lived maharajah style. At the head of our locality, there was a cantonment area for an Indian Army company. There was a hospital and dispensary even for the locals—my mother used to take us there for medication.

We saw parts of cars being carried to Lhasa, to be reassembled there. And we saw Tibetans carrying jerry cans of petrol all the way from Kalimpong to the Potala. They had a motor road around the Potala for the pleasure of the lamas and aristocrats to ride their motorcycles and cars. The rest of Tibet had no motor road. Either you walked, or if you were wealthy you moved on horseback.

I have lots of memories of my life in the valley. I was the first son after two girls. Then after me were two more boys. One sister died, so then we were four children.

When I went to Manali in 1978, along the Beas River, we used to look for rocks for bouldering. I smelt a familiar smell. I said, "I know this smell;

this plant I know." I brought down the plant and smelt it again. Memories took me back to Chumbi Valley. My sister, who was six years older, knew this plant was sold in the cantonment. She would make a train [single file, like railroad cars] with all of us, jump up, and pull some stalks down. The whole valley filled with the scent. We would rub the stalks, and we had fun doing that. We had black sap collected on our hands. Then she would hold up her baku and everybody would rub and drop the sap— there would be a big, black lump, like tar. She carried this to the cantonment, and we waited as she went up to the gate. Nothing would happen for a long time. Finally, one of the soldiers would come down, followed by another, and there was negotiation. They took the lump, and she came back with coins. She gave us one coin each. It was great fun. In Manali, I [learned] this was ganja!

WHEN MY FATHER DIED, EVERYTHING was completely over. I was six years old.

There was a threat of the bungalow-caretaker job being given to somebody else. My mother stuffed extra straw into my boots to make me a little taller. We were going to meet a very big sahab, she said. And I remember this man—he was kind—a gentleman with specs and a felt hat. I had seen him earlier on horseback. He said in Tibetan, "No, he is too small—he can't be a *chowkidar* [caretaker]." She said, "I do most of the work. When my husband was there, I was looking after the bungalow." It was so. She was a strong woman—physically and mentally. My father was older, much older. She explained, but this man kept shaking his head. My mother was crying; I was also crying. He is supposed to have promised to give the job to me when I grew older—eleven or twelve years old. And she held that as a promise. So, she wanted me to grow fast.

I saw how my mother, being a widow, was subjected, how people tried to take advantage of her. When you read about Tibetans and Buddhists as holy, pious, religious—it is hypocrisy, propaganda. I say, "You haven't seen Tibetans." We four children would go cling to her, and some ruffians would try to pull her away from us. We would scream, and my sister would go running to the neighbor for help.

So, my mother stopped [the serai] altogether. Our front yard and backyard, where there used to be fifty to sixty mules, tethered, watered, and given fodder—all that stopped. She got a man called Engineer to write letters to her brother to come and take her to Darjeeling. Finally, one evening, my youngest uncle and a friend came with six horses. My sister whispered, "We are going to Darjeeling." My mother loaded whatever she could on four horses. Two horses were kept for riding. My youngest brother was nine months [old] or so.

This is how we came. I came walking over the Nathu La pass. It must have been in October [or] November—orange season. I remember my mother saying that we walked for nine days. I walked all the way. My mother used to flatter me, and [my uncle and his friend] would also say, "He's a strong boy—he doesn't like to ride a horse." I didn't want to ride because of my ego! But I was so tired that I slept while walking, I'm told. One day, I remember my uncle went under this rock with a knife and I followed, out of curiosity. He was cutting the leg off a dead sadhu. The sadhu was naked, and one leg was already gone. My uncle was trying to cut the other one for the thigh bone, to take it as a gift to his brother-in-law, who was a Tantric lama. My mother got off the horse and dragged him away. "There are children here. Are you going to carry a dead man's leg?" [she said.] That was Tibet.

Nine days from Yatung to Bhutia basti in Darjeeling. [Back in Yatung,] I had seen pieces of newspapers, magazines that came with the sahabs who stayed in the *dak* bungalow. After they left, as a kid, I would quickly go and look in the rubbish bin and pick up all those papers. There used to be pictures. I had seen in these papers motorcars, aeroplanes, and a number of modern things, but I hadn't [yet] seen a solid assembled motorcar, leave aside a moving one.

I saw my first electric bulb in Gangtok! We were staying in a lodge, and there was this switch. My sister knew everything! Not that she had seen anything, but she was much more informed and she was six years older than me. She told me not to touch it: "If you touch it, you will be thrown back there." I used to be scared but I was curious. You do clack here and there is a light there! I was so very tempted to do it, so I turned it off and it went dark and nothing happened to me—so I quickly turned it on and the light came on! Now it became a plaything for me. I wanted to see how fast it travels! There was a water hydrant—when people came to fill water, I would go and open the tap and then close it for them. [And] the first car I saw was in Gangtok. I would see people getting on the side and the car moving in the middle, minding its own business with big eyes and all! We stayed in Gangtok for two nights and saw lots of things of the twentieth century.

Yatung has changed. Often when I have nothing to do, I go on to Google Earth and look at Nathu La and Chumbi Valley. I went in 2001 with National Geographic from the Nepali side, but we were not allowed to descend beyond Khampa Dzong. How much I wanted to see Chumbi Valley. I hope someday they open the passes for tourism at least. I feel before I die I must go—my childhood was there. My good childhood was there.

IN DORJEE LHATOO'S WARM, WOOD-PANELED living room, plate-glass windows provide wonderful views of the valley below—forests with tall deodars interspersed with bright red rhododendron, as well as walnuts and oaks. The bookshelf that covers a wall is crammed with mountaineering books, while his medals and awards are hidden away in an alcove. Strains of Indian classical music fill the air. The difference between his childhood conditions and the beautiful home he has created is stark. What his stories tell us is that he has an almost photographic memory and an insatiable curiosity. The child Dorjee Lhatoo once was is still evident in the man—indeed, this is what sets him apart.

When we reached Darjeeling, we stayed for a few months in my uncle's home in Toong Soong. But we were overstaying the welcome. We were four of us plus their two—six kids. In those days, uncle had two rooms. He stayed with his family in one room, and we were given the other room. My mother decided that we should move out and have our own place. Ajeeba was her cousin; we moved below his house. I was to go back to Yatung to get back my father's job, so I was sent to a Chinese school.

Those were hard times. It was soon after the Second World War and India's independence. You could not get anything in the open market. With a ration card, there would be long lines every week for sugar, rice, kerosene. It was hungry yesterday, hungry today, hungry tomorrow. My mother used to buy beef—the only meat we could afford. In those days it was six annas a kilo for good meat. But she used to bring scrap. Poverty. We were refugees so my mother wanted to go back. We were better up there. We had our own home, we had tenants, and we had a plot of land where she grew vegetables and barley.

She was an expert brewer of chang, the local brew. When she came here, she thought she would start with the same business. But this was a different world—you needed a license. If you wanted to drink, you had to go to a licensed shop. You could not brew at home. Men in khakhi [policemen] would come, confiscate everything, and pour all the brew into the drains. There would be yelling, screaming, my mother begging with folded hands, "Please, please." They would crush the pots and drag her to the police station, me running behind. My sister would go to a relative's house. Ang Tsering or someone would bail her out. There would be a case pending—no brewing. Later she learned that you had to bribe the uniformed people. She was on the list of illicit brewers, and there would be collection every month. Then it became semi-legal so she was advised to make a license. For that too she had to pay.

My mother also brewed a special alcohol for herself—100 proof! Not chang; much stronger. And she smoked sixty to seventy cigarettes a day. Ang Lhamu (Tenzing's second wife), who was never without a cigarette either, would visit and they would sit together and drink, chatting all afternoon. I was a small kid but I remember those events. I remember people saying that we are now independent. Chong Rinzing was one of my close cronies at the time. I remember him telling me that Gandhiji [Mahatma Gandhi] had been shot and killed in Delhi. My mother used to be amazed by my childhood memories. But "he has a black heart" she would say in a negative way. "He remembers all the wrong done to him."

She kept in touch with those who came from Yatung. She had many acquaintances among the traders, and she impatiently watched me grow. In 1952–53 we went back. She went to see the sahab who had promised to give my father's job to me. I don't know what transpired, but my mother was crying. She made arrangements with the lama of Thungka gompa for our home and our household goods to be bought by the monastery. I had to go and sign as the eldest son. There were two lamas: one was writing and drawing, and every now and then I was made to put my thumb impression on one paper after another. That was the selling of our property, and we never went back to Yatung.

WHEN LHATOO SPEAKS, IT IS always in impeccable, measured English. Life has taught him to be careful and cautious. Never was he unguarded enough to reveal anything of himself that he didn't want to. Of his early years in Darjeeling, he spoke little, preferring to talk of happier times. We heard, however, that even as a child of seven or eight, Lhatoo worked on roads as a laborer. Money was tight in the family, so every bit of income helped. It was his curiosity and love for music that made him wander into a church one day. This led to him being employed as a houseboy to some missionaries and then to Rita Skillbeck, an Australian missionary. Though he went to her as a servant, Skillbeck soon became like a mother to him. She taught him Nepali and English. When she went on sabbatical to Australia, Skillbeck recommended him as a servant to the Schoonmaker family in Tezpur, Assam. Dr. Schoonmaker, an American doctor and missionary, had three sons.

We met the youngest, Marlin, in 2015. He spoke fondly of Lhatoo, and made it sound like he was part of the family. "When I first saw Dorjee, I was six," he told us. "And Lhatoo was twelve, thirteen, something like that." Lhatoo stayed with the Schoonmakers for eight months. Marlin remembered them as happy times, though Lhatoo, in his role as a servant, recalled struggling with some unhappy incidents that he was reluctant for us to share. He wrote to Skillbeck to take him away, so she arranged for him to go to Ghaziabad near Delhi, where there was an occupational facility. He was to study and learn a trade. The young teenager made a five-day journey all alone from Assam to the capital city. He left Ghaziabad a few years later, having learned the skill of carpentry. Marlin Schoonmaker reconnected with Lhatoo in 2007, and the two have been in occasional contact ever since. With Rita Skillbeck, Dorjee Lhatoo remained fondly in touch, visiting her bedside in Australia as she lay dying in 1991.

He never told us whether he was ever religious, but he is now an agnostic—unwilling to commit to any god and yet unwilling to anger any of them either. He remains a proud, complex man, as fiercely loyal in his relationships as he is unforgiving of those who he feels have slighted him.

> I left home definitely when I was twelve or thirteen, and I was then an occasional visitor to my mother. My sister had left home for Calcutta to work as domestic help. My two younger brothers were schooling in Darjeeling. The youngest contracted TB and never recovered—he died in his

teens. The middle one joined the army; he was doing very well—he was a *havaldar* [the equivalent of a sergeant]. My mother passed away in 1976. She was sixty-six years old. When she died, my brother decided to leave the army and look after my mother's business. My sister now lives in Delhi. She has three daughters. I have nothing to do with her, and we have no relationship. That's a sad story, but I don't want to go into it.

Lhatoo was still a minor when he decided to enlist in the British Army. He went to Dharan in Nepal, passed the tests, and was selected. He was waiting to be deployed to Malaya when he was told that his mother and sister had arrived to take him home. A loud altercation followed—and ended when he was grabbed by the hair and dragged away!

Now what do I do? I couldn't stay home and I couldn't stay in poverty; I needed to go and look for my fortune. I was getting to be a good footballer. We went to [the Gurkha Regimental Recruiting Center] Katapahar to play a match. As soon as we finished playing, tables and chairs were laid out, and one of the soldiers made us take off boots and shirts and run—we did it for the heck of it. I had no serious thought of now joining the Indian Army. Then we were lined up and they put crosses and numbers on our chest, and I happened to be selected. In the afternoon we were taken to the barracks—there was a harmonium playing, music was on, and Nepali boys were dancing. It was a gay, lovely atmosphere. In the evening, there was food. We were given a plate and a mug, and we formed a line for dal, meat, and rice. After washing plates, there was more music and dance. This is life! Next day they taught us how to do parade. This was in early 1957, and after a few days of this I did not go home. I disappeared, like the last time when I went to Dharan. My mother came to know after a year where I was, when I wrote her a letter from Dehradun that I had become a soldier.

I was a combatant soldier in [the 11th] Gorkha Rifles. It was a peacetime army. So, we would dig the officers' mess garden, carry supplies to the regimental kitchen, and peel potatoes. But I was fortunate. I was playing hockey, football, and basketball for the regiment. My monthly salary was Rs 39 and 60 paise [$0.49]. From this, I used to give my mother Rs 15 [$0.18]. Rs 6 [$0.074] was pocket money, so when I came home on leave I had about Rs 300 [$3.70]. That was in 1959, '60, '61. In

'62, I left the army to join the Himalayan Mountaineering Institute, where my salary was Rs 180 [$2.21] to begin with.

[My family] got me engaged in 1961. Doma [the niece of Tenzing Norgay] was my older sister's friend. [My family] said, "She is a good girl; we must keep her in the family." I said, "I will not marry until I earn enough to support a wife and, maybe, children." The CO called me one day and said, "Young man, I am sending you home to get married. I have got phone calls from Tenzing Norgay."

I resented it at that time. But then there was something called "falling in love gradually." I joined the army thinking I would educate myself, that I would become somebody, make lots of money, but things took a different turn once I got married. Doma understood that bettering myself would be bettering her, as we were married for life. After marriage, I went back to the army, but I could not take Tenzing's niece to the base and live in the lowest-ranking family quarters. I wanted to get out. The HMI became my way out, because the army could [have kept] me for fifteen years before they let me out with a pension.

As soon as I arrived in Darjeeling, I met the principal [of the HMI], Colonel Jaswal. To hire me as an instructor, he had to show that he was increasing the number of courses, the number of students, and therefore needed one more instructor. This is how he cleverly created a vacancy for me. I have met very kind people in my life. I did strive for bettering myself, but good came to me. I had a wife—a good wife; and I had a job—a good job!

Lhatoo didn't enter the profession the way most Sherpas did in those days. He was never a cook or porter. It was indeed a backdoor entrance to a life and environment in which he thrived. His first teachers of mountain craft were Tenzing Norgay and Lhatoo's brother-in-law Nawang Gombu, but everything else he learned was driven by his interest in people and their lives, and a thirst to soak up each and every experience.

I may have been teaching the rudiments of mountain climbing to students that came from all over India in those days, but now when I think of it, I learnt more from them. I taught them how to climb mountains, how to wear crampons, how not to wear a sweater over a windproof—in many cases, I taught them how to tie laces even. But then most of the people who came in those days were educated, and I was keen to learn. Mountaineering I knew; it's in my genes. I would gain knowledge from these other people, talking in English, improving my language skills. If you see any goodness in me, it has rubbed off on me by those people. In my community, we had good humor and good campfire stories; we exchanged stories about each other's expeditions. My philosophical approach to life is more from reading and from meeting people. I met all sorts of people.

LHATOO REMAINED AT THE HMI from 1962 to 2000. As a teacher, he captured both hearts and minds. On his courses, he would play the harmonica, sing ghazals—lyric poems—and quote poetry, all while explaining the history and geography of the regions they were passing through. He climbed lightly, airily—almost like a cloud—and inspired many accomplished climbers of today.

In the mountains, Lhatoo came to be known as the "Peak Bagger." Every expedition he was on was successful. His very first climb was to Frey Peak (5,889 meters), Sikkim, as an instructor. The training for Everest 1965 took place on Rathong Peak and Glacier. Lhatoo and another instructor, Ang Kami—both of them too junior to be in contention for the actual expedition team on Everest—found the way to the top when other, more experienced climbers failed. As a reward, they were allowed to be on the first summit team. It was Lhatoo's first ascent and the first ascent of Rathong. After that, he climbed Bandarpunch, Tirsuli, and Hardeol. And then came Chomolhari in 1970, on a joint HMI-Bhutan expedition. Chomolhari is considered a holy peak, so the expedition was positioned as a pilgrimage to make an offering to the gods. The King of Bhutan presented a holy pot, blessed by a high lama and containing gold, silver, diamonds, and holy prayers, all sealed with the king's seal, to be placed on the summit.

In five days, we reached basecamp, which was immediately below the northeast face of the mountain. From there, it took just two camps to the shoulder. This was the watershed boundary between Tibet and Bhutan, the crest of Chomolhari. I was amazed by what I saw from the shoulder. There was this mud fort, Phari Dzong. And on top of the fort was something red and prominent. I later learnt it was a big portrait of Mao Tse Tung. And by the side of it a straight, long road disappeared on the horizon. Premchand, Thondu Sherpa, Santosh Arora, and I got to the top. I placed the holy pot there with all reverence—I felt rather sentimental.

Tragedy unfolded when the second summit team, comprised of captains G. S. Kang and Dharampal and Sherpa Ang Nima, disappeared from view on the way to the summit the next day. Lhatoo led a search party, but it turned up nothing. A second search team turned back when the would-be rescuers felt that they were being shot at from the Tibetan side. The team leader's concern was that the Chinese would come over the pass to arrest the expedition for trespassing into Tibetan territory, which they had entered earlier on the expedition.

> I had felt satisfaction, having gone to the top, but when I saw the tragedy, I thought, "Was it worth it?"
>
> Doma was eight months pregnant when I left for Chomolhari in April 1970. We already had two kids—Samden and Yongden—and I was hoping for a daughter. When we arrived at basecamp, there was a telegraphic message for me: "Congratulations! Son born. Son and mother well." I had made up my mind that my daughter was going to be named Chomolhari. *Chomo* is an honorific term for "lady." *Lha* is "deity." And *ri* is "mountain." So "Lady Goddess Mountain" or "Deity Mountain." But I thought, "I must keep my promise [to myself], so it will be Lhari." If you delete *chomo* then Lhari means "Holy Mountain"; it is a rare name.
>
> Doma was a very good mother, a good wife, a good homemaker. The children are very close to Doma. I was the bread earner. Whether children come out good, much depends on their mother. Father has to put food on the table.

In 1975, Lhatoo was on Nanda Devi, with the French. He got to see the famous Chamonix guides in action for the first time. He was impressed by their democratic style of functioning and the sheer skill with which they overcame alpine obstacles. The task was to make the traverse between Nanda Devi's twin peaks. Although the team climbed both peaks separately, the traverse was put off due to the impending monsoon.

> But the very next year, '76, the Japanese came and accomplished the traverse. As soon as the French expedition was over and [the Japanese]

learned that the traverse was not accomplished, they came to everyone connected with Nanda Devi for information. I was invited, and I was in that expedition also.

Dorjee Lhatoo climbed Everest in 1984. After that achievement, he was awarded the small plot of land on which he started building his house. We interviewed his eldest son, Dr. Samden Lhatoo, a neurologist practicing in America:

I grew up in HMI. I didn't see my dad very much—he went to the mountains a lot. They were either on climbing courses or on expeditions, but there was always a sense of flux, of transition and movement on the campus. It was difficult for the kids because sometimes people didn't come back . . . we went to funerals—we knew the score. He would be back for a week, two weeks, and then would be gone again. He understood that he had no opportunity to be an influence in our lives unless he took us climbing with him. So, when the hill schools shut down between November and March, he would take us to the courses—Basic, Adventure, or Advanced—where we would get maybe three or four weeks at a time with him, and during that time, we would talk nonstop.

He was a role model for me in many ways because he carried himself in a way that was very different from the other instructors. He was a lot more polished, more refined—he read books; he could talk about books, you know. He knew Indian classical music and things like that. He spoke Hindi and Urdu fluently, English too, whereas other instructors spoke broken everything. So yeah, he was somebody to look up to, and when we saw him climb—when he was climbing rocks or ice climbing on Rathong Glacier—he was a very graceful, stylish climber. We heard from him climbing stories, the pride that he had about our relatives from the 1920s and '30s, the climbs with the foreigners—Nanga Parbat and places like that. We had this library in the mountaineering institute— a tremendous library. Nobody used it, and I was introduced to it by my father. My mother, though, was the rock. I look back at those days and I find a very strong woman. Uneducated. But with great common sense, courage, a lot of dignity.

Samden Lhatoo knew the sacrifices and hardship that Dorjee Lhatoo put himself through to give his sons the finest education anyone could hope for. Dr. Samden Lhatoo, MD, FRCP, is based at UT Health Houston, McGovern Medical School. Here, he is the John P. and Kathrine G. McGovern Distinguished University Professor of Neurology; executive vice chair, Neurology; director, Texas Comprehensive Epilepsy Program; and co-director, Texas Institute of Restorative Neurotechnologies. Lhatoo's second son, Yongden, is chief news editor at the *South China Morning Post*. He had worked as a television news anchor and editor in Hong Kong for nearly two decades before joining the *Post* in 2015. And as for Lhari, he has been a senior police official for several years, recently taking charge as inspector general of the North-West Frontier of the Indo-Tibetan Border Police.

Dorjee Lhatoo reflects on his lifetime:

> I've been in the middle. I knew the old climbers who participated in history-making expeditions. I came after them. And now I am before this new lot of Sherpas who climb Everest like it is a walk up the hill! Among these new people I am too old. So I don't fit anywhere.
>
> At the age of nine, I was doing all sorts of things. I had to support my mother, my brothers. And later, I had a wife and three kids to support. My salary was not enough so I went on expeditions. I went to Germany and Switzerland to do manual labor in farms, cleaning pig sties, cowsheds, working in factories, cleaning, and sweeping. I was not skilled. I did the most menial jobs for extra money during the HMI vacations. A director of Unilever employed me in his plastics factory in Germany. On the weekends, I would take the executives climbing in the Alps. It was hard work. I taught rock climbing in a school in Australia. All my life, I have worked under someone; for someone. I have given my own children, even Doma, happier parts of my life. The other parts remain private.
>
> Now, I have enough. I've not become rich, but in my old age I don't need any more. In my lifetime, we struggled. We were very austere. Two-thirds of my life I would worry how to put food on the table tomorrow for the five of us. Now we are comfortable. Our children are very comfortable. I don't intend to live with them. Not leaving this room even. Not going anywhere. We travel a bit, go around the world, but Darjeeling is home.

IN ONE SENSE, LHATOO IS all Sherpas who struggled and did everything they could to provide their children with a better life than their own, while working in one of the most dangerous professions on Earth. In another sense, he is of course unique, because he succeeded where many others failed. He hasn't become a household name like Tenzing, nor has he garnered the medals that his brother-in-law Gombu did. He cannot boast of having climbed the most peaks, but this quiet man most certainly symbolizes the Sherpa story of vertical ascent.

Through the ten years we have known Dorjee Lhatoo, it has been his intellect and deep thirst to learn that have shone through. Very early in our project, we began to feel that Dorjee Lhatoo should take center stage in our narrative. "I'm not important," he told us in alarm. "I'm no one." So he potters about his home, finding things to occupy himself, while his wife, Doma, divides her time between Darjeeling and her youngest son's family, based in New Delhi and now Leh, Ladakh. His is a story you will hear nowhere else, and he would probably be annoyed and embarrassed to read about himself on these pages. But to Dorjee Lhatoo we owe our immense gratitude—for sharing his story and those of so many others, for answering every query, and for being a wonderful friend and an enlightened mentor.

PART THREE

The Flight of the Garud

Captain M.S. Kohli (front row, fifth from left) with his Everest expedition team in 1965
(Captain M.S. Kohli Collection)

CHAPTER 16

The Great Indian Dream

Satish Ranjan Das, advocate general of Bengal in the 1920s, envisaged an educational institution modeled on traditional English public schools. Thus was born the Doon School, nestled in Dehradun in the foothills of the Garhwal Himalaya. It opened in 1935 with seventy boys.

Nalni Jayal, an eminent Himalayan expert, environmental crusader, and Doon School alumnus, wrote, "Fortunately, its first Headmaster, Arthur Foot, a member of the Alpine Club, was a keen climber, and perhaps his love for the mountains influenced him in recruiting three house masters, John Martyn, Jack Gibson and R L Holdsworth (Holdie) who were all experienced alpinists. Indeed, Holdie had climbed Kamet in 1931 with Frank Smythe's expedition."

These housemasters played a crucial role in encouraging their pupils to first venture into the forests and hills around the Doon Valley and later take on more adventurous trekking and climbing outings. One of the first expeditions the school led was in 1942 to the nearby Arwa Valley. John Martyn and Holdie, with two Sherpas, took three boys to climb some nearby peaks, as an introduction to mountaineering. The trip was frustrated by persistently bad monsoon weather; nevertheless, one of the boys, Narendra (Nandu) Dhar Jayal, wrote of his experience, "The hills have claimed another willing slave." In the years to follow, the association of the Doon School with the Himalaya continued to grow, and the school became a cradle of Indian mountaineering.

In 1945, a young man called Gurdial Singh joined the staff, and very soon mountains became part of his life too. Harish Kapadia told us, "In 1947, when the British left, people thought that mountaineering would not hold up in India. Then, in 1951, Gurdial Singh and a few others went up Trisul peak [7,120 meters] in the Kumaon region. That's how Indian mountaineering took off." Reaching the summit of Trisul was a great achievement, as it was the first Indian ascent of a peak of repute. Leading the porters was Sherpa Dawa Thondup.

Gurdial said, "Gasping for breath, [Roy] Greenwood and I tugged at the rope. Dawa turned around and, with a mixture of firmness and politeness, emphasized that time was pressing; therefore, we must quicken our pace. What prodigious energy he had!" They stood atop the summit—or rather, Gurdial expressed his joy with head in the snow and feet in the air. Greenwood, a physical training instructor at the Indian Military Academy Dehra Dun, it is said, felt the headstand lacked technique!

The triumph on Everest in 1953 led to the establishment of the HMI, which imparted the basics of mountaineering education in India. There was a flurry of successful climbs in that period. The same year as Everest, the Germans climbed Nanga Parbat, the "Killer Mountain." The Austrians claimed Cho Oyu in 1954, while the Italians reached the top of K2 that same year. And, in 1955, Kangchenjunga and Makalu were both climbed. Indian climbers were also honing their skills. The Kamet expedition in 1955 was launched in collaboration with the Bengal Sappers—an Indian military unit. The team included Gurdial Singh and five HMI instructors led by Nandu Jayal, the starry-eyed ex-student of the Doon School, who was now an officer in the Bengal Sappers and the principal of the HMI. A failed first attempt was followed a mere week later by another attempt, in which four Sherpas summitted. That same year, Jack Gibson and boys from the Doon School achieved the first ascent of Kalanag (6,387 meters), a peak in Uttarakhand. All the while, the Sherpas of Darjeeling were accompanying not only the foreign expeditions but the ever more numerous Indian ones as well.

In 1956, a fresh HMI laureate named Mohan Singh Kohli took part in an attempt on Saser Kangri (7,672 meters) and its surrounding peaks in the Eastern Karakoram. The expedition did not achieve all its objectives, but M. S. Kohli (later a naval captain) went on to lead the first Indian ascent of Everest in 1965 and played a very important role in the careers of many Darjeeling Sherpas.

In 1958, the ascent of Cho Oyu was another landmark in Indian mountaineering. It was planned by a Mumbai solicitor named Keki Bunshah, who approached a government secretary for funding (the secretary in turn created a group to sponsor the expedition). The flamboyant Pasang Dawa Lama—along with Sonam Gyatso and John Dias—ascended Cho Oyu (8,188 meters) for his second time. (The Austrians Josef Jochlër and Herbert Tichy, along with Pasang Dawa Lama, had made the first ascent of Cho Oyu in 1954.)

Although the 1958 expedition led to victory, it began in tragedy. Nandu Jayal, who was to be part of the team, had just resigned his post as principal of the HMI. Leaving Darjeeling after his handover to the new principal, he rushed to catch up with the other team members, who had left days earlier. On the way to basecamp, he collapsed and died of pulmonary edema caused by overexertion. Jayal was just thirty-one years old.

On the heels of the 1958 climb came the Indian ascent of Nanda Kot (6,861 meters) in 1959. These achievements excited bureaucratic hearts, and the group that had initially raised funds for Cho Oyu metamorphosed into a Sponsoring Committee for Everest and other mountaineering expeditions, finally becoming the Indian Mountaineering Foundation in 1961. This body now sponsors, organizes, and issues permits for every expedition that wishes to climb a peak in India.

In this manner, Indian mountaineering, filled with fresh energy and passion, was set to conquer Everest. A new sahab was emerging, more egalitarian perhaps and with the same skin tone as the Sherpa. With HMI instructors being invited as team members, another distinction was born—Sherpas who climbed instead of working as high-altitude porters.

SEVERAL EXPEDITIONS FOLLOWED—NOT ALL OF which were successful. There was Everest in 1960, on which the team members turned back a mere 100 meters from the summit, followed in 1961 by the first ascent of Annapurna III by Captain Kohli and others via its Northeast Face. Nilkantha (6,500 meters), an impressive peak in the Garhwal Himalaya, had resisted seven attempts before an Indian team claimed the first ascent, led by the eminent mountaineer Colonel Narinder Kumar, also in 1961. (Their climb was, however, widely discredited, and the acknowledged first ascent of Nilkantha went to Sonam Palzor and his Indo-Tibetan Border Police team in 1974.) Another unsuccessful Indian attempt on Everest was made in 1962. With these milestone climbs as well as others, Indian mountaineers were inching

HMI instructors in 1971: Standing left to right are Phu Dorji, Pasang Temba, Dorjee
Lhatoo, Nima Tashi, Chewang Tashi, Nawang Phenjo, Da Namgyal, and Ang Temba.
Seated left to right are Nawang Gombu, Principal A. S. Cheema, and Tenzing Norgay.
(Dorjee Lhatoo Collection)

closer to achieving their dream of hoisting the Indian flag on Everest. Thus,
in 1964, Indian climbers began preparing for the peak in earnest, with three
successful expeditions—to Panchachuli (6,904 meters), Nanda Devi (7,816
meters), Tirsuli (7,074 meters), and Nanda Devi East (7,434 meters) in the
North Indian state of Uttarakhand.

It was Mohan Singh Kohli who led the Indian team on Everest in 1965,
a large expedition with twenty-one core members and fifty high-altitude
Sherpas. Nawang Gombu (who had stood atop Everest in 1963 with the
Americans) and Ang Kami from the Sherpa community were full members
of the expedition. Other climbers included proven men of the mountains:
Narendra "Bull" Kumar, A. S. Cheema, Sonam Gyatso, Sonam Wangyal, and
C. H. S. Rawat, among others. It was the third Indian attempt, and every

effort was made to see it succeed. By all accounts the expedition was happy, the team was cohesive, and the planning immaculate. An effort to climb Lhotse was stymied by strong winds, but the team waited patiently for the weather to clear so they could achieve the main objective.

On May 20, 1965, Lieutenant Colonel Avatar Singh Cheema and Nawang Gombu stood on the summit, followed by Sonam Gyatso and Sonam Wangyal on May 22, C. P. Vohra and Ang Kami Sherpa on May 24, and finally, on May 29, some twelve years after the first ascent of the mountain, Phu Dorjee Sherpa, Major H. P. S. Ahluwalia, and C. H. S. Rawat—nine atop Everest! Kohli wrote:

> The Sherpas beat all their own splendid records by putting up an unprecedented performance. Out of the 44 high-altitude Sherpas, one reached the top, 19 carried loads to the last camp and 22 others to the South Col. Many of them carried loads four times, one even five times. Whether a Sherpa or a member, each one had done his best. How honoured and privileged I feel to have led a team of such fine men!

Spy Story

Another event in 1965 needs to be mentioned here. Immediately after Everest, an Indo-US secret mission was launched to place a spying device on top of Nanda Devi. In those days before satellites, both countries were paranoid about China's growing nuclear capability, and the American-made plutonium capsule was meant to track the position of China's missiles. Kohli, fresh from the success of Everest, was chosen to carry out the mission, and recruited many Sherpas from Darjeeling to help with the task. Because it was a military exercise, the selected Sherpas had to be inducted into the Indian military. Thus, several men got pensionable jobs for which they would otherwise not have qualified, creating an immense sense of goodwill and gratitude. Kohli is still remembered fondly in Sherpa homes today.

Ultimately, a blizzard prevented the plutonium device from being placed, and it was temporarily lodged at a lower point. When the expedition returned the next season, the device was missing. Kohli and his men spent three years searching for it. The capsule was never found, leading to fears that it may be leaking nuclear material into the glacial waters of North India. Kohli published this tale of intrigue and horror as the book *Spies in the Himalayas*, cowritten with Kenneth Conboy.

The success of this expedition generated much excitement in India. Several mountaineering clubs and schools opened. From five expeditions in 1965, India mounted fifteen in 1966. Finally, by 1984, 101 expeditions were recorded.

ON THE EVEREST EXPEDITION OF 1984, Bachendri Pal became the first Indian woman to summit the mountain. This expedition was noteworthy not only because of Bachendri's achievement but also because of the assertiveness of the Sherpas and the breakdown in sahab-Sherpa relations.

Starting in 1982 as a lead-up to the expedition, the IMF held pre-Everest exercises, which included expeditions to other Indian peaks, mainly Satopanth in the Garhwal Himalaya, during which members were chosen. Colonel Balwant Sandhu was strongly expected to be chosen as the leader, but his name was dropped at the last moment. In his place was chosen Darshan Kumar Khullar, principal of the HMI, by his own admission "a gentleman climber" who had only been "on moderate Himalayan expeditions." The plan was to place Indian women mountaineers on the summit of Everest.

Six women were chosen for the climb: Chandraprabha Aitwal, generally regarded as the strongest and most likely to make it to the top; Harshwanti Bisht; Rita Gombu; Rekha Sharma; Bachendri Pal; and Sharavati Prabhu. There were also nine men on the climbing team, not including the leader, deputy leader, doctor, and signal operator (who coordinated wireless communications between camps). Among the climbers were N D Sherpa, Phu Dorji, Sonam Paljore, Magan Bissa, and Dorjee Lhatoo.

Trouble began at the HMI itself. Lhatoo told us, "Long story in short, I did not get along with Khullar." Khullar claims that he had to banish Lhatoo to the Nehru Institute of Mountaineering for six months for having an affair with another instructor's wife. Whatever the reasons, the relationship between these men only worsened as preparations for the climb progressed.

The early days of the expedition saw tragedy. One Sherpa, Ang Ringzin, was hit by an avalanche while en route to the Khumbu Icefall, barely fifteen minutes from basecamp. No sooner was his funeral finished than one of the kitchen boys, Jang Bir, collapsed halfway down to Lobuje. Khullar wrote, "We now had two dead men and the expedition had hardly begun."

The trouble was not only between Khullar and Lhatoo. In general, the expedition's planning and execution also fomented discontent. The food was bad; equipment failed; there were altercations with the porters, who had issues with payments and rations; and Khullar lost the confidence of his deputy, Lieutenant Colonel Prem Chand.

When the summit parties were announced, Dorjee Lhatoo was assigned to the last party, and neither he nor the woman climber he was assigned to figured in the summit teams. He would get a chance only if other summit teams failed to make the attempt during the time assigned to them.

What happened after that? Lhatoo told us, "It became contentious. Khullar did not want me to climb Everest, and therefore I had to climb it. I'm a professional, I'm excluded from the summit team, I'm in my element, I will go."

Manik Banerjee, a highly respected Bengal climber who was initially tapped to be on the expedition, told us that "there was an ego problem between the two of them. Khullar as a mountaineer was not the same level as Lhatoo. No way." Banerjee indicated that when subordinates see that the leader is not up to the task in terms of planning, route-finding, and figuring out systems, there is a problem—a big problem. Lhatoo disobeyed direct orders when he decided to try for the top, but Khullar had let his personal bias keep one of his ace climbers out of the summit bid.

Rita Gombu, who was chosen for the first summit team, told us in an interview in Delhi, "The only reason Khullar was selected was because the other person was too expensive [implying that the latter's expedition budget was much higher], so they agreed on Khullar. This is a fact, okay." Relying on sketchy information down at basecamp, Khullar would suggest routes to Rita and Bachendri, who were already up on the mountain. The expedition leader's lack of practical experience was proving costly. When asked what became of her summit bid, Rita Gombu told us that Khullar sent her and Chandraprabha with Phu Dorji and another Sherpa, Ang Dorji, from basecamp to Camp II in one day. "Nobody does double camp in one day," said Rita. "And on Lhotse Face he told us to share one cylinder." Finally, Rita proceeded without supplemental oxygen. She ultimately turned back without attempting the top.

Chandraprabha's case was different. Even though we met her in 2019, thirty-five years after the expedition, she still refused to talk about what had happened. Deeply bitter, she felt she had lost her chance at fame through no fault of her own. Chandraprabha was climbing with Lieutenant Colonel Prem Chand. Manik Banerjee told us that they turned back from the South Summit because gas cylinders—critical equipment—that were supposed to have been sent from basecamp did not arrive on time. Banerjee said, "When their gas didn't reach them, Prem took a decision. Being a true mountaineer, he said, 'I will stay back.' He also asked Chandraprabha to stay back. Otherwise, Chandraprabha would have made the summit—not only made the summit, [but] would have been the first Indian woman to make the summit. Anyway, this is luck."

Lhatoo's decision to try for the summit ultimately saved the expedition, although few people will admit it. Rita said, "If Lhatoo had not rebelled, Bachendri may not have reached the summit. Ang Dorji did not have a rope and Lhatoo had a rope; if you read carefully, Bachendri and Ang Dorji were on that rope."

On May 23, 1984, Bachendri Pal, Ang Dorji, Dorjee Lhatoo, and Sonam Paljore stood on top of Everest. Khullar had earlier threatened, "I am going to send you to jail!" Then he pleaded, "Lhatoo, please take the girl." In the publicity that followed the climb, Bachendri's name figured prominently as the first Indian woman to ascend Mount Everest, while Ang Dorji was applauded for having climbed the peak without supplemental oxygen. The other climbers were barely even mentioned.

In 1992, a book by Khullar about the expedition was published that rendered scathing opinions of several people, particularly Lhatoo. He also wrote a letter to *The Himalayan Journal*, to which Dorjee Lhatoo responded. When we met Khullar in 2017, he admitted, "Now, if I were to write [the book] again, I would make a few changes. I would be a little more sober. I would give a benefit to certain human judgements and errors of behavior and try to understand why things have happened." But the damage was done. Lhatoo came in for his share of criticism—for being openly rebellious on the mountain and for a wholly inappropriate affair with one of the climbers. The story of Everest 1984 made for thoroughly distasteful reading and overshadowed what should have been a joyful achievement.

Meanwhile, in the larger climbing world beyond Everest, expeditions to different areas in the Indian Himalaya were not only increasing but trends were shifting. Two types of Indian climbers were emerging. Harish Kapadia led one sort of explorers during the 1980s and 1990s. He was interested in exploring one valley after another, writing books and articles on his travels. Like Smythe and Shipton, his idea was not to climb peaks but to open new valleys with endless possibilities. With him walked many Darjeeling Sherpas. The other sort of climber that emerged was men and women who saved for years, sacrificing luxuries and even necessities to achieve their goal of climbing Everest in the hope of becoming famous overnight. Many of these climbers came from West Bengal and Maharashtra; they were blue-collar workers and daily-wage earners who often put everything at risk, placing their faith entirely in Sherpa guides they could ill afford to take them to the top and bring them back safely.

Mountaineering changed and so did the role of the Sherpas. No longer content to be porters, the newer Sherpas of Darjeeling began to rapidly branch out into the larger climbing world—some of them starting their own agencies, others specializing as personal guides on Everest, and yet others concentrating on 8,000ers.

Prime Minister Jawaharlal Nehru inaugurating the Himalayan
Mountaineering Institute in 1954 *(Himalayan Mountaineering
Institute Collection)*

CHAPTER 17

The Lost Legacy

Scanning the HMI website imparts a sense of the ongoing pride that the institute derives from the two personalities who started it: Pandit Jawaharlal Nehru and Tenzing Norgay. The masthead quotes Nehru: "The Institute trains young men not only to climb Himalayan peaks, but also creates in them an urge to climb peaks of human endeavor." The website also pays tribute to Tenzing for having sparked the flame of adventure in Indian youth. The HMI online photo gallery depicts primarily the Nehru family and Sherpas with other mountaineering celebrities of that era. Sadly, this is the only legacy left, for Sherpas have little to no influence at the HMI today. As the HMI nears seventy, the Sherpa, once the backbone of this institution, is missing in action.

The governments of India and West Bengal run the HMI jointly. The prime minister is no longer involved; the defense minister is the president of the HMI's Executive Council (EC), and the chief minister of West Bengal is vice president. Other officials comprise representatives from the bureaucracy and ministries. All these executives are often far removed from the institute's activity, many probably unaware that the HMI is even in their portfolio. A serving or retired army officer is principal, and other instructors are also deputed from the army. Although courses are subsidized to make them affordable for civilian students, several special programs are designed for army cadets from different corps.

When sports journalist Rudraneil Sengupta interviewed Harish Kapadia in 2012, Kapadia told him, "The nationalistic attitude generated by the Everest climb of '65 meant that climbing quickly became an institutionalized pursuit, monopolized by the armed forces. The spirit of Gurdial Singh—just four or five friends going out looking for adventure—that did not go forward." The army had money to spend, and it was soon recognized that expeditions helped boost soldiers' morale during peacetime while also becoming a show of strength to neighboring countries.

During this era—the 1970s and 1980s—the Indian Mountaineering Foundation was at its peak in sponsoring Indian, foreign, and mixed expeditions; however, the increase in red tape and unnecessary controls also made the process of applying for permissions frustrating and time consuming. Somewhere along the way, mountaineering activity and expeditions slowed down significantly—if not for everyone, certainly for the Darjeeling Sherpa. The generation that founded the HMI had begun to age; Tenzing lost his sheen and relevance, and the army began elbowing out the Sherpas as instructors as well as load carriers in expeditions. New institutions run by the armed forces were launched in other parts of the Himalaya. Many porters from Darjeeling began shifting to Nepal and its myriad climbing opportunities. As Dorjee Lhatoo wrote in *The Himalayan Journal* in 1979, "At present we are 27 Climbing Sherpas of sorts on record. Of these 3 are retired and 12 of us, including Tenzing and Gombu, are permanently employed in the Himalayan Mountaineering Institute. The younger lot are all educated . . . The other Sherpas are not permanently employed by any concern. They are employed once or twice, if very lucky thrice a year, for periods of one month to two months during the climbing seasons."

As the children of the Sherpas became educated, they did not want to climb or teach climbing. They aspired to secure jobs in the army or administrative sector or to other white-collar jobs. The army was also tightening its grip on the institute, a development related to the rise of the Gorkhaland movement in the 1980s. "Gurkha" or "Gorkha" refers to the indigenous people of Nepal, groups comprising various tribes that live in the country. Their name is said to have been derived from a legendary warrior saint named Gorkhanath, who lived in the area more than 1,200 years ago. The Gurkhas pride themselves on their military prowess and became famous as a regiment in the British Army in the mid-nineteenth century. The Gorkhaland movement began as a mass movement for a separate state of Nepali-speaking people in Darjeeling, as well as the surrounding districts of Kalimpong and the Dooars region (an area covering roughly 7,500 square kilometers), on the grounds that this population is culturally and ethnically different from the rest of West Bengal. The movement has seen several changes in leadership and taken many violent turns, engulfing Darjeeling and the surrounding areas in flames that rekindle every few years.

By 1999, when Anindya Mukherjee, one of India's finest mountaineers and a professional guide, completed the Basic course, "The army was running pretty much everything other than the field activity," he told us. The Sherpas who worked at the HMI, either permanently or as stringers, didn't like being led by army officials. Mukherjee continued, "But you need the army there to keep things in order. What happened during Gorkhaland agitation? There were two surges—one in the '80s, the other in the 2000s—and both times, there was this huge unruliness and there were attempts to take over HMI. If there was a civilian running HMI, the institution would have been finished."

Whatever the reasons, the shift of power since the 1980s was neither subtle nor temporary, and among the Sherpa instructors, it was seen as an attempt by the state machinery to evict them from their rightful position. Subsequent principals at the HMI made no bones about what they thought was unnecessary catering to Sherpa sentiment.

D. K. Khullar (principal at the HMI from 1981 to 1985) told us, "You know when Nehru, B. C. Roy [then chief minister of West Bengal], and Tenzing would have sat together, a lot of things may have happened verbally. It might have been said that Nehru set up HMI for the Sherpas. But this is not on record. These people were good instructors, and what made HMI so unique was the Sherpa element. But then a stage came that the Sherpas who did well, whether it was Tenzing, Gombu, or even Lhatoo and Nima—their children went into education, not into mountaineering; the other Sherpas who started coming, their quality went down. You are literally getting now the uneducated riffraff or the guys who couldn't make it."

Dipti Bhoota, a Mumbai-based lawyer and avid mountaineer, completed the Basic and Advanced courses in 1985 and 1990, respectively. It was a different HMI. Tenzing had retired in 1976 and passed away in 1986. Nawang Gombu was director of field training, and Dorjee Lhatoo occupied the post of deputy field director. Bhoota described the courses, which included classroom training, films on climbing, rock climbing demos on nearby rocks named after Gombu and Tenzing, expedition planning, and equipment use. Field training included a ten-to-twelve-day trek to basecamp and carrying weight such as tents.

Bhoota recalled, "During the Basic course, teachers kept to themselves; they restricted themselves to teaching us. As a lot of local people were students, they would speak Nepali. Sometimes I would tell the teachers, 'Please speak in Hindi.' If they—the local students—needed something, it was always provided. There was discrimination [against non-Nepali/Sherpa students]. My friends who went to [Nehru Institute of Mountaineering] did not see that kind of discrimination."

Bhoota had a vastly different experience in the Advanced course. Her Basic course included sixty women, but her Advanced course had around twenty-two. She recalled, "Lhatoo was our field trainer. Because of Lhatoo, the environment was totally different. He carried a lot of books, poems, etc. He had an amazing singing voice. As we would be walking, he would be singing, he would play the flute, talk about his climbs. When I met him, he had already done Nanda Devi East and West. He had climbed Chomolhari in Bhutan."

Anindya Mukherjee agreed with Bhoota. "[The well-known instructors] Chewang Tashi and Lhakpa were there," he told us. " But we were all in awe of Lhatoo. In general, I was very unhappy with the course structure. It really doesn't allow any candidate to learn something. But I was in Dorjee Lhatoo's last Basic course. I was so lucky to have Lhatoo sir as my instructor, and that remains the best memory ever. Almost every day in basecamp after the day's training, he would gather some of us and tell us stories. He made us fall in love with mountain adventure, which is more than lugging a load of twenty-five kilos. For me, the stories of the mountains told by Lhatoo in those days were immortal. I fell in love, and knew that I was not going to work in any other job. I was working in a pharmaceutical company, and after that I quit my job."

By the time Lhatoo left in 2000, the HMI was well into a downward spiral. The chasm between the bureaucracy and the Sherpas widened; a corruption of sorts seeped into the institution—not material, but in terms of the power equation. Aspiring instructors were now required to have high school diplomas. They went through the gamut of institutionally provided courses—Basic and Advanced, Search and Rescue, and Methods of Instruction. The army was in charge, imposing their own system on the HMI's teachings, a far cry from the old days when the instructors went on expeditions during which they were constantly learning from an international body of climbers.

If the Sherpas learned anything outside the courses, it was strictly through personal effort. If they went on expeditions with foreign teams, it was on their own time on holidays or on leave without pay. Institutional insurance did not cover them. When they retired, they did not receive a pension—or if they did, it was just a pittance. Naturally, they wanted better lives for their children. When Khullar announced that he was getting only "riffraff," it begged the question: what was the institution doing in these later years to develop instructors to the earlier standards of excellence?

One day in the early 1990s, Harish Kapadia and Dorjee Lhatoo were walking on Mall Road in Darjeeling when they came across the famous mountaineer brothers and ex-HMI instructors Gyalzen Mickchen and Da Namgyal selling sweaters on the pavement. Kapadia took a photograph of the three men, which he published in *The Himalayan Journal* as "Two sweater sellers and one future sweater seller" to draw attention to how the HMI had treated these highly respected teachers, not offering them a pension or benefits when they retired. That photo, it is said, led to changes in the rules regarding the HMI's terms of employment.

The year 2003 saw the golden jubilee of Hillary and Tenzing's ascent of Everest, an occasion the Sherpas of Darjeeling looked forward to eagerly. The Sherpa Association had planned a program, and it was expected that the HMI would also do something suitable to honor their hero. But what eventually transpired showed how unimportant the Sherpas had truly become to the managers of the institute. *The Statesman* carried a report in May 2003 mentioning "the alleged failure of the Himalayan Mountaineering Institute to organize a function befitting the 50th anniversary of Mt. Everest's first conquest." The institute offered clarifications, stating that they would soon hold grand celebrations to mark the event.

A year and a half later, *The Statesman* published an update: "Last year, the institute, with a glorious legacy, was in the news for having failed to organize a celebration of its 50th anniversary. Today, it was again, for having failed to meet its promise to hold one at the end of the anniversary year. It was a small affair today at the institute: put together by the staff. Both the principal and vice principal were absent. One of the senior staff recalled that to celebrate the 25th anniversary of the institute the then prime minister, Indira Gandhi, was herself present."

In 2012, the HMI's principal was Colonel Neeraj Rana. During our interview with him, the management's complete disconnect from and disinterest in the history and traditions of the institution became quite evident. He spoke almost entirely about himself and what he had done for the HMI to increase numbers and expand the institute, including the building of a Hindu temple on the premises.

Rana became belligerent when we asked him about Sherpas' interests. He said, "I have given jobs to them. This institution does not belong to Sherpas. Let's be very clear about it. This is on record, off record, you can play it anywhere. This institution was opened for a purpose by Panditji. It was opened to make way for young people to get into mountaineering. I do not tell them that the Sherpa community did this or did that. The moment the word 'community' comes into being, then it is politics. Pandit Nehruji was a politician. I am not a politician. I've been given a set of guidelines, which I follow. So how does the community come into play, I do not know; I would not like to comment."

Sangye Sherpa was a senior instructor whom we met on the HMI campus. Under a beautiful spreading oak, Sangye shared his plans to emigrate to the United States as soon as he retired. He was even willing to emigrate before he retired if his papers came through. Although a well-respected instructor, he was embittered and disillusioned with the institution and its administrators. As he told us, "They retire us at forty-eight. Earlier, instructors like Nima Norbu got extensions of seven years. Ang Tsering was retired suddenly without receiving his pay. They called it 'golden handshake.' They promised him seven lakhs, or about $8,500, plus pension. He has not received anything. They gave him a year's extension and then retired him. They don't give a reason. They just say that there is a letter/order from Delhi."

Sangye Sherpa, forty-six at the time, was neither able to emigrate to America nor look forward to retiring from the HMI. A few months after this interview, he died of a fall at home. His unfulfilled dreams evaporated with the end of his life. He left behind his wife, two daughters, and a mother who had already lost her younger son as well.

Nima Norbu, the younger brother of Tenzing's third wife, Daku, is an Everester. He was rewarded for this feat with a piece of land opposite the Darjeeling railway station. Here, he has built a small hotel, which he leases out. He lives the good life with his socially active and worldly wife, Doma Norbu. The couple have a daughter who works for a famous restaurant chain based in New York. Their beautifully appointed home adjoining the hotel offers stunning views of Darjeeling. When we met him, although he'd retired from the HMI after several extensions, he continued to conduct treks for his nephew Jamling's (Tenzing Norgay's son) agency. "Sherpas stopped coming to Darjeeling after 1970," Nima Norbu told us. "The commercial and tourist activity in Nepal increased. Sherpas started working there, opened travel agencies and became rich, got a lot of work. What was there for them in Darjeeling? The only options are working in HMI or joining the army. Ninety-nine percent [of the] educated Darjeeling Sherpas are not going into mountaineering. Our children will not take up this profession.

"There is no future for the climbing Sherpas of Darjeeling. When HMI opened—that was a different time. The whole system has changed. There are very few Sherpa instructors in HMI, and none in other institutes like Uttarkashi and Manali!"

The few Sherpas left at the HMI nevertheless remind us of the qualities that made the Sherpas who they are.

We interviewed a young filmmaker, Arpita Roy, who'd completed her Basic course in 2017. During training, she was part of a summit push when the weather turned bad. Their instructor, Lhakpa Norbu Sherpa, insisted they turn back. The students were disappointed, but Lhakpa gently encouraged them to think differently. He taught them that life is more important than the summit and that there would always be another chance.

Roy added, "They respect the mountains. The kind of respect they show is very genuine and you can feel it." After her course, Roy followed and filmed a team of instructors as they did the traverse from Kang Yatse II to I in Ladakh. Although they were not officially part of the team, Lhakpa Sherpa closely monitored Arpita and her climbing partner. She told us, "It was evening. The instructors had already come down, and we were following slowly. Lhakpa Sherpa came to look for us. My partner said, 'Look, this is why the Sherpas are what they are . . . it is in their blood.'"

When Lhakpa retired in September 2021, Pasang Tenzing was the last remaining Sherpa instructor at the institute they once defined.

Some contemporary climbers in Darjeeling with Dorjee Lhatoo. Standing, from left to right, are Lhakpa Sherpa, Kusang Sherpa, Dorjee Lhatoo, Pemba Sherpa, Mingma (Hapshi) Sherpa, Mingma Sherpa, and Samgyal Sherpa. Kneeling, from left to right, are Nima Thendu Sherpa, Dawa Norbu Sherpa, Lhakpa Sherpa, and Nim Dorji Sherpa. *(Photo by Dilip Banerjee)*

CHAPTER 18

New Men in Town

The fifth-highest mountain in the world is Makalu (8,463 meters), a four-sided pyramid on the Nepal-Tibet border just 19 kilometers southeast of Everest. According to most sources, its name is derived from the Sanskrit Maha Kala, a name for the Hindu god Shiva. However, people from the area translate it as "Summit Mother" (from *ma*, meaning "mother," and *kalu*, meaning "summit," in the local language). The peak is in Makalu Barun National Park, a remote, wild, and beautiful area, sheltering one of the world's last pristine mountain ecosystems.

In the high foothills of Makalu in Nepal lives a community of Sherpas with the same ethnic background as the Sherpas of Solu Khumbu. The ancestors of the Makalu Sherpas were probably part of a later wave of migration from Kham in Tibet. Instead of settling in Khumbu, they traveled east to the Barun Valley in Nepal.

The villagers in the Barun Valley till subsistence plots with oxen and wooden ploughs or raise small quantities of livestock. Except on the routes to Makalu Basecamp, foreigners are a rare sight. The mountain, with its knife-edged ridges and steep pitches, presents one of the most challenging climbs in the world. In the more remote villages, month-old newspapers occasionally arrive at the local government office—but no one knows how to read them. Even Kathmandu belongs to a faraway world. One or two members of each family may take a trip to the nearest town each year to get salt, to plead a land-dispute case at the district court, or simply to see the market.

It is from this isolated place that the first Makalu Sherpas began moving to Darjeeling in the 1970s and 1980s. Since then, there has been a steady trickle, and now, they dominate the climbing profession. Like the older Sherpas of Darjeeling, these men want to provide a better life for their children, but they also want to be taken seriously as climbers. They attend courses at the HMI and are constantly upgrading their skills. Many work with international companies and climb nine or ten months of the year. They have among the best climbing records in the world.

The two communities of climbing Sherpas are said to have a good relationship. Many Makalu Sherpas continue to visit the Toong Soong gompa—although they have one of their own in Alubari basti—and festivals and marriages are a time for them to get together. However, the older Sherpas tend to treat Makalu Sherpas, even those who have been in Darjeeling for the past three decades, as newcomers. Though this inevitably leads to some friction, there is also real warmth between these new men in town and some of the old families.

In early 2018, we finally had the opportunity to meet some Sherpas who are still actively climbing. All of our previous trips to Darjeeling had been in spring and autumn, when the climbers were away working. So it was with great excitement that we attended a program organized by the HMI to celebrate Everest climbers on January 26, India's Republic Day.

The HMI auditorium was full. Neatly dressed families—parents in jackets, cardigans, and shawls, children bundled in colorful anoraks—sat in ordered rows, talking softly among themselves. Harish Kapadia, for whom the Sherpa community has high regard, gave a slide show on his association with early climbers. There was much excitement as photos of great Sherpas were projected. After Harish's presentation, we talked about our project and our desire to know more about the assembled Sherpas and their lives.

At lunch in the canteen afterward, children ran around and there was the laughter, smiles, and easy camaraderie of people who live, work, and worry together. Two Sherpas we had met earlier were there, but the names of the rest were a blur. "Do you have a list of everyone here?" we asked Pasang Tenzing, a young guest instructor at the HMI and son of the senior instructor Kusang Sherpa.

"Why, yes," he replied and disappeared. Fifteen minutes later he returned with a printed list. "I thought the handwritten list wasn't good enough," he said, grinning. The list contained neat columns for names, addresses, and Everest climbs—Everest five times, seven times, nine times.

"What about other peaks?" we asked.

"Those are too many. These are just successful summits of Everest," he replied.

ONE OF THE EARLIEST OF the Makalu Sherpas to come to Darjeeling, Kusang Sherpa has continued to be a role model for others. He established a world record by climbing Everest from three faces (southwest, north, and east), has had a successful career at the HMI, and serves as president of the Sherpa Trekking and Mountaineering Association, an organization created in 2010 to boost the welfare of the Makalu climbers and their families. He also narrated his life story to the writer Susanta Kumar Das, with whom he published his autobiography, *The Long Walk from Darkness to Light*, in 2018. About 5′5″ (average height for a Sherpa), broad-chested, and brawny, he is a compact powerhouse, and his weathered face is topped by a head of curly jet-black hair. He moves with economy, and his speech is earnest and measured, with a throaty chuckle punctuating every few sentences. He is yet another Sherpa who has struggled to earn every advantage he now enjoys.

In 2013, Kusang was living at the HMI instructors' quarters. The apartments are ill designed and cramped—surprising given how much land the institute owns. His tiny home was filled with the stuffed animals from China that flood the local markets and are so favored in Darjeeling. Kusang told us:

> I came here from Makalu in 1975. I was fifteen years old. My father was a farmer, and I did not like the work, so I came by myself, then my two brothers followed. I first started doing a porter's job in HMI, and I was a kitchen [helper] at basecamp. I would quickly help the cook to prepare food, then run to watch them do crampon training. I watched secretly, and my heart was with them. Then I thought, "They go with all these small rucksacks; one day, I want to carry a rucksack too." After I had been as a porter two or three times, Gombu sahab asked whether I wanted to go on an expedition, and I said, "Yes, yes, I'll go!"

Kusang's first expedition was in 1989 to Kangchenjunga. In 1990, he went to Makalu with a Japanese team; the next year, he was with the first Indian expedition to Nanda Devi East. Kusang recalled, "I climbed to the top; it was most satisfying and challenging. I was in full *josh*. After that it was one peak after another, and in most cases successful." He participated in two or

Kusang Sherpa is one of the earliest and most accomplished of the Makalu Sherpas in Darjeeling. *(Photo by Dilip Banerjee)*

three expeditions every year. It was when he climbed Everest in 1993 via the Southeast Ridge on the southwest face that Kusang got his recognition and a permanent job at the HMI. He climbed the peak a second time from the north in 1996, once more from the south in 1998, a fourth time via the eastern Kangshung Face in 1999, and yet once more from the south a few years later. Kusang was the first person to climb Everest from three directions. He was also the first citizen of India to climb Makalu in 2009. When we met him in 2013, he was slated to retire. "But I am trying to get an extension," he said. "I am not tired; I am still strong. I can still run."

Kusang and his wife, Pinky, have three children. The oldest son is a lama; their daughter is married and has moved away; and their youngest, Pasang Tenzing, was the one who gave us the Sherpa list at the HMI function. We met Kusang's wife on that first visit in 2012 in Nawang Gombu's house, where she was helping with the puja. She had a shy smile and the pinkest cheeks we had ever seen.

Kusang is a Makalu Sherpa very much in the mold of the old climbers. He was taught by them and shares the same values. As he told us, "Education is

Phuchung: A Young and Articulate Sherpa

Phuchung is not from Makalu, but he is an example of the newer Sherpas. He was born in Manebhanjan, a village close to Darjeeling, and his grandparents were traders on the India-Nepal route. When Phuchung was in his first year of college, his father died and the responsibility of looking after his family fell on his shoulders. He left for Dubai, where he worked as a salesman for three years before returning to Darjeeling. Back home, he completed all the HMI courses and started working with expeditions. His brother-in-law Sangye Sherpa helped him get a job at the HMI, where he rose through the ranks from guest instructor to permanent instructor. At first, he had intended to finish college and get a government job, but Phuchung had grown to love what he was doing and he wanted to learn more. "I want to climb all fourteen peaks above 8,000 . . . Not [possible to climb] K2 on an Indian passport, but at least the other thirteen. And I am thinking of doing some new courses like ski courses and rescue courses," he told us enthusiastically.

Phuchung climbed Everest in 2012. He told us that many older Sherpas lament the fact that Everest has become an easy climb: "People say it's like a road, but no matter that there is a fixed rope, you have to climb by yourself; nobody is going to push you or carry you." His ascent was tough at times, but he reminded himself, "You are a Sherpa—you can do it." It's this confidence that helps Sherpas lead others up the mountains. Phuchung explained, "People don't climb alone. They take Sherpas who usually look after their clients very well. That is their duty: to climb mountains, look after their clients, and bring them back safe. Unfortunately, after they come down, only the members' names will be on the list of those who summitted. Not the names of the Sherpas—that still happens." What Phuchung said is important. Every year we encounter several expedition accounts in which Sherpa summiteers are not listed. In fact, there are often claims of "solo" ascents in which Sherpa support is conveniently left out.

Phuchung had recently married a Darjeeling girl. He told us, "My wife knows nothing about the mountains. I tried to explain to her that even during a course we have to look at the safety of the students, sometimes risking our lives. There is no phone network; we have to stay for twenty to twenty-five days in the mountains. But she doesn't understand. I am thinking of making her do one course so that she can understand."

important. I have educated my son, but it's his decision to follow this line. If he gets a permanent job here in HMI, then it is good; otherwise to earn just from expeditions is dangerous. I would not encourage youngsters." Kusang meant that a permanent HMI job offered greater security in terms of employment and pay than expedition work. Climbers without the safety net of the HMI face the risk and uncertainty of undertaking three or more expeditions each year in order to support their families.

If Kusang is old-school, his son Pasang Tenzing is at the other end of the spectrum. Born in 1986—at the HMI—Pasang Tenzing is already in the second generation of Makalu Sherpas to take up climbing. He earned a bachelor's degree in computing, but was not keen to make a career in software engineering. As he told us, "I enjoy mountaineering and decided to do it. My father keeps telling me that it is not right, that mountaineering is dangerous, that I am educated and should not be climbing mountains But I feel with my education I can go further. I want to tell those who are educated, 'Come and let's do something for those who are working.'"

In 2001, Pasang Tenzing completed his Adventure course at the HMI. In 2009, he completed the Basic and Advanced courses, and in March 2010 he completed the Instructor's course. Pasang Tenzing got straight As in all his courses and won several medals. In 2018, he was employed as a guest instructor at the HMI on a contract basis, but since then he has accepted a permanent position. He has been on expeditions with British, French, and Spanish groups. Pasang Tenzing described his experience: "At first, when they see how young I look, they think I couldn't be a climber. And they are very proud of their alpine style of climbing, while ours is the traditional style. But going alpine above 7,000 meters is very difficult. When they acknowledge the difference, they feel, 'Yes, these people are climbers too.' It is necessary to prove oneself. I wait for such opportunities because they do not come easily."

When Pasang Tenzing was just starting out, his father took him to Mamostang Kangri, a remote peak in Ladakh. "I watched him," said Kusang. "One day, I gave him a load of fifty-five to sixty kilograms, and even with that load he managed well. Then I thought to myself, 'Okay, this boy is fit to join this line!'"

Ambitious, articulate, and confident, Pasang Tenzing is set to go places. In 2022, he married his college sweetheart, a non-Sherpa girl from Delhi—a departure from tradition among the Sherpas, who rarely marry outside the community. So what does being a Sherpa mean to this younger generation? Pasang Tenzing reflected awhile when we asked him this question, and then said, "This is a special word for me. Because of this name and the family I belong to, I am where I am today. We have to change the concept of Sherpas as porters. This is also what I tell people when I deliver my lectures: 'Look at Sherpas as friends and companions without whom you cannot climb mountains. It is important to respect them.'"

When we asked him whether the HMI teaches students about the great climbing Sherpas, he responded, "Ah no, never! There are very few Sherpa instructors left in HMI. After them, there will be no more Sherpas and nothing taught about the Sherpas in the courses either. If I get to be chief instructor . . ." He then hesitated shyly for a fraction of a second before continuing, "I will change this."

During the off-season, house repairs occupy many Sherpas, like Pemba Chorty, pictured here months before his fatal fall in 2019. *(Photo by Dilip Banerjee)*

CHAPTER 19

Shadows on the Mountain

Ghoom is a small settlement situated on the highest point of the ridge that leads down to Darjeeling. Four brothers, best known as the "Ghoom Brothers," live in adjacent homes in this settlement. From the outside, each home looks like a single-room cottage, but as with most buildings in the area, you enter at the top and work your way downward to rooms that cling to the hillside.

As we sat inside the small home of the eldest brother, the wind whistled through its wooden panels and icy fingers crept up through the double layer of wool carpets on the floor. "My full name is Pasang Phutar Sherpa," he told us. "We are four brothers, but only three do mountaineering. One brother doesn't climb. He cooks for trekkers."

Pasang Phutar is a slender, shyly smiling man with smudgy brown eyes. He was born in 1962 in Taamku village, in the Makalu region of Nepal. He came to Darjeeling in 1984 at the age of twenty-two and worked for two years as a porter for the HMI Basic courses. Then, starting in 1986, Dorjee Lhatoo took him on as a cook's helper on his Advanced courses. Before that, in 1985, Pasang Phutar also started working at Tenzing Norgay's trekking agency. Expedition work came a few years later in 1990. "I went with a Maharashtra team to Bhrigupanth. It was the first Indian climb and my first summit," he told us, regarding climbing the 6,772-meter peak in the Garhwal Himalaya. After that, Pasang went on expeditions regularly; in between, he continued working for the HMI.

In 1991, Pasang Phutar's father died back home in the village. His brothers and mother soon followed him to Darjeeling, and his sisters married and moved away. The small plot of land his father had cultivated was abandoned. "It has all become jungle now," he said.

Pasang Phutar married Kipa Lahmu in 1989. She too was born in Nepal, but had come to Darjeeling to live with her uncle and cousin who own a sporting-goods store. "We lived close by," he explained. "My friends would say, 'Marry this one, marry that one [suggesting various eligible girls],' and so we finally got married."

Pasang and Kipa have two children. When we met in 2018, the daughter, Phuri Yangtze, had just turned eighteen and was preparing for her Class 12 board exams. The son, Pemba Norbu, is two years younger and was completing his Class 10. Pasang Phutar told us, "If they study well, they will get a job anywhere. If they don't study well, then they will be forced to do this job. My son is not saying anything right now. He is too young. But if the boy says, 'I want to become a mountaineer,' I'll say do it."

In 2012, journalist Rudraneil Sengupta wrote that Pasang Phutar and his younger brother Pemba Chorty, along with the Kolkata-based climbers Basanta Singha Roy and Debashish Biswas, formed the most formidable climbing team in India at the time. And indeed, a brief glance at Pasang Phutar's biodata in early 2018 showed fifty-one expeditions. Very few of the climbs did not have the word "summit" recorded beside them.

Since his first expedition, in 1990, Pasang Phutar had been to Everest twelve times and summited twice. He said, "Apart from Everest, I have been to Kangchenjunga three times, summited once; Cho Oyu I went five or six times and summited thrice. Among the good peaks in India, I have summited Shivling three times—once in 2005 and twice in 2007 with different teams. And I have summited Thalay Sagar twice—in 2008 and 2012. Indrasan, I went thrice, but we could summit only once. And then I have summited Nun."

When Pasang Phutar goes to Nepal, it is mainly with foreigners and sometimes with the "Calcuttawallahs" (people from Kolkata), as he calls the active West Bengal climbers. During the monsoon, he always goes with Indian expeditions. (Although the monsoon is the slow season for climbing, several areas in the states of Kashmir, Ladakh, and Himachal Pradesh are in the rain shadow and receive little rain. However, as foreign expeditions don't climb in the region during this time, it's almost always Indian groups on expedition.)

On the whole, Sherpa climbers are ambivalent about their work. They are naturally suited for it and the money is good, but fear and death are always looming, like shadows on the mountain. "Because it is a dangerous job my wife sometimes tells me to stop," said Pasang Phutar. "But this work is my habit so she cannot say, 'Don't go.' I can't do any other work. I have to educate my children, and that's why I have to go."

Other climbers expressed similar sentiments. "On Jonsong," one Sherpa told us, "an avalanche took me down twenty-five meters and I was stuck. I was alone but roped." At such times, these climbers feel the risks they incur acutely.

But it is important to foster and maintain camaraderie. Another Sherpa told us, "When we reach the Khumbu Icefall, in order to be safe, we move one by one—someone ahead and someone behind. Nobody turns around to see who is lagging behind. It is only when we reach a safe place—when we are sure the ice will not break, when there is no fear of avalanches from above—[that] we all come together, talk, drink some water, eat a little if we want. We make tea, someone sings . . . we have our Sherpa songs."

While it is still dangerous to cross the Khumbu Icefall, conditions were even worse in previous decades. Pasang Phutar told us, "In '92–'93 when going to Everest, if there were ten teams, then each day two Sherpas from two teams would make the path in the Khumbu Icefall: 'Today your and my team will send four Sherpas, tomorrow another four Sherpas'—turn by turn, the path was made. After '94, the contract system started. Now the climbing Sherpas do not have to make the route. The Sherpas making the route through the Khumbu Icefall are different. The climbers continue climbing, the load bearers continue carrying, the road is there. If the route becomes bad, we call the Icefall Doctors [Nepali Sherpas who specialize in creating and maintaining the route over the Khumbu Icefall]. Now the need for technique is less, as you only have to carry the load; earlier, you made the route as well."

These men talk lightly of their hardships. It may be that climbing capricious peaks and skirting dead bodies helps put their lives in perspective. "I have seen many deaths on Everest," said one of them. "There are dead bodies everywhere—we walk around them, drink water, we rest with bodies around. On Kamet also there are bodies." Belief in destiny helps them overcome grief in the mountains, assuages anger, and enables many to find solace when coping with death. In many ways, this belief has allowed them to function and move on with their lives.

PASANG PHUTAR HAS SEEN HIS share of avalanches and death through the years. In 1993, he supported an all-women Indo-Nepalese Everest expedition led by Bachendri Pal, the first Indian woman to ascend the peak. The expedition set a few records: Santosh Yadav became the first woman to climb

The Tiger Is Dead, Long Live the Garud

The last Himalayan Club Tiger Badges were awarded in 1965. For many years afterward, although thoughts of reinstating the badge in a different form may have been discussed, nothing came of it. Then, in 2013, the Jagdish C. Nanavati Garud Gold Medal was instituted to recognize and honor outstanding Indian support staff on explorations and expeditions in the Himalaya.

For all his accomplishments in the mountains, Pasang Phutar was recommended by several teams for the Garud Medal. In Mumbai in March 2018, at the annual Himalayan Club seminar and award function, the unassuming Pasang Phutar received his award. Dressed in a jacket and clearly out of his environment, Pasang Phutar seemed overwhelmed by Mumbai, which even at the best of times is a climatic shock for people from the hills. The shy man had to also contend with the standing ovation he received and the many people who milled around him.

The Garud Medal bears the likeness of an eagle and carries a cash prize of Rs 11,000 ($135). The awardees to date have been:

2013—Harsingh Harkotia, Uttarakhand
2014—Pemba Norbu ("King Kong"), Darjeeling
2015—Ringzin Ladakhi, Ladakh
2016—Naveen Panwar, Uttarakhand
2017—Skalzen Rinzing, Ladakh
2018—Pasang Phutar, Darjeeling
2019—Samgyal Sherpa, Darjeeling
2020—Nim Dorjee, Darjeeling
2021—Konchuk Thinles, Ladakh
2022—Mingma Hapshe, Darjeeling

Everest twice. Dicky Dolma at age nineteen was the youngest to summit. That expedition placed a record eighteen climbers on top, including seven women. Pasang Phutar, however, did not summit because he was involved in a search-and-retrieve operation for another group. As he told us, "Tenzing sahab's nephew Lobsang died at South Col and he had to be brought to basecamp. Rita *didi* [Nawang Gombu's daughter and deputy leader of the expedition] said, 'You are all from Darjeeling; you should help him,' so we got together. But it still took a week to bring the body down."

In 2014, Pasang Phutar was on Everest with an international group when a catastrophic avalanche hit. He recounted, "We had set out, but one ladder broke in the Khumbu Icefall, creating a jam of people there until the ladder was fixed. If the avalanche had come at that time, fifty or sixty people would have died. I was about twenty or twenty-five minutes ahead when the avalanche hit. I did not see it; I did not hear anything. It is only when my friend said, 'Dada, see an avalanche . . . ,' that I looked. We were at Camp I, and the avalanche came between Camp I and basecamp." Pasang and his friend were the only two Sherpas from their team on Everest that morning. The rest of the Sherpas and members had gone to Island Peak on an acclimatization climb.

Pasang Phutar said, "Among the dead were two people from our village in Nepal. All the Sherpas who died were from Nepal, not from Darjeeling." Pasang Phutar and his friend assisted with the rescue and body recovery. "Sixteen people had died," he told us, as he remembered that awful moment. "We were able to pull out thirteen bodies. We laid them out, and a heli came to take them. After seeing the dead bodies and all the blood, I stopped going to Everest and Kangchenjunga. I will continue doing 6,000-meter peaks for the next two or at the most three years."

After meeting with Pasang Phutar, we went next door to meet his brother Pemba Chorty, a thinner and younger version of his older sibling.

He told us, "My name is Pemba Sherpa. Actually, my full name is Pemba Chorty Sherpa. I am number three, forty-seven years old. Mountaineering starts with portering. That means we go as porters on treks, then we go as cooks. In '94–'95, I was the chowkidar at HMI basecamp for two years. In '96, I left the job and I started mountaineering with my older brother. I have three children—two girls and one boy. All three go to school."

Pemba Chorty had summited Everest seven times. Apart from that, he had also climbed the 8,000-meter peaks Kangchenjunga, Makalu, Manaslu, and Cho Oyu. Below that height, he had done too many peaks to remember. "I am out for eight or nine months of the year," he said. "Actually, rather than our own families, we make outsiders our families and live with them. This is because of our work."

Our interview with Pemba Chorty was cut short when a flurry of people arrived. It was getting late, and we promised to talk again when we returned to Darjeeling. But we would never resume our conversation. On July 13 of that same year—2018—while on an expedition to Saser Kangri IV in the Karakoram Range, Pemba fell into a crevasse. His brother Pasang Phutar was also part of the team. Pemba Chorty's body was never recovered.

We returned to Ghoom the following year and heard about the terrible ordeal the family had been through. Pasang Phutar told us that the ill-fated expedition comprised a joint Maharashtra-Bengal team led by Anil Retawde and Basanta Singha Roy. Though there were thirteen members, only two, led by three Sherpas including Pemba Chorty, went to the summit. The accident happened on the way down. Pasang Phutar was not with the summit team, as he had brought an ailing member from Camp II to basecamp. When the summit team did not reach Camp I as planned, a worried Pasang Phutar headed up to search for them. He saw only four people returning: the two expedition members with two Sherpas—his nephew Pemba Tsering and Lhakpa. His brother Pemba Chorty was not with them. Pasang told us:

> Pemba Tsering started crying, "Pemba uncle has fallen in a crevasse. We did not have any rope so we could not do anything. We could hear him for about ten minutes; after that, there was no sound." I rushed to the crevasse with some rope and made an anchor. I went down about six meters and flashed my light but could not see anything. By then it was very late. He had fallen at around 8:30 a.m., and now it was 1 or 2 p.m. He was so deep inside that he would have survived for only ten or fifteen minutes.

Unable to reach his brother, Pasang Phutar frantically returned to basecamp, looking for help to retrieve Pemba Chorty's body, but no one offered to help. Despite his persistence, the team leaders discouraged Pasang, and the expedition returned to Darjeeling. Reliving the encounter, Pasang Phutar shook with sorrow and impotent rage.

Retrieving dead bodies from the mountains is always a dangerous business. Most bodies are allowed to lie where they fall—heartbreaking for families, particularly when family members work with the same team. Pasang Phutar must have felt every agonizing second of Pemba Chorty's last minutes, the latter helpless and knowing that death was imminent.

While talking to the Sherpas, the subject of death always came up. Sometimes we asked, and other times a climber would volunteer his experience. One young Sherpa, Mingma Hapshe, cried uncontrollably while telling us his story.

This particular tragedy happened in 2009 on a small peak called Tingchen Khang (6,010 meters) in the Sikkim Himalaya. The expedition comprised five members of a climbing club from near Mumbai. The official report states that two of the members and two Sherpas reached the summit. While descending, the four slipped and fell. Both members died, and both Sherpas were severely injured. (An expedition in 2010 to retrieve the bodies proved unsuccessful.)

Mingma Hapshe was the lead Sherpa on the 2009 expedition. He recalled:

> It was not good. To climb one needs experience. It is not like walking on the road. In work I will not cheat you, and you should not cheat me. After the accident, I found out that three people were climbing [on the expedition] without doing a course. I had climbed with the leader before. He was a very good man. On the way to the summit, I told them we would go no further, as it was dangerous. We had almost finished our rope, and it was getting late. I said that I would fix more rope the next day. But one member started shouting at the leader in Marathi.
>
> Finally, the leader gave in to him and said, "Why stop so close to the summit?" We had about seventy meters of rope left. I said that we would go as far as the rope and then return. They agreed. After [I fixed] about fifty meters of rope, they again insisted we continue. So, I cut the remaining twenty meters, and we roped up. It was a big risk, but they had to reach the summit. We reached it at 1:30 p.m. At the summit, the member slipped twice and opened his jacket fully, and I understood that his brain was changing. So I zipped him up and put him in the harness. I told him that the summit is not done till we get down safely. We needed to go carefully back to the fixed rope.

The other Sherpa on the rope team, Ang Dorjee, was in front, followed by the expedition leader, then the climber, and lastly Mingma Hapshe. They were anchoring each other as they came down, but the climber was acting as if he were drunk. Suddenly, recalled Mingma Hapshe, "He slipped and took us with him. We fell in a crevasse. He fell in first, and his head must have hit the ice. When I regained consciousness, I saw that he was dead and I went mad." At this point in his story, Mingma Hapshe broke down completely. "I was thinking, this dead man must have a wife and children . . . I was not married at the time. Why did some have to live while others died? I sat and cried," he said.

The leader was still alive, and though the Sherpas could not see any visible injuries, he did not respond. Mingma and Ang Dorjee began warming ice in their mouths and transferring it to the leader's mouth. They rubbed his hands and feet and covered him with their jackets, but it was no use. "What to do?" said an anguished Mingma Hapshe. "He didn't live."

It was only when the two Sherpas made it back to camp and the adrenaline had worn off that they realized they'd suffered cuts and bruises too. Other repercussions on Mingma's life were devastating. He said, "For four or five years, I drank and spoiled my life. Everyone said it is my fault. My friends made fun of me. Even among Sherpas there is jealousy. If one of the members had survived, he could have told the truth. But because I could not save them, everything came on me. They said, 'This man is careless.'"

Mingma Hapshe finally took control of his life again. With no alternative to climbing and with the encouragement of his brothers Samgyal, Nim Dorjee, and Mingma Thendup, he started expedition work again. Mingma has since grown to be one of Darjeeling's finest mountaineers. In 2022, he climbed Annapurna I, Kangchenjunga, Everest, Lhotse, and Makalu in the span of one month—April 28 through May 28.

Dorjee Lhatoo told us, "Present-day climbing Sherpas are different from those of the earlier times. In those days, the British led climbs and the Sherpas carried loads. [The Sherpas] did not even know how to cut steps. But *now*, these are lead climbers. Logistics planning, they may not do; however, from basecamp onwards, they lead the expedition. They fix rope, make [the] route, [and] decide where to make camp, how much equipment to carry, and when to wind up. If a Sherpa says, 'This is too risky; we should not go,' you think twice." Mingma Hapshe and many of the young Sherpas of Alubari basti are certainly representative of the climbers that Lhatoo described.

In 2016, the mountaineers Debraj Dutta, Pradeep Sahoo, and Sahoo's wife, Chetna, were on Everest with a Sherpa named Phurba. Debraj and

Phurba Sherpa is a true example of the new generation of climbers—ambitious, informed, and hard-working. *(The Sherpa Project)*

Pradeep reached the summit and then descended to the South Col, while Phurba was traveling slowly up the mountain with Chetna, who was not well. They made it to the top, but while descending, they got stuck just below the South Summit. Chetna's oxygen mask was malfunctioning, and her condition was rapidly deteriorating. "Phurba could have left her," Dutta told us. "He had run out of oxygen too. But he didn't leave her. He climbed down some distance and communicated [on] the walkie-talkie and went back to stay with her until Sherpas could be arranged to take oxygen and bring her down." Around midnight, Phurba staggered into the South Col camp, where Debraj Dutta and Pradeep Sahoo waited, saying that Chetna was being brought down. Then he fainted. Pradeep could hardly believe it when his wife was brought to the South Col camp at 2:15 a.m. She was badly frostbitten and would need months of treatment, but she was alive—"Thanks to Phurba," said Dutta. "If Phurba had left Chetna, it would not have been possible to locate her. Phurba has the values of older Sherpas: he understands the ethics of mountaineering—that a Sherpa should not leave his client behind."

"We were the ones to bring Chetna Sahoo down," said Nim Dorjee, Mingma Hapshe's brother. "We don't abandon people," added Lakhpa

Tenzing. "The members you have gone with, you summit with them and come back with them."

But once in a while, mountaineers have said uncomplimentary things about the Sherpas as well. Alpinist Debabrata Mukherjee has been vitriolic in conversations with us in his condemnation of the current Sherpas, for whom he says money is everything and who he believes have no qualms abandoning clients on the mountainside. But Kuntal Joisher, a mountaineer who climbed Everest in 2016, had a different take: "Don't blame the Sherpas," he said with agitation. "My Sherpa does not babysit me. He expects me to be in top shape and prepared. Commercialization is not new, but I have seen clients go from couch to Everest. They don't know right from left crampon. Nepali operators do not inquire into the résumé of climbers. As long as people can pay, they are promised success. What are the Sherpas expected to do?"

Umesh Zirpe, a veteran mountaineer who has led several expeditions to 8,000ers in Nepal, was even more specific. "I have heard of Sherpas taking advantage of climbers," he told us, "but not the Darjeeling men. . . . In fact, the Darjeeling Sherpas get bullied by the Nepal ones."

The issue of abandonment on the mountain is a complex one. Several interviews with climbers indicated a deadly combination: a government, in this case Nepalese, eager to milk the Everest cow by giving out too many permits in a given season; unscrupulous operators preying on clients who are often technically, physically, financially, and emotionally unprepared to face the challenge; and Sherpas themselves, who see their jobs these days as a purely commercial transaction. News reports of stress, scuffles, overcrowding, and rope- and route-sharing grab headlines every season, and yet the allure of Everest remains undiminished for both climbers and Sherpas alike.

WHEN SHERPA CLIMBERS DIE, THEIR widows, many of them young themselves, are left with children to look after. In 2019, we met Pemba Chorty's widow, Chokpa Sherpa, and daughter, Lhakpa Dolma Sherpa, then eighteen. Lhakpa Dolma told us that her father always described the peaks he was going to climb and brought back stories and videos of his expeditions. His last words to her as he left for Saser Kangri IV were "Study well."

Pasang Phutar, Pemba Chorty's brother, explained that Basantdada (Basanta Singha Roy) was collecting money for the family, but he did not know how much. There would also be a payout from Pemba Chorty's life-insurance policy, but in the absence of a dead body, it would take several years. "This is the problem in India," Pasang Phutar told us. "We'll get it after seven years, they say. Sometimes the nominee is not alive after seven years."

Phurba told us, "For every expedition, we get separate insurance. When we sign the papers before leaving for an expedition, we think, 'How long will this go on?' But we don't share our fears with our families. And we never share with our children the possibility of what could happen to us."

One late October day in 2012, Dorjee Lhatoo had brought a widow named Mohmaya to the cottage where we were staying. Her husband had died on an expedition only two months earlier. She was a pretty young lady with dimpled cheeks and downcast eyes. "I am twenty-five years old," she told us. "My husband, Nima Sherpa, was thirty years old. We are from a village in Makalu. I have

Mohmaya Sherpa and Yangje Sherpa both lost their husbands to the mountains. *(Photo by Dilip Banerjee)*

two sons: Pema Sange Sherpa, seven years old; and Pemba Rinzing Sherpa, five years old. They go to school." She explained that when her husband left for the expedition, he had promised to call on August 25, but the agency that had hired him rang her up before then with grim news of his accident. "He had left in July with a friend, but they went on different jobs so I don't know how the accident happened," Mohmaya told us. Nima Sherpa's body was not recovered, so Mohmaya would have to wait seven years for his insurance. In the interim, the Swiss team that he was with apparently promised either a lump sum of $6,000 or Rs 6,000 ($73) a month for her children's education. Mohmaya was confused. She did immediately get Rs 50,000 ($612), which was owed to her husband as his pay. She said the woman at the Delhi agency who had hired her husband told her they would find her a job if she put her children in a residential school. "How can I?" Mohmaya sobbed. "They are so young!"

The insurance papers that we examined stated that the accident happened on August 17, 2012, at 6,900 meters on Kun in Ladakh. Two Sherpas were swept away in an avalanche, while a Swiss-German climber was evacuated by helicopter. Curiously, we could not find any mention of the accident or even the expedition on the company's website. They appeared to have deleted all traces of the Kun expedition. There were reports of expeditions before and after, but not of this one.

According to the other Darjeeling Sherpas, the family of the Nepalese Sherpa who died in the expedition got full compensation. Dorjee Lhatoo said, "In Nepal, the Sherpa union is very strong so nobody can mess with them. All the Sherpas there go on strike if anyone is dealt with unjustly. Darjeeling Sherpas have no union and are exploited because of this."

We spoke several times to a belligerent woman at the agency who insisted that Mohmaya was being paid. In 2019, when we met with Mohmaya again, she said that the agency had not sent her any money. The Swiss, however, had been sending $2,000 a year for her children. That August, seven years would have passed, at which point she'd be entitled to her husband's insurance too. "The madam gave me the insurance papers, but she has not called to ask about them or tell me what to do," said Mohmaya.

She seemed quite upset when we asked why she doesn't work. The Khumbu Sherpanis had always worked, even when their husbands were earning. It had never been considered below their dignity, and remarriage was also a given. The Makalu women, we realized, were closer to their Hindu sisters, for whom family roles are clearly demarcated; working outside the home is seen as an abandonment of children and respectability. Mohmaya admitted that she sometimes made and sold chang from her home, but the income was uncertain and meager at best. "And will you get married again?" we asked. "No, why should I?" she shot back, offended.

We also met thirty-five-year-old Yangje Sherpa, who was born in Alubari and had married a climber called Ang Dorjee. She was pregnant with her third son when her husband died in 2015 on an Indian Army expedition to Frey Peak in Sikkim. He fell into a crevasse, and the other Sherpas were able to retrieve the body. Because there was a body, she got an insurance payout three months later, but it was only Rs three lakh ($3,673). The agency who employed her husband gave her nothing. "Half the amount is already over," she lamented. "How long will three lakhs last? That is why I have given one son to the monastery to become a lama. I can't afford to bring up three sons."

In 2018, Phuri Yangtze, Pasang Phutar's daughter, told us, "On the first few days of the expedition, Dad calls constantly at dinner, breakfast, and lunch. Then he tells us that he is going up and won't be able to call. Sometimes before summitting he calls and says, 'I have my summit today.' Then everyone prays that they summit. We hope the weather is good, and my mom cries because it is so very risky out there. I am proud of my dad because it is not a simple job and not everyone can do it. In school, when they ask, 'What does your father do?' I proudly say that he is a mountaineer."

Samgyal Sherpa *(Photo by Dilip Banerjee)*

CHAPTER 20

In Every Home an Everester

Google "Alubari" and the search engine displays an ad for a board game called *A Nice Cup of Tea*. The game begins with a brief history of Darjeeling, and you learn that the Kurseong and Darjeeling Tea Company opened a tea garden in Alubari in 1856. To play the game, participants compete to cultivate their own tea estates and assist in building the railway and town. At the end, the player who contributes the most to the development of the hill station is declared the winner.

The background is correct—Alubari is a village in the Phulbari subdivision of Darjeeling. The whole area was once filled with tea gardens, but now only a few remain. To reach Alubari, you first walk past the Toong Soong Sherpa gompa and then Ang Tsering's house on Dr. Zakir Hussain Road (also called T N Road), eventually reaching a broad footpath that leads down the hillside. The fairly steep path, dotted with benches for rest stops, leads to a small, neat basti called Lamba Dara in Alubari. Lamba Dara is the settlement of the Makalu Sherpas in Darjeeling, just as Toong Soong is for the Khumbu Sherpas. It has perhaps fifty or sixty well-constructed, well-maintained houses, most of which have two stories and are brightly painted. Several of the homes have at least one family member who has reached the top of Everest.

On a crisp morning in March 2019, we descended along the footpath, our guide Phurba openly amused at our mild panting. "If I had told you how far down Lamba Dara is, you would never have come!" he joked, adding that he'd been here eighteen years or so. "I have Indian citizenship but Nepali papers too. The Nepali papers are necessary for those who go to Nepal on expeditions. The permit (for Everest) otherwise costs $11,000. Who is going to give $11,000 in order to take us? But we cannot go to Pakistan, and Nepal Sherpas are not allowed in certain areas in India like North Sikkim."

We had first met Phurba in 2013. A handsome young man in a black jacket, he was at ease, confident, and articulate—a great example of the new generation of climbers. By then, Phurba had already reached the summit of Everest ten times. "I have climbed no other mountain in Nepal," he told us. In India, he had been up Kamet in Uttaranchal three times and to Satopanth, Kabru North, and Thalay Sagar five times. He had also climbed Mamostang Kangri, Saser Kangri IV, Dharamsura, Jonsong, and Nanda Devi East, among others. He told us that there were fifteen to sixteen high-altitude Sherpas of his caliber in Alubari and far more who did trekking work.

Born in the Makalu area of Nepal in 1982, Phurba heard of men climbing mountains when he was about thirteen years old. The idea fascinated him, and so he came to Darjeeling, where he didn't know anyone. "I . . . started a milk business and also sold vegetables in the basti for two or three months," he told us. Then he heard about the HMI. He met Dorjee Lhatoo, who offered him work as an orderly and kitchen boy on the courses. "I was about fifteen or sixteen when I got my first expedition in 1998. I told the sardar to take me with him; in return, I worked in his house. The peak was a small one, but the sardar liked my work and said that I would perform well in the mountains," said Phurba.

The brothers Samgyal, Nim Dorjee, Mingma Hapshe, and Mingma Temba are also high-altitude Sherpas living in Lamba Dara. Like Phurba, these brothers came to Darjeeling separately when they were between ten and twelve years old. Hapshe is the third brother's nickname. He was named Mingma, as he was born on a Tuesday (Mingma means "Tuesday" in the Sherpa language; see appendix 4 on Sherpa names), but when the next brother was also born on a Tuesday and given the same name, his family started calling the older Mingma "Hapshe," which means "dark," as his skin tone is slightly darker than that of his brothers.

All four brothers were born in Makalu. Their parents left them with an older sister and came to Darjeeling in search of work. It seemed terrible to us that such young children were left in the care of one who could not have been much older. "People from mountain areas are poor," said Samgyal softly. "My parents could not look after us, [so] that is why they left—to get some livelihood. Then they started living here and we followed." Life in Darjeeling was not much better, though. They all lived together in one small room.

Samgyal continued, "Then after five [or] six years I could work. I looked after my brothers for a year or two, and then they also grew up. At the beginning, it is always trekking. They worked with me, and then they started on their own."

"Everyone has built separate houses now," chimed in Nim Dorjee.

"It's been many years," continued Samgyal. "I married twenty to twenty-two years ago and went separate. Arrange your own marriage and lives; there is no property from the parents to divide."

We heard similar stories from other climbers we interviewed. "I came in 2000 at the age of thirteen," said Lhakpa Tsering. "I was born in 1987 in Makalu," said Nima Thendup. "I came at sixteen." They all started very young, which explains why most of them in their mid-thirties have expedition lists that are several pages long. Lamba Dara is a settlement of youngsters.

We asked them how easy it was getting their first jobs in expeditions. Samgyal (around forty-five at the time of the interview) told us, "First I was in the HMI course. There were just a few trekking companies then: Gombu sahab's, Lhatoo sahab's, and Tenzing Jamling's companies [this would have been in the early 1990s]. We used to get jobs with great difficulty. I worked in HMI for five years."

Dawa Norbu Sherpa, another young climber, agreed. He told us, "When I came to Darjeeling, at first I was doing all jobs but I was unhappy so I thought I would leave. Then a friend from Nepal told me that mountaineering is good. If a man can climb then he can send some money home. I did the courses and joined groups whenever I got a chance. But you don't get climbing jobs immediately. Any company will tell you that technique is necessary. No company will take the risk with clients. So they see how much work you have done, how many expeditions you have been on. They look for experienced climbers, those who have climbed before." The companies Dawa Norbu referred to are the better-known trekking and expedition agencies based in Delhi or Kathmandu. The Sherpas mentioned names like Rimo Expeditions, Artou Voyages, Shikhar Travels, White Magic, and Seven Summit Treks. Most current Sherpas are employed by one or the other, and those company websites feature many photos of them. Apart from such agencies, the Sherpas also climb with teams from the Indian armed forces, the Indo-Tibetan Border Police, and climbing clubs across the subcontinent.

All the Alubari Sherpas have taken at least the Basic course at the HMI. After that, they learn on the job. Phurba said that he goes to Nepal to learn new skills. He has friends who are instructors; they teach him techniques that are constantly evolving. He told us, "HMI instructors teach old techniques. They have no idea of the new ones!" Once the Sherpas have been on a few climbs and proven their worth, word gets around and they are asked for by name. Now that everyone owns a cell phone, getting in touch has become easy. They also build contacts by word of mouth, and when one of them is booked for an expedition, they suggest others who may be available.

In some ways, these young men are like their older counterparts. They have had very little formal education. Some have studied up to Class 6 or 7, but none have graduated high school. And, like the Khumbu Sherpas, they are at ease in the mountains. "We don't have problems of altitude," said Dawa Norbu, another high-altitude Sherpa from Lamba Dara, grinning. "We live at high altitudes; we walk barefoot on snow and ice." And, as Pemba Chorty told us during our only meeting with him, "One or two years ago, Tibet mountaineering banned the entry of Nepali Sherpas, saying climbing guides will be provided from Tibet. But the foreigners did not agree; they said they only wanted Sherpas. 'If a Sherpa takes us, we will be successful' is the faith people have. Climbing mountains is very difficult. We were born in the mountains and can tolerate it; we can climb, we can guide."

During our visit in 2019, Phurba took us to his home and introduced us to his wife, Mingma Diki—whom he had met and married in Darjeeling—and two daughters, Dawa Doma Sherpa and Lhakpa Yanji Sherpa. After a tasty home-cooked meal, we were joined by Dawa Norbu and Kusang Sherpa, who had retired from the HMI by then. Phurba and the others seemed fairly comfortable. Surely, they must be getting paid reasonably well on expeditions. Dawa Norbu, who works for a big trekking agency, told us, "We don't get paid by the month. We get paid when we are in the field, by day. I get Rs 500 to 600 [$6–7] a day. I am in the field about seven or eight months in the year. I am at home for about five months, and during that time the company pays expenses of Rs 3,000 [$36] a month. It's not much, but when work is on, we get food, accommodation, travel. Everything is taken care of."

Phurba does not work with any one agency. Most of his clients are from Kolkata. He does around four to five expeditions a year. He said, "We work out the pay and a summit bonus in advance, depending on how technical the peak is. We take Rs 40,000 to 50,000 [$490–610] on reaching the summit.

If not, we get our daily wages. Kolkata teams are now my friends. We eat together and climb as a team. I am included in the meetings after basecamp. I am always consulted, and I take decisions along with the leader." Phurba pointed to a different approach between foreign and Indian expeditions in terms of budget, food, equipment, and so forth, noting that the foreign expeditions often had major corporate sponsorship, which meant more money, as well as an ample supply of gear.

"Equipment is also supplied, so they do not feel a loss at leaving it behind or if it gets swept away by an avalanche," he told us of the foreigners. "Indian expeditions struggle a lot. They keep aside money every month, live on very little in order to be able to go on an expedition, so there is a big difference. Indian expeditions feel very strongly about reaching the summit, as they have struggled hard to put the expedition together. The attitude is 'We will definitely reach the top, no matter what!'"

Phurba said that on expeditions in India, he never gets to keep the equipment, but in Nepal—on Everest—he always does. "Common stuff like tents, ropes, etc., [comes] from the teams, but ice axes, crampons, boots are our own. For 8,000-meter expeditions, we are given $2,000 for equipment. If I have the necessary equipment, then I save all that money," he said. "If I take a new Sherpa along, who has nothing, then even $2,000 is not enough to equip him. Boots, crampons, ice axe, balaclava, sleeping bag, and bodysuit have to be bought. Equipment lasts around five years; sleeping bags last two to three years."

Lhakpa Tenzing said, "The summit bonus comes from every member. But some foreigners pay more. The Indian teams may say, 'We will pay you two lakhs, three lakhs [$2,450–3,670] if we summit,' but after summitting they want to negotiate. Now there are far fewer teams coming from European countries and more Indians and Chinese. The Chinese tip even better than the Westerners, who have started bargaining—'This is a lot of money; why is it so much?' They are not as they used to be earlier."

Plus, Dawa Norbu said, "There is one rule for all, whether from India or Nepal. For climbing one peak, this much has to be paid; summit bonus has to be paid. For the big peaks, the insurance is also decided. The government has laid down rules, and what is said has to be paid by the company." He added that the rate for small peaks is up to the team, and that likewise there aren't fixed peak bonuses for these smaller mountains. Dawa Norbu noted that the Darjeeling Sherpas earn the same as their counterparts in

Nepal: "There are more Sherpas there, but they also have a strong union. Our Darjeeling Sherpas have not made a union yet. But we do have a committee and we decide things together."

We went back to talking about Everest. In a busy season, the men told us, there might be 1,500 people at Everest Basecamp, including team members, Sherpas, and kitchen staff. The Khumbu Icefall changes all the time. "There is [often] no ice on the mountain," said Samgyal, referring to how climate change has affected the quality and quantity of ice on Everest.

"Does that make it less dangerous?" we asked.

"No, the icefall is still dangerous," Mingma volunteered. Samgyal continued, "There is less danger of ice falling from above, but in the middle it breaks and boom!" "Crevasses form," ended Nim Dorjee.

Dawa Norbu and Nima Thendup joined in the conversation. There is not much chance of an avalanche on the north side of Everest, they informed us, but the wind was terrible. All these Sherpas had been up from both the north and south. The Khumbu Icefall was the most dangerous part of the South Col route, they agreed, but they got more work from that side. Getting visas for China is difficult.

We asked them how many times they had to cross the Khumbu Icefall per expedition. "At least ten to twelve," said Samgyal, giving a nod. "And sometimes more than that," agreed Nim Dorjee.

IT WAS LATE AFTERNOON BY the time we left Phurba's house that March day. There were signs of activity everywhere in Alubari basti—plants being tended, construction work going on, children playing. Phurba looked around and said, "The newer lot is very different from the earlier Sherpas. From start to finish of an expedition, we do not touch alcohol. I have heard that in earlier days, much of the earnings were spent on drink. If they earned Rs 10,000 [$120], they would bring home Rs 2,000 to 3,000 [$24–36] and drink away the rest. Now if a Sherpa earns Rs 10,000, then he brings the whole sum home and gives it to his wife." Phurba said that he and his peers might drink at parties, but that the alcoholics you see around are Nepalis from other tribes—not Sherpas. "Nowadays, our people are health and body conscious. Older people in our families drink, and I try to tell them that it is wrong—'Give yourselves a better, longer life'—but then the next afternoon, it's the same thing!"

"What else do you do for time pass [the Indian phrase for passing time] when you're at home?" we asked some of the Sherpas. "When not on expedition, I just rest," said Dawa Norbu.

What about gambling, drinking, and chasing after girls, we asked. "It happens," said Nim Dorji. "Because that is the time pass," added Samgyal. "It has become less now," chimed in Mingma. "We eat well—soup and fruit," continued Samgyal. "Exercise is not necessary," said Nima Dorjee. "Because there is always some work to do at home," finished Mingma.

These Sherpas are also active on social media. All of them have Facebook accounts, though few manage them as well as Phurba. He constantly uploads pictures of all his climbs and posts information about expeditions online. All of them have chat accounts, which they use with varying familiarity; even from Mumbai, it was possible for us to send messages that read, "Please send us your biodata!"

Our final stop that day was the new gompa being built in Lamba Dara by the Sherpa Trekking and Mountaineering Association that these climbers had formed. "There are fifty-six members," said Kusang, who had been quiet until now. "And Everest summiteers would be forty-seven out of these fifty-six." The road to and land for the gompa had been donated by the chief minister of West Bengal from a discretionary fund, possibly in hopes of keeping the Alubari Sherpas away from any thoughts of joining the Gorkhaland agitation. She may not have much to worry about on that score: Most climbers professed no interest at all in local politics, and our conversations never led to deeply held political convictions. The Makalu Sherpas were too busy raising funds for the ongoing construction.

"Why a new gompa?" we asked. There was already a Sherpa gompa in Toong Soong.

For the first time that day, a flash of disdain crossed Phurba's face. "You ask why we built a separate monastery from the Toong Soong one?" he said. "Firstly, those who are senior have a certain attitude. When Mohmaya's husband died in 2012, the Buddhist association there asked for Rs 10,000 [$120]. And there was so much expense [for] the lamas and rites and rituals. So, we thought we should have our own arrangement. We decided that we needed our monastery. Now we can have ceremonies and weddings here. Our monastery is almost ready. We have built a place where our children can get tuition and computer training."

"We will make a museum," said Kusang. "We will have photos of all Sherpas working in HMI and of the mountaineers here. Then future generations will know what we did."

We sat for a while on the steps outside the gompa. A remark that Phurba had made earlier that day came to mind. "Do no Sherpas from Alubari go to the peaks in Pakistan?" we asked. "Or is it done surreptitiously?" He shook his head vigorously.

Dawa Norbu piped up. "Since the last ten or fifteen years, no one has gone from here. It is too risky."

"We are Indian citizens," added Phurba. "Nepali Sherpas can go there."

When asked the same question, Pasang Phutar from Ghoom had been more forthcoming. "I have not been to Pakistan," he'd told us. "But my younger brother has been to K2. He is young, so he has kept his Nepali identity." It is sad because any dream to climb all the 8,000-meter peaks will remain unattainable for these ambitious Sherpas for the foreseeable future, just as it is for their Pakistani counterparts.

"My parents were not climbing, and the generation after us will not do it," said Phurba. "In five to ten years, it will be difficult to find climbers in Alubari. Everyone's sons are studying. They are doing small businesses. Right now, each and every Sherpa house in this village has a climber. The generation of Darjeeling-born Sherpas [has] not and will not take up this profession. Only the ones who have come from Nepal do this work." Meanwhile, Sherpas like him were already planning for the future. Phurba had managed to save some money from twenty years of climbing, and had just registered a company for trekking and expeditions. Kusang had built a small house in Siliguri, and as part of the Sherpa Culture Board—an organization set up by the West Bengal government to preserve the culture, language, and traditions of the Sherpa community—he made trips to the HMI basecamp as an unpaid observer. He was enjoying the status and respect that his community gave him.

As we got ready to huff and puff our way back up to Toong Soong, we asked Phurba what he dreamed about. He replied, "I would love to climb a virgin peak, one that no one has ever climbed before. The idea of there being no route, that a route has to be planned along the face—this needs a different kind of thinking. The mystery of the unknown—that is a different pleasure!"

Doma, PemPem, and Nima in the late 1950s *(Dorjee Lhatoo Collection)*

Epilogue
LUNCH AT GLENARY'S

A lot got packed into our final visit to Darjeeling. Our journey had begun at the wake of Nawang Gombu in 2012. It ended with a wedding that we attended with our friend Doma Norbu in 2019, at the beautiful, old, palatial Sonada Monastery, about an hour from Darjeeling. We were in our dowdy everyday best. Everyone around us was resplendent.

A large tent had been erected on the temple grounds. Inside sat the bride and groom and their families. A gentleman seated at a table at the entrance was accepting cash and gifts on behalf of the couple and meticulously writing down amounts in a large register.

Opposite the tent, a hall had a thermocol sign that read "BAR" in large, shiny letters. Even before meeting the couple, we were whisked straight to a counter laden with every variety of alcohol and rakshi possible. We settled for tea and Coke and met the bride, adorned in a beautiful Tibetan hat, and the groom in his suit. We placed our khadas around their necks, which were already burdened by several dozen.

All the men wore elegant bakus, tied with cloth belts at the waist from where they flowed like stiff skirts. A shirt with a high collar was worn underneath. The garb looked strangely Western, perhaps because it was paired with headgear of all kinds—fedoras, Stetsons, yak-wool hats, berets, and the Mongolian type with fur lining. Leather boots, spit polished, some knee high, some closed at the ankle, rounded out their attire.

The women also wore bakus, pieces of art made of thick, patterned silk, worn over fine silk blouses and colorful aprons with silver buckles. (Married women wear the aprons at the front and back, while maidens wear them only at the back.) Heirloom turquoise, coral, and pearl necklaces completed their ensembles.

The front courtyard was the dancing area. It began with gentle, hypnotic swaying with synchronized hand and foot movements—the day was still young, and much alcohol would be required to get the party going. Everyone in the gompa, including its maroon-robed monks, was drinking and dancing gracefully. There were enough high-quality lunch dishes to feed royalty. We were amazed at the variety of meats in the Buddhist temple. The food was a mix of Indian and Tibetan—lentils, rice, momos, rich meat, potato stews, and Tibetan breads, noodles, and pancakes. Meanwhile, the ever-present dogs and cats took their role of cleaning crew seriously.

Astrological charts are central to the events leading up to a traditional marriage. Sherpa children are born under one of twelve animal signs, and when a man's and a woman's birth charts are compared for compatibility, the animals are also matched. Then, an auspicious date is selected, and on that day, close relatives of the groom (all but the parents) accompany him to the woman's house. The ceremony known as *sodené* ("to ask") is a simple offering, by the man's family, of a jar of chang. If the woman's family accepts the jar, it means the marriage proposal is accepted. From that day onward, the woman is considered a member of her fiancé's family.

Sherpa society is based on a clan system called *ru*. It literally means "bone" and is believed to have originated way back in Kham. According to most sources, there are a total of eighteen Sherpa clans. Clan identity is inherited from the father, and marriage within a given clan is prohibited, as all members of a clan consider themselves closely related. The older Sherpas of Darjeeling are aware of their ru and will tell you, for instance, that they are Chusherwa or Murmincho, but younger Sherpas seem to be unaware. The ru, however, is considered when the horoscopes and astrological charts are brought out to arrange a wedding.

Back at the wedding, the dancing was getting energetic and almost hyp-notic. We left after lunch, knowing that the celebration would go on until the wee hours, for it had only just begun.

Over those last few days, we also completed some unfinished business. Glenary's on Mall Road, Darjeeling, was the obvious choice when we took our friends—the cousins Doma and PemPem—for a long and lazy ladies' lunch. American chop suey is a version of noodles that is hard to find now-adays. For the uninitiated, it is fusion food from a time before the term was coined. The description makes it sound unappetizing: deep-fried noodles in a bowl, topped with miscellaneous vegetables and meats cooked to death in a sweet sauce of cornflower mixed with a lot of tomato ketchup, all topped with a runny fried egg (the ketchup is what makes it American!). For many people our age from Mumbai, Kolkata, and Delhi, chop suey is comfort restaurant food from a time when choices were few and eating out was a prized treat. When we discovered it on the Glenary's menu, we decided that it had to be the dish that the two cousins reconnected over.

For most of the lunch, we were ignored. These women had much catching up to do. Though they lived barely three kilometers apart, Doma and Pem-Pem had not spoken in twenty-five years—they had a falling out in the 1990s. Now, in that not-so-quiet moment, a piece of history was being written.

Doma and PemPem had a shared youth and had been extremely close at one point in their lives. Tenzing Norgay brought Doma to Darjeeling when she was a young girl—thirteen or fourteen—and she lived in his household, growing up with his daughters PemPem and Nima, until she married.

Doma shared happy memories with us: "Mrs. Tenzing senior—Ang Lhamu—was a number of years older than Tenzing. She was a big personality. She was very nice; she loved me a lot. We would always be together; picture, movie, somebody's party. After she died, then of course Daku was brought in, but I was the housekeeper." When we asked Doma whether she regretted not going to school, she said, "I don't really know if I wanted to go to school. At that time, we didn't have the sense. I left everything to my uncle, and he decided my entire life."

Doma was the first female student at the HMI. She told us, "I was very interested in doing the Basic course . . . so Tenzing arranged it for me. First, I went to Sandakphu on a trek. It was a new thing, Indian girls, going to the Himalaya, trekking, climbing. In the Basic course, all boys! They called me 'Mr. Doma'!" PemPem and Nima also trained; eventually, they and Doma were the three Indian women selected to go on an all-women's expedition to Cho Oyu, the world's sixth-highest peak, in 1959. The expedition ended in disaster when an avalanche killed the leader and another member, along with their Sherpa. Doma, PemPem, and Nima returned without advancing beyond basecamp.

The cousins had other reminiscences from their youth. They talked about picnics with Tenzing and parties that he organized for celebrities and film stars from everywhere. Every now and then they would slip into Nepali—

gossiping about all those who had passed through their lives. It was a heady afternoon. As to why they had fallen out, that story we reserve for the end.

But here on Mall Road, the two women embraced and posed happily for photos. It was just as well that these two old friends and relatives found closure, for PemPem passed away only two years later.

AS WE SAY, OUR LAST days were packed. Darjeeling has a carnival that features several events, including drama and music performances and poetry reading at Chowrasta and Bhanu Bhavan. It is an effort by the government to cheer up this hill town, promote a sense of shared identity, and downplay the simmering Gorkhaland agitation. The grand finale is a parade that starts at Chowrasta and winds down the market, past the railway station, and finally to the end of town, where people disperse to continue partying. We walked along the parade route. Every community in Darjeeling was here—some walking, some dancing, some with floats, but all in costumes that represented their life and work. There were Gurkhas in saris and suits and the typical headgear; there were other Nepali tribes, such as Limbus, Tamangs, Gurungs, Murmis, and Rais, in their colorful dresses and scarves, waving rumals (decorative handkerchiefs); tea-plantation workers with their baskets; the graceful Lepchas with beads; Tibetan Khampas dressed like cowboys; and so many others—the Bengali and Marwari merchants included. Bhutia lamas also joined in, wearing elaborate silks and demon and animal masks.

A lump formed in our throats when we saw our Sherpas. Phurtemba was in his honey-colored jacket and hat. All the gentlemen and gentlewomen were in their bakus, much like at the wedding, and then came the Everesters like Phurba and Nim Dorjee from Alubari. Dressed in bodysuits, mittens, and snow goggles and boots, they were boiling in the Darjeeling sun, yet still smiling while holding their ice axes high.

Now it really was time to leave, but as we do, we offer you one last story: It was May 1993. Tenzing Norgay's grandson Tashi Tenzing was leading an Australian-Macedonian expedition to commemorate the fortieth anniversary of the first ascent of Everest. Two climbers—Michael Groom and Tashi's uncle Lobsang Tshering Bhutia—reached the top. Tashi Tenzing himself turned away 400 meters from the summit, suffering from snow blindness. On the descent, Lobsang Tshering fell to his death. The handsome, charismatic Sherpa was in his forties, an instructor at the HMI, and married with a young son. The tragedy made the international news, and Tashi Tenzing was accused of bad leadership. Some family members like Gombu felt that Lobsang Tshering's family should be compensated, and there were also arguments about how much compensation they deserved. The situation became ugly. Two camps—PemPem and Tashi Tenzing in one, and Gombu, Sita, Doma, and Dorjee Lhatoo in another—traded charges, which led to a huge rift in the family. Even twenty-five years later, memories of the accusations would elicit an angry outburst from PemPem—until that afternoon in Glenary's.

It was, perhaps, our last interview in Darjeeling. Tenzing Lobsang, son of Lobsang Tshering, was all grown up. After an education in Delhi, he had returned to be closer to his mother and run a homestay, a private home that lends a room to a paying guest. He remembered his childhood at the HMI as happy and uneventful until their home and life were rudely disrupted by his father's death. His well-educated mother was a senior income-tax officer. She had continued her studies after she married and got a job; she had started moving up in the department and was now an officer. Tenzing Lobsang spoke about his father's death, which had happened when he was thirteen years old, and the fallout that ensued:

> On May 10, we got word that my father had climbed the mountain and we celebrated. The very next day, coming back from school, I met Lhari Lhatoo [Dorjee Lhatoo's youngest son]. He was coming to get me. I noticed his face was a bit sad. When I came home, everyone was crying and sobbing. I knew instantly what was happening. Later, we were asked to move out of the HMI quarters. We didn't have a place to go. Lhatoo uncle talked to the principal and extended our stay for about a year, I think. One of the members from the Tashi Tenzing expedition decided to sponsor my education till I finished Class 12. There was a lot of discussion, and finally Tashi and PemPem gave us a house. Then they totally cut us off from the family. I think the difference was about the compensation and the insurance for my father on the expedition.

Kusang Sherpa, who was with the 1993 Indian Everest team, said that he had met Lobsang Tshering on the way down. He needed supplemental oxygen, but Kusang did not have any. "After that there was nothing. He fell down the slope . . . ," Kusang recalled. Rita Gombu and Bachendri Pal were also on the mountain at the time. The body was brought down to Thyangboche Monastery, where they performed the last rites.

Tenzing Lobsang told us, "Ritaji told me Tashi was very distraught and sad. I don't think he met us after the tragedy. He came once to take a photograph for the sponsor who was paying for my education. Tragically, my grandfather had a stroke and passed away within a month of my father's passing."

The young man spoke wistfully about his father, with whom he'd shared a love of mountaineering, trekking, rock climbing, and canoeing. Lobsang Tshering was not strict about studies, he said, but he was particular about behavior and values. Of his father, Tenzing Lobsang recalled, "He was a family man—in touch with everyone, helping them, visiting them . . . not everybody in the family did that. He went jogging at five every morning and came back and exercised. I think at that time in HMI he was the fittest instructor. He drank alcohol only on the day of our new year—Losar. On Losar, he was drunk at eleven in the morning, but the rest of the year, not a single drop. That is the discipline he had throughout his life."

Tenzing and his wife run a small school in Toong Soong—a kindergarten next to the gompa. Most of the children who attend are from Alubari and Lamba Dara.

As he told us, "I don't have any grudges against anyone. The sad thing is that it could have ended on a much happier note . . . there is no reason to keep grudges against each other. Yes, it would have been nice if it had been handled better. But it's time for a change and moving on."

We left the interview with light hearts. We had helped bring together two old friends and learned that Lobsang Tshering's son had made peace with this tragedy. Tenzing Lobsang is well spoken and well educated, as are the children of other Sherpa climbers around the world, and down in Alubari, a new generation of Sherpa youngsters is growing up and going to school. Their fathers climb mountains so they don't have to. Darjeeling's Sherpas are still on the move!

ACKNOWLEDGMENTS

The Himalayan Club, founded in 1928, continues to be the authority on all things Himalayan. We are proud, honored, and grateful for its support.

Thank you, Dorjee Lhatoo—without your continued involvement this book would still have been just an idea. Most of all we value your friendship. Thanks also to Doug Scott, Harish Kapadia, and Monisha Ahmed for guiding us in the early days.

We are grateful to Kate Rogers for recognizing the value in our book—and to Erin Cusick, Matt Samet, and Laura Shauger whose sharp eyes and deft editing helped make this book. Thanks to creative director Jen Grable for an appealing design. Our thanks to Katie Ives for a foreword that captures the essence of our book and is a clarion call for more inclusive histories.

The many months we spent in Darjeeling and other cities required funding and equipment. We are grateful to Cyrus Guzder, David Somerwell, Deepak Bhimani, Dinesh Purandare, Gautam Khanduja, and Tomatsu Nakamura for their kind donations and to Cox & Kings for buying us air tickets.

A host of people shared information, documentation, and technological expertise. Thanks to Ann Walsh, Bob Whyte, Chandranath Das, David Somerwell, Dilip Banerjee, Glyn Hughes, Helen Thornton, Kunzes Goba, Laurent Padoux, Mikhael Shah, Norman Hardie, Olivia Wylie, Rupert Pullee, Siddharth Meghani, Tim Healey, Tony Smythe, Amanda Karpinski, and Aparna Joshi. Thanks to all the photographers and individuals who have shared photographs with us. We have tried to trace copyright wherever possible and will be happy to acknowledge any copyright holders in future editions if brought to our notice.

We are grateful to all the institutions and libraries that allowed us to access material, rare books, and newspaper archives, including The Himalayan Club Library, The Himalayan Mountaineering Institute, The India

International Centre, The Indian Mountaineering Federation, the Alpine Club, and The National Library of India in Kolkata.

Your feedback helped us hone our story, and your participation in our journey invaluable. Thank you to Bernadette McDonald, Dinesh Purandare, Meher Marfatia, Stephen Alter, Joanna Croston, and Uttara Purandare.

Everywhere we traveled we were welcomed into warm homes and hearths. Thank you to Dilip Banerjee; Dinesh Purandare; Doma Norbu; Dorjee Lhatoo; Dr. Sunaina Rai; Kallol and Sudeshna Das; Michelle Le-Fevre; Mousumy Bhattacharya; M. S. Kohli; Phurdiki, Pemadiki, and Lakhpa Chamji; and Seema Bhatt for the wonderful meals and conversations while you shared your homes.

We pestered so many people for stories and information who responded patiently—the list is long, as you will notice. Thank you: Amitava Sain, Anindya Mukherjee, Ang Doma, Ang Nimi, Ang Phuti, Ang Tserap, Arpita Roy, Brig Mulkraj, Brig. D. K. Khullar, M. S. Kohli, Chanchal Mitra, Chandranath Das, Chokpa Sherpa, Chong Rinzing, Col. Narendra ("Bull") Kumar, Col. Chauhan, Col. Neeraj Rana, Col. Paul, D. K. Sherpa, Da Norbu, Da Tenzing, Daki, Daku Sherpa, Dawa Norbu, Dawa Sherpa, Dawa Tsering, Debabrata Mukherjee, Debraj Dutta, Deepak Dutta, D. I. G. Tsering, Dipti Bhoota, Divyesh Muni, Doma Lhatoo, Doma Norbu, Dorje of Sonada, Dorjee Lhatoo, Dr. Lala Telang, Dr. Srikar Amladi, Durga Das, Ed Douglas, Gurdial Singh, Gyalzen Sherpa, Harish Kapadia, Jamling Norgay, Kami Tsering, Khurshid Elavia, Kuntal Joisher, Kusang Sherpa, Lakhpa Chamji, Lakhpa Doma, Lakhpadiki, Lakhpa Norbu, Lakhpa Temba, Lhakpa Dolma, Lhakpa Tenzing, Lhamu Iti, Maane Sherpa, Malatiben Jhaveri, Malvika Chari, Manik Banerjee, Marlin Schoonmaker, Meher Mehta, Mingma Hapshe, Mohan Das, Mohmaya, Nalni Jayal, N. D. Sherpa, Nim Dorjee, Nim Tenzing, Nima Dorje, Nima Norbu, Nima Thendup, Nima Tsering, Norbu Tenzing, Ongmu Gombu, Pasang Phutar, Pasang Sherpa, Pasang Tenzing, Pemadiki, Pemba Sherpa, Pemba Tsering, PemPem, Phinjo Sherpa, Phuchung Sherpa, Phurba Sherpa, Phurdiki, Phuri Yangtze, Phursumba, Phurtemba, Rabin Banerjee, Rekha Shroff, Rita Gombu Marwah, Samgyal, Samden Lhatoo, Sangbo, Sangye Dorjee, Saraswati Krishnan, Sarkini , Sona ("King Kong"), Sonam Chotay, Sonam Wangyal, Stephen Alter, Tenzing Lhotay, Tenzing Lobsang, Tenzing Tharkay, Tharchen, Thendup, Topgay Sherpa, Umesh Zirpe, Urgen, Yangdu Gombu, and Yangje.

And finally, it's you guys who make us go on. Thank you Dinesh, Parth, Uttara, Tara, and Kahan for being there for us—now and forever.

Appendix 1
TIMELINE

1480: Sherpas leave Kham and settle in south-central Tibet.

1533: Sherpas cross into Nepal and settle in Khumbu.

1835: The British acquire Darjeeling from the ruler of Sikkim for a hill station and sanatorium. More land is annexed in 1850 and 1865.

1852: The first tea estates are planted.

1855: The first leg of rail line is opened from Kolkata to Raniganj.

1860s onward: People migrate from Nepal and the plains of India to work on the tea estates and building the town and railways.

1881: The Darjeeling Himalayan Railway is completed.

1880s: The first Sherpas migrate from Khumbu to Darjeeling in search of work as porters and dandi bearers.

1900–1910: Carl Wilhelm Rubenson and Ingveld Monrad Aas and then Alexander Kellas discover the superior qualities of the Sherpas and Bhutias as expedition porters.

1921: The British perform Everest reconnaissance from the Tibet side.

1922: The first Everest expedition is led by Gen C. G. Bruce. Seven porters die in an avalanche.

1920s–1930s: Toong Soong develops as the Sherpa settlement in Darjeeling. The number of expeditions increases every year.

1928: The Himalayan Club is formed.

1929: The first issue of *The Himalayan Journal* is published.

1934: Six porters die on Nanga Parbat. The Himalayan Club starts to issue numbers and porter books to the expedition Sherpas and Bhotias.

1937: Pasang Dawa Lama becomes the first Sherpa to summit a peak (Chomolhari, 7,326 meters).

1937: Nine more porters die in an avalanche on Nanga Parbat. The Himalayan Club announces the intention of awarding Tiger Badges to select porters with a proven ability on the mountains.

1939: Three porters die while attempting a heroic rescue on K2. Thirteen Sherpas and Bhutias receive the first Tiger Badges.

1947: India gains independence from Great Britain.

1950: Nepal opens its borders to expeditions. The first explorations of Everest from the southern approach begin.

1951: *The Himalayan Journal* publishes a list of porters along with personal and expedition details.

1953: Edmund Hillary and Tenzing Norgay climb Everest via the South Col route.

1954: The Himalayan Mountaineering Institute is set up in Darjeeling. The first batch of Sherpa instructors, along with Principal Nandu Jayal, are sent to Switzerland for training.

1960s: The base of expeditions in the Himalaya starts shifting from Darjeeling to Nepal.

1965: Nine men summit Everest on the first Indian expedition to climb the peak. Nawang Gombu becomes the first man to climb Everest twice. The last Tiger Badges are awarded.

1973: International mountaineers meet in Darjeeling.

1976: Tenzing Norgay retires from the HMI and Nawang Gombu becomes the director of field training.

1980s: Gorkhaland agitation flares up in Darjeeling. The Indian Army tightens its hold on the HMI. Fewer Sherpas in Darjeeling pursue climbing work as the children of Sherpas get educated and seek safer, more stable jobs. The first Sherpas start coming from the Makalu region to Darjeeling in search of jobs; they form the next wave of climbing Sherpas in Darjeeling.

1984: Bachendri Pal becomes the first Indian woman to climb Everest.

1986: Tenzing Norgay dies.

1990s: More Sherpas migrate from Makalu to the newer Sherpa settlement in Alubari.

2000: A celebration is held for the last three Sherpa Tigers in Darjeeling.

2012: We visit Darjeeling for the first time. Nawang Topgay, the last of the Sherpa Tigers, dies.

2022: There is only one Sherpa instructor left at the HMI.

Appendix 2
SHERPA CLANS

Sherpa society is divided into clans, or *ru*. Most accounts list eighteen ru. In a study conducted in the early 1960s, however, anthropologist Christoph von Fürer-Haimendorf listed no less than twenty-one such clans in the region comprising Khumbu, Pharak, and Solu in Nepal, including:

Chiawa
Chusherwa
Gardza
Gole
Goparma
Jongdomba
Khambadze
Lakshindu
Lama
Lukhpa
Mende
Munming
Nawa
Paldorje
Pankarma
Pinasa
Salaka
Shangup
Sherwa
Shire
Thaktu

The reason for the discrepancy, according to von Fürer-Haimendorf, is that, though known by different names in different regions, some clans are identical. Thus the clan known as Paldorje in Khumbu is known as Salaka in Solu, thereby constituting a single *ru*. The word *ru* translates as "bone," indicating that children inherit their father's bones. All descendants of one ancestor in the male line are therefore of "one bone." All clans are considered equal and no clan has precedence or superiority over the others.

There is also the notion of brother clans, whose members are forbidden from marrying each other—Sherpa society being exogamous—and therefore such clans could also be counted as one. Three recognized groups of brother clans are Gole, Pinasa, and Thaktu; Paldorje and Salaka; and Nawa and Lukhpa.

Appendix 3
FAMILY TREES

ANG THARKAY AND PASANG DAWA LAMA FAMILY TREE

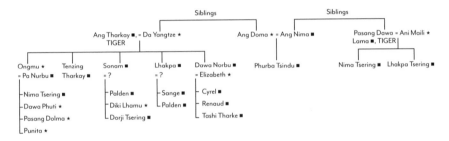

GYALZEN MIKCHEN AND DA NAMGYAL FAMILY TREE

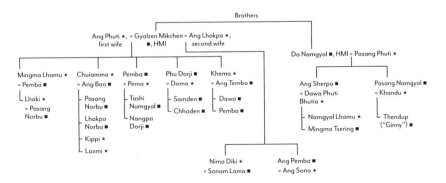

■ indicates male

★ indicates female

= indicates marriage

NAWANG GOMBU, DORJEE LHATOO, AND ANG TSERING FAMILY TREE

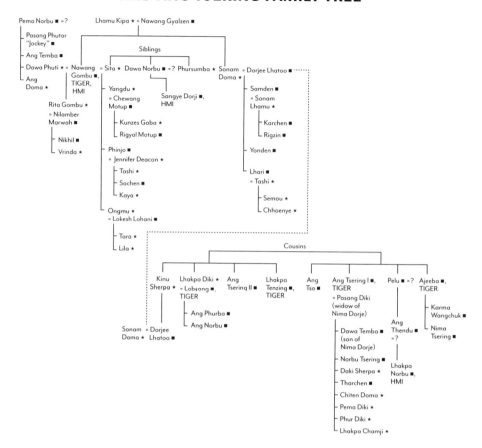

ANG TSERING "PANSY" AND AILA FAMILY TREE

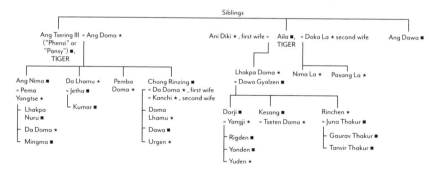

TENZING NORGAY FAMILY TREE

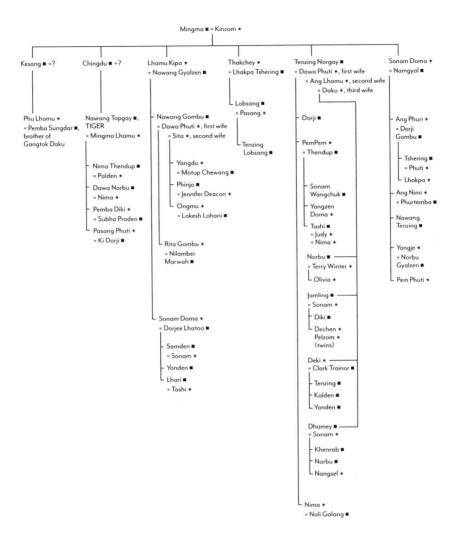

Appendix 4
SUGGESTED EXPLANATIONS OF SHERPA NAMES

Note: Reproduced with permission from *The Himalayan Journal,* Archives of The Himalayan Club, Volume 20, 1957, www.himalayanclub.org/hj.

WE GIVE BELOW A LIST of the common, or better-known Sherpa names, together with suggested explanations of meanings and derivations. Column A is by Ludwig Krenek; Column B by Johannes Schubert, who also provides philological corrections.

We do not propose to enter the controversy over the meanings, still less over the variety of spellings and pronunciations, which appear to be legion.

Generally, however, the pronunciation of Tibetan names deviates considerably from the original Tibetan spelling. For example, the Tibetan 'p' and 'ch' are often pronounced 'b' and 'ts'. The prefix 'Ang' is always stressed, e.g. Ang Tsering is pronounced Angts(e)ring, with an almost inaudible e. The same applies to the prefixes Da and Pa, e.g. DaN (or) bu, PaN (or) bu; the or being practically inaudible.

It is interesting to find that in some cases there is perfect agreement between the two versions; whilst in others, the opposite seems to be the case.

Mr. Krenek says that he has been helped in his interpretations and spellings by Rai Bahadur Tenduf La, son-in-law of the late Sirdar Bahadur Laden La, one of the best-known figures of his time in Darjeeling.

DAYS OF THE WEEK	
Monday	Dawa
Tuesday	Mingma
Wednesday	Lhakpa
Thursday	Phurba (Purba)
Friday	Pasang
Saturday	Pemba
Sunday	Nyima (Njima)

Name	A	B
Ajiba	The fourth son	Tib. bzhi-pa = the fourth, i.e. son.
Ang, Anga	Infant, baby. As in similar cases (cf. Nullu) the name given to the small child is retained throughout life.	The meaning 'baby' is doubtful.
Changba	The youngest. This is not a Sherpa name. It derives from the Thamang; another branch of Nepalese Buddhists.	Tib. chun-ba (also chun-nu) = the small or young one. The youngest in the case of many children.
Chettan, Tsetan	Che = life, ten = safe, sure, hence an assured or long life.	Tib. tshe-brtan = enduring, eternal, long life.
Chodi		Tib. chos-ldan = having religion, pious.
Chicade	One who prattles unceasingly.	
Chung	Small	(Cf. changba; Tib. chun-ba).
Da or Dawn	Born on a Monday	Tib. zla, zla-ba = moon, month Pronounced da.
Dakshi	Perhaps the same as Dawa = born on a Monday.	
Dorji	Thunderbolt	Better with e (Tib. rdo-rje) = Dorje.
Dukpa	A native of Bhutan	Tib. 'abrag-pa' = the man from Bhutan. The Bhutan woman would be ' abrug-ma'. Pronounced dukpa and drukpa.
Genden Amdo	Genden (?) from the province of Amdo, a region on borders of China and Tibet.	Genden may be Tib. dge-ldan = virtuous. Uncertain. Amdo is Tib. a-mdo.

Name	A	B
Gna (better Nga)	The fifth son	Tib. Ina = five. Is, of course, an abbreviation of Ina-pa (nga-ba, nga-wa), the fifth.
Gyalgen	Gyal = king, chen = great, hence great king.	Not 'great king' (Tib. rgyal-/po/chen/po), but 'emblem of victory' (Tib. rgyal-mtshan), pronounced djalchen.
Gyali	The victor (often in fisticuffs between brothers).	Tib. rgyal-ba, or rgyal-la, or rgyal-le, or jal(l)e/i.
Hishe or Yishe	The son of a priest	Tib. ye-shes = absolute wisdom = Sskr. [Sanskrit] jnana. A very popular Tibetan name and, owing to the spread of Lamaism, also in Mongolia (Ishi).
Jigme	Designation of a low caste. When the first son dies, the parents often call the second son by the name of a low caste or an animal, hoping thereby to confuse death or the god of death, as if to say: It is not worth while taking him, for he is only an animal.	Tib. 'ajigs-med = fearless.
Karma	Star	Tib. skar-ma = star. Perhaps associated with Karmi and Kami?
Karsang		Tib. skar-bzan = favourable star (born under a favourable star?).
Kesar Singh		Tib. ge-sar. By popular etymology also skye-gsar or ke-sar. Name of the hero of the Tibetan national epic. Skr. [Sanskrit] simha = lion.
Kikuli	Name given to a dog (cf. Jigme)	Contains Ki, Tib. khyi = dog.
Kitar	One who leads a carefree life.	
Lewa (better Leba)	Of good looks.	
Lhakpa	Born on a Wednesday	Tib. lhag-pa = Wednesday.
Lobsang	Lob = heart, sang = good or big, hence kind, generous.	Tib. blo-bzan = of good understanding. The meaning 'heart' for lob is an error. It is a very frequent name.
Mingma	Born on a Tuesday	Tib. mig-dmar = Redeye = Mars = Tuesday.

Name	A	B
Namgyal also Norbu (the r almost inaudible).	Nam = heaven, Gyal = king Precious stone, jewel	Tib. rnam (par) rgyal (-ba) = thoroughly victorious. No connection with 'heaven' or 'king'. A name often met with in Sikkim.
Naspati		Probably Hindustani from Persian naspati = pear.
Norsang	Nor = riches, sang = much, great	Tib. nor-(bu) bzan(-po) = fine jewel.
Nullu	One who always cries. Name given to an infant (cf. Ang).	
Nyima (Njima)	Born on a Sunday	Tib. nyi-ma = sun, Sunday.
Palden		Tib. dpal-ldan = having fame = famous.
Pasang	Born on a Friday	Tib. pa-sans or wa-sans = Venus, Friday.
Pemba	Born on a Saturday	Tib. spen-pa = Saturn, Saturday.
Phensing	Not a Tibetan name. Mr. Kydd of Darjeeling nicknamed Angtsering III 'Fancy'. Angtsering pronounced it 'Phansi'. On later expeditions this became 'Pansy'.	
Phu (pronounced more like pu)	Son	Not Tib. bu = son, but abbreviation of Phurba.
Phu or Phurba (Purba)	Born on a Thursday	Tib. phur-pa = peg, nail, magic dagger. Also = Jupiter, Thursday.
Pintso		Tib. phun-(sum)-tshogs(-pa) = perfect, excellent; very common for men and women alike.
Rinsing		Tib. rigs-'adzin = understanding science, having great talents.
Samdup	Reliable, true	Tib. bsam-'agrub = executing the will.
Sanglu	Good singer. His voice may have been good when he was a child.	Tib. bzan-glu = good song.
Sarki	Leather merchant (a very low caste, cf. Jigme).	
Sona, Sona(m)	A happy one	Tib. bsod-nams = luck.

Name	A	B
Tashi	One who lives happily	Tib. bkra-shis = blessing, happiness.
Temba	Equable, reliable	Tib. brtan-pa = sure, certain.
Tensing (better than Tenzing) Tewang (more correctly Tewing)	About the same as Temba Name of a monkey (cf. Jigme)	Tib. bstan-'adzin = understanding the teaching. A frequent name.
Tharke	A name without a special meaning	
Thondup	Successful in life	Tib. don-grub = one who has reached his goal; Skr. [Sanskrit] Siddhartha.
Thundu		
Tendrup		
Thondup		
Thupden		Tib. thub-ldan = having strength, endurance.
Tinle	One who works fast	Tib. phrin-las = the busy one. Better Thinle. Also occurs as Thinlay.
Tobge	Very strong	Tib. stobs-rgyas = extended power.
Tse (I)	Tibetan che = life	Tib. tshe = life. Better aspirated with h.
Tse (II)	Mountain top, summit	Tib. rtse = summit.
Tsering	Long life. Abbr. Tsin	Tib. tshe-rin = long life (same as Chettan). Abbreviated to Tsin.
Tsong	Name of a Tibetan province near the borders of Nepal.	Tib. gtsan = pure. Name of one of the chief provinces of Tibet, the Sherpa pronunciation being tsong.
Urgent	A Bhutia name of unknown meaning	Tib. o-rgyan or u-rgyan = Skr. [Sanskrit] udyana = garden.
Wangdi also Ongdi (more correctly Wongdi)	A powerful or mighty one	Tib. dban-ldan = having power, strong, mighty
Wangyal also Ongyal		Tib. dban-rgyal = powerful.
Yila, Yula, Yil	A local god in the Khumbu district	Tib. Yul-lha = a national god.

Appendix 5
HIMALAYAN PORTERS

Note: Reproduced with permission from *The Himalayan Journal*, Archives of The Himalayan Club, Volume 16, 1950–51, www.himalayanclub.org/hj. List compiled September 1950.

OF THE 175 PORTERS MENTIONED 51 have died and 24 were killed in the mountains. Twenty-nine, still fit for mountaineering, are at present available in Darjeeling.

This list does not include the names of the young porters now working on small treks in Sikkim, who have no high altitude experience. Nor does it include the names of the seven porters killed on the slopes of the North col on Everest in 1922. Their names were not given in the official report.

[As we go to press information has come in of the names of the seven porters killed on Everest in 1922. They are inscribed, alongside those of Kellas, Mallory, and Irvine, on the Memorial Cairn at the Base Camp. Their full names and numbers have not yet been ascertained.—Ed.]

Abbreviations	
Annap	Annapurna
Ev	Everest
Garh	Garhwal
Kanch	Kangchenjunga
KK	Karakoram
N.P.	Nanga Parbat
Rakap	Rakaposhi
Sik	Sikkim

* The best porters available (eight).
‡ Died—killed in the mountains.
† Now available at Darjeeling.
D. Died.

Himalayan Cl. No.	Name	Date of birth	Expeditions	Remarks
61*	Aila Sherpa	1913	36: Ev. 37: Shaksgam. 38: Gangotri (Austr). 39: Sik (Grob). 49: Pyramid Pk. 50: Annapurna.	One of the best Sherpas available at present. Tiger's Badge.
10*	Ajeeba	1911	33: Ev. 35: Kabru. 36: Ev. 37: Sik (Grob). 38: Rakap. 39: Sik (Grob). 47: Gangotri. 49: Pyramid Pk. 50: Annap. 50/51: KK (Marsh).	Very experienced. One of the best Sherpas now available.
43 †	Ang Babu	1915	30: Kanch. 33: Ev. 35: Ev. 36: Ev. 39: Lahoul (Krenek).	Good only for minor expeditions.
40	Ang Dawa I (Thamay)		36: Ev. 37: Sik (Grob). 38: Ev. 39: Garh (Roch). 47: Garh (Roch).	Now at Sola Khumbu.
41†	Ang Dawa II	1915	36: Ev. 47: Rakap. 50: Garh (Dittert).	Still going strong. Reliable sirdar and excellent cook.
42	Ang Dawa III (Luckla)		36: Ev. 38: Gangotri.	Now at Sola Khumbu.
152 †	Ang Dawa IV (Chota)	1928	49: Pyramid Pk. 50: Annap. 50: Garh (Dittert).	Promising young porter.
	Ang Dawa V	1929	49: Pyramid Pk.	Did quite well.
D. 116	Ang Karma	1913	36: Ev. 38: Ev. 42: Lama Amden. 43: Bandarpunch.	Died during the war.
1†	Ang Nima	1907	33: Ev. 34: N.P. 34: Sik (Gourley). 36: Simvu. 36: Fluted Pk. 39: Lahoul. 49: Pyramid Pk.	Willing, but slow to grasp things.
	Ang Nurbu		47: Garh (Roch).	Now at Sola Khumbu.
D. 24	Ang Pasang	1912	33: Ev. 34: Sik (Gourley). 36: Tibet (Martyn).	Died in 1943.
D.	Ang Pemba		38: Kanch.	Died in 1942.
103	Ang Phuri		36: KK (French).	?
D. 44	Ang Phurwa		36: Ev.	Died in 1937.
89	Ang Yemba II		36: KK (French).	Too old now.
155 †	Ang Temba III	1932	49: Pyramid Pk. 50/51: KK (Marsh).	Did well in 1949.
D.	Ang Tenzing I	1908	24: Ev. 34: N.P. 35: Garh f Auden).	Died in 1936.
3 ‡	Ang Tenzing II	1912	29: Kanch. 30: Kanch. 33: Ev. 35: Ev. 36: Ev. 37: Shaksgam. 38: Gangotri (Aust) 46: Nun Kun.	Died in 1949 whilst on tour with Wood in Lhonak. Malaria. Tiger's Badge.
	Ang Tenzing III	1922	47: Rakap.	Now at Sola Khumbu.
13	Ang Thari	1915	35: Kabru. 36: Ev.	Now at Sola Khumbu.
19*	Ang Tharkay	1909	31: Kanch. 33: Ev. 34: Nanda Devi. 36: Ev. 36: Garh (Osmaston). 37: Shaksgam. 38: Ev. 39: KK (Shipton). 45: Pauhunri. 49: Kanchenjau. 50: Annapurna.	Very likely the best and most experienced Sherpa, now working. Highly praised Tiger's badge.

Himalayan Cl. No.	Name	Date of birth	Expeditions	Remarks
36 †	Ang Tsering I	1910	24: Ev. 30: Kanch. 31: Kamet. 33: Ev. 34: N.P. 36: Ev. 39: Lahoul (Krenek).	German order of the Red Cross (Nanga Parbat, 34). Works as sirdar on treks below snow-line.
15 ‡	Ang Tsering II	1909	33: Ev. 35: Ev. 35: Kabru. 36: Ev. 37: N.P.	Killed in avalanche on Nanga Parbat 1937.
51 †	Ang Tsering III ('Pansy')	1907	36: Ev. 37: Garh (Gardiner). 38: Sik (Grob). 39: Sik (Grob). 49: Pyramid Pk. 50: Annap. 50: Nepal (Madgavkar).	Rather old now but still going strong. Tiger's Badge.
101 †	Ang Tsering IV	1915	36: KK (French). 47: Garh (Roch). 49: Pyramid Pk. 50: Nepal (Madgavkar).	In 1949 employed as Post Runner only.
16	Champa Lama	1913	34: Tibet (Bell). 35: Sik (Twynam).	Left Darjeeling 1937, returned 1949. Excellent cook and sirdar, inexperienced climber.
.. ‡	Chettan		22: Ev. 24: Ev. 26: Kumaon (Ruttledge). 27: Garh (Ruttledge). 29: Kanch. 30: Kanch.	In his time one of the most famous of the Tigers. Killed in avalanche on Kanch.
104 †	Chong Karma		36: KK (French). 37: N.P.	Killed in avalanche on Nanga Parbat.
100	Chung Tsering		36: KK (French).	?
76	Chung Chung	1900	33: Ev. 36: Ev.	Now cook in Alubari monastery.
92	Chumbi		30: KK (French)	?
. ‡	Dakschi		33: Ev. 34: N.P.	Died on Nanga Parbat.
D. 33	Da Namgyal	1895	29: Kanch. 30: Kanch.	Died 1938.
157 †	Da Namgyal II	1925	49: Nepal (Tilman). 50: Nepal (Tilman).	New man, no reports received so far.
	Da Nurbu	1925	50: Nepal (Madgavkar).	New man.
D. 105	Da Tenzing		36: KK (French).	Died 1939.
49*	Dawa Thondup	1907	33: Ev. 34: N.P. 35: Garh (Auden). 36: Ev. 37: Sik (Gook). 38: Masherbrum. 39: K.2. 47: Gangotri (Roch). 50: Annap. 50: Garh (Dittert). 45: Ghomo Yummo. 43: Bandarpunch.	Though rather old is still really excellent. He reached the summit of Abi Gamin in 1950. Order of German Red Cross. Tiger's Badge.
D. 53	Dawa Tsering Bhutia	1916	36: KK (French).	Died 1946. Him. Journal, 1940, p. j141, states No. 53 received Tiger's Badge, an error: Dawa Tsering Sherpa received it.
D.	Dawa Tsering Sherpa		33: Ev. 36: Ev. 38: Ev.	Died in 1939. Tiger's Badge.
113	Dhunbir Lepcha		36: K.K (French).	?
122	Dongri		36: Ev.	?
55	Dorji Mistri		36: Ev.	Works now as Mistri at Kalimpong.
D. 14	Dupha	1909	21: Ev. 22: Ev.	Died 1935

Himalayan Cl. No.	Name	Date of birth	Expeditions	Remarks
D. 91	Genden Umdu		36: KK (French). 39: Sik (Grob).	Died in 1943.
.. ‡	Geyley		22: Ev. 34: N.P.	Died on Nanga Parbat 1934.
84	Girmey Chakki Bhutia		36: Ev.	Too old now.
59	Gna Temba		36: Ev.	Gone to Sola Khumbu.
118 ‡	Gombu		36: Ev. 39: Garh (Roch).	Killed in avalanche on Chaukamba 1939.
56	Gyalgen I Khumiung		36: Ev.	Gone to Sola Khumbu.
57*	Gyalgen II Mikchen	1915	36: Ev. 38: Ev. 39: KK (Shipton). 46: Nun Kun. 49: Pyramid Pk. 50: Nepal (Tilman).	Excellent sirdar. Highly praised.
58‡	Gyalgen III Monjo		36: Ev. 37: N.P.	Killed in avalanche on Nanga Parbat 1937.
115	Gyalgen IV		?	Now doing business at Darjeeling.
125	Gyalgen V (Bhutia)		36: Ev.	Working m Sikkim.
145	Gyalgen VI	1918	38: Ev.	Gone to Yarkand.
	Gyalgen VII	1931	49: Pyramid Pk. 49: Panch Chuli. 50: Garh (Ch-Thomas).	Very young. Promising.
.. ‡	Gyalgen VIII	1930	50: Nepal (Madgavkar).	New man.
D. 142	Hawang Sherpa	1909	37: Sik (Hunt).	Died 1941.
D. 111	Hishey Bhutia		37: KK (Hunt).	Died 1941.
159 †	Ila Namgyal	1923	45: Sik (Tilley).	Not much experience.
18	Ila Kitar		29: Kanch. 30: Kanch. 31: Kanch. 33: Ev. 35: Ev. 36: Ev.	Now at Sola Khumbu.
D. 85	Ila Tenzing	1916	36: Ev.	Died, date uncertain.
D. 97	Injung Bhutia	1911	36: KK (French).	Died, date uncertain.
D. 22	Jayung Nakpa	1904	29: Kanch. 36: Ev.	Died 1941.
23‡	Jigmi		29: Kanch. 30: Kanch. 31: Kanch. 33: Ev. 34: N.P. 35: Ev. 35: Kabru. 36: Ev. 37: N.P.	Killed in avalanche on Nanga Parbat 1937.
52 †	Jigmay Tsering	1911	34: N.P. 36: KK (French).	Ten years as cook at Bellevue Hotel, now available again.
117‡	Karmi		36: Ev. 37: N.P.	Killed in avalanche on Nanga Parbat
156 †	Karsang	1928	49: Pyramid Pk. 50: Nepal.	New man.
83	Kijaipa		36: Ev.	?
63	Kirken		36: Ev.	Gone to Sola Khumbu.
35‡	Kitar	1905	24: Ev. 31: Kamet. 32: Kumaon (Ruttledge). 33: Ev. 34: N.P. 35: Kabru. 36: Gurla M. (Tichy). 36: Nanda Devi.	Died on Nanda Devi in 1936.
120	Kitar II		36: Ev.	?

Himalayan Cl. No.	Name	Date of birth	Expeditions	Remarks
D. 9	Kusang Namgay		33: Ev. 34: Nanda Devi. 36: Ev. 38: Ev.	Died at Sola Kumbu 1950. Tiger's Badge.
20 ‡	Kusang Siter	1906	31: Kamet. 33: Ev. 34: N.P. 35: Ev.	Drowned on returning from Everest 1935.
126	Kusang Temba		36: Ev.	Gone to Sola Khumbu.
34	Lhakpa Chedi	1903	24: Ev. 33: Ev.	Now in Calcutta.
30	Lhakpa Tenzing	1915	33: Ev. 35: Kabru. 36: KK (French). 37: Shaksgam. 38: Ev.	Gone to Yarkand. Tiger's Badge.
D. 46 †	Lewa	1902	33: Ev. 34: N.P. 31: Garnet. 35-37: Tibet (Kaulback). 38: Kaulback.	Died in 1948. Tiger's Badge.
64	Lobsang Sherpa	1903	29: Kanch. 33: Ev. 34: N.P.	?
D. 144	Lobsang Sherpa II	1909	38: Ev.	Died 1945. Tiger's Badge.
D. 21	Lobsang Tenzing	1904	33: Ev. 34: N.P.	Died 1935.
132	Manbahadur Sherpa	1901	36: Sik (Bauer). 37: N.P. 38: Tibet (Shepheard).	Works with P.W.D., Gangtok.
D. 96	Mapchi Topgay	1906	36: KK (French). 37: Koluhoi.	Died, date uncertain.
128	Mingma		36: Ev.	?
69	Mingma Gyalgen	1915	36: Ev.	Now at Sola Khumbu.
112	Mingma Kaprak	1903	36: KK (French).	?
D. 87	Mingma Neithen		36: KK (French).	Died, date unknown.
D. 31	Mingma Thu Thu ('Alice')	1900	22: Ev. 24: Ev. 31: Kanch. oik (Osmaston). 39: Kumaon. 47: Rakaposhi.	Disappeared on the Return journey from Srinagar to Darjeeling.
68 ‡	Mingma Tsering		36: Ev. 37: N.P.	Died in the avalanche on Nanga Parbat 1937.
D. 62	Namgyal		33: Ev. 34: N.P. 35: Ev. 36: Ev.	Died 1938.
D. 5	Narsang ('Policy')	1891	22: Ev. 24: Ev. 29: Kanch. 30: Kanch. 31: Kanch. 32: Sik (Osmaston). 33: Ev. 36: Ev.	Died 1942.
D.	Nima	1914	33: Ev. 34: N.P. 39: Garh (Koch).	Died, date unknown.
D.	Nima Dorje I	1903	24: Ev. 29: Kanch. 30: Kanch. 31: Kamet. 32: Nanda Devi. 33: Ev. 33: Sik (Gourley). 34: N.P. 34: Sik (Auden). 35: Tibet (Kaulb).	Died on the way back from Gyanste in 1938.
.. ‡	Nima Dorje II		33: Ev. 34: N.P.	Died on Nanga Parbat.
.. ‡	Nima Nurbu		33: Ev. 34: N.P.	Died on Nanga Parbat 1934.
65	Nima Sherpa	1909	31: Kamet, 33: Ev. 34: N.P.	?
D.	Nima Sherpa II	1912	38: N.P.	Died 1942.
.. ‡	Nima Tashi		29: Kanch. 33: Ev. 34: N.P.	Died on Nanga Parbat 1934.

Himalayan Cl. No.	Name	Date of birth	Expeditions	Remarks
149 †	Nima Tenzing	1921	49: Pyramid Pk. 50: Garh (Tichy).	Reliable sirdar.
D. 67	Nima Thondup	1894	21: Ev. 22: Ev. 24: Ev. 29: Kanch. 30: Kanch. 31: Kanch. 33: Ev. 34: N.P. 35: Tibet (Kaulb).	Died in 1949.
17 ‡	Nima Tsering I	1908	33: Ev. 35: Ev. 36: KK (French). 37: N.P.	Killed in avalanche on Nanga Parbat 1937.
110 ‡	Nima Tsering II		36: KK (French). 37: N.P.	Killed in avalanche on Nanga Parbat 1937.
D. 129	Nima Tsering III	1907	36: Nanda Devi. 37: Sik (Grob). 38: Masherbrum.	Died in 1939.
70 ‡	Nukku	1910	36: Ev. 37: Shaksgam. 38: Ev. 39: Assam (Tilman).	Died of malaria in Bhutan in 1939.
D. 27	Nullu	1894	24: Ev. 31: Kamet. 34: N.P. 36: KK (French).	Died at Sola Khumbu in 1938.
D. 71	Nutbu Bhutia		36: Ev. 37: Garh (Smythe). 38: Ev.	Died 1941.
124	Nurbu II		36: Ev.	Now in Kurseong.
D.	Nurbu Sonam	1912	33: Ev. 34: N.P.	Died in 1935.
	Nuri	1917	36: Ev. 39: Garh (Roch).	?
	Nuri Sikkimi		44: Trisul (Goodfellow).	?
81	Oocheri		36: Ev.	Now at Sola Khumbu.
121	Ongyal		36: Ev.	?
D. 7	Pasang Anju	1910	29: Kanch. 30: Kanch. 31: Kanch. 32: Sik (Osmaston). 33: Ev. 33: Sik (Gourley). 34: Sik (Auden). 35: Garh (Auden).	Died in 1936.
D. 86	Pasang Chkikadi	1903	36: KK (French). 37: Kolahoi. 38: N.P.	Died May 1950.
.. ‡	Pasang		31: Kanch.	Killed on Kanch. 1931.
D. 39	Pasang Bhutia		33: Ev. 34: Nanda Devi. 35: Ev. 36: Ev. 38: Ev.	Died in 1948.
	Pasang Dawa	1925	50: Nepal (Tilman).	New man.
139*	Pasang Dawa Lama (or Pasang Sherpa)	1911	38: Masherbrum. 37: Ghomolhari. 39: K.2. 37: Sik (Cook). 49: Pyramid Pk. 50: Garh (Snelsen). 44: Nanda Ghunti.	Reached 24,450 feet on K.2. Able organizer and very good climber. Tiger's Badge.
D. 28*	Pasang Dorji	1894	31: Kanch. 33: Ev. 34: N.P.	Died 1947.
11	Pasang Gaken	1908	30: Kanch.	Too old now.
8 ‡	Pasang Kikuli	1911	29: Kanch. 30: Kanch. 31: Kanch. 33: Ev. 34: N.P. 36: Nanda Devi. 38: K.2. 39:	Excellent reports throughout. Died on K.2. in 1939. Tiger's Badge.
.. ‡	Pasang Kitar		39: K.2.	Killed on K.2. 1939.
2	Pasang Lama	1892	24: Ev. 34: N. P.	too old now.
29 ‡	Pasang Nurbu (Picture)	1907	29: Kanch. 31: Kanch. 34: N.P. 36: Ev. 37: N.P.	Killed in avalanche on Nanga Parbat 1937.

Himalayan Cl. No.	Name	Date of birth	Expeditions	Remarks
79	Pasang Phuttar	1910	29: Kanch. 33: Ev. 35: Sik (Stoddart). 35: Kabru. 36: Nanda Devi. 38: Masherbrum.	No longer fit. Lost 7 fingers on Masherbrum, now has heart trouble.
D. 127	Pasang Sherpa		36: Ev. 38: Gangotri (Austr).	Died, date unknown.
D. 78	Pasang Tsering (Okaraya)	1906	29: Kanch. 30: Kanch. 33: Ev. 34: N.P.	Died in 1936.
98 †	Pasang Urgen	1908	36: KK (French). 38: Gangotri (Austr). 47: Garh (Roch).	Now working as rickshaw coolie.
54	Palden	1903	33: Ev. 34: N.P. 35: K. 36: Sik (Heim).	Now working at Kurseong. Tiger's Badge.
D. 146	Pemba Bhutia	1910	38: N.P.	Died, date unknown.
D. 147	Pemba Kitar (Sherpa)	1915	38: K.2.	Died in 1946.
150 †	Pemba Nurbu		38: Gangotri (Austr). 38: Garh (White). 49: Nepal (Tilman).	Quite satisfactory.
D. 90	Pemba Sherpa		26: KK (French).	Died, date unknown.
72	Pemba Sundar		36: Ev.	Gone to Sola Khumbu.
158	Penuri	1928	47: Garh (Roch). 49: Pyramid Pk. 49: Panch Chuli (Thomas). 50: Garh (Dittert).	Strong, reliable, and slowly gaining experience.
45	Phurba Tashi		36: Ev.	Business at Lhasa.
D. 66	Phurba Tenzing		33: Ev. 35: Ev. 36: Ev. 38: Ev.	Died during the war.
131	Phur Temba		36: Ev.	Gone to Sola Khumbu.
155 †	Phu Tharkey	1922	45: Pauhunri. 47: Rakap. 49: Nepal (Tilman). 50: Annap.	Very satisfactory.
.. ‡	Pintso Nurbu		33: Ev. 34: N.P.	Killed on Nanga Parbat 1937.
141 ‡	Pintso Sherpa	1913	38: K.2. 39: K.2.	Killed on K.2. 1939.
D. 32	Ringsing Bhutia		33: Ev. 35: Ev. 36: Ev. 36: Garh (Os- maston). 38: Ev.	Died in 1947. Tiger's Badge.
119	Rinsing II		36: Ev.	?
D. 74	Samden		36: Ev.	Died in Simla 1948.
93	Samdup		36: KK (French).	Gone to Tibet.
D. 77	San Dorji		35: Ev.	Died, Sola Khumbu, 1945.
D. 37	Sanglu Sirdar	1885	20: Kanga La (Kellas). 21: Ev. 22: Ev. 24: Ev. 29: Kashmir (Noel). 31: Kanch. 36: KK (French).	Died in 1941.
80	Santu		36: Ev.	?
D. 88	Sanu Pasang	1913	36: KK (French).	Died, date unknown.
151 *	Sarki	1920	46: Nun Kun. 46: Ghomo Yummo (Braham). 50: Annap. 50: Nepal (Madgavkar).	Reached Camp V on Annapurna. Possibly the most promising of the younger Sherpas.
82	Sona(m)	1915	36: Ev.	Now Police Dept., Calcutta.
D. 94	Sonam Bhutia	1909	36: KK (French).	Died, date unknown.
143	Sonam Sherpa		39: K.2.	Now too frail.

Himalayan Cl. No.	Name	Date of birth	Expeditions	Remarks
75	Sonam Tenzing		35: Ev. 36: Ev. 36: Garh (Osmaston). 37: Shaksgam. 38: Ev (Tilman).	Gone to Sola Khumbu.
D.	Sonam Topgay I	1903	34: N.P.	Died in 1935.
102	Sonam Topgay II		36: KK (French).	?
106	Sonam Tsering	1917	36: KK (French). 46: Sasir (Roberts).	Left Darjeeling.
107	Tarke		36: KK (French).	?
D. 47	Tashi Thondup	1897	22: Ev. 24: Ev. 29: Kanch. 30: Kanch. 31: Kanch 33: Tibet (K. Ward). 34: N.P. 35: Tibet (K. Ward).	Died in 1944.
6	Tehley (Socogem)	1888	27: Gyantse (Gourley). 29: Kanch. 32: Chomo Yummo (Spence). 34: Sik.	Too old now.
48*	Tenzing Bhutia	1917	36: Ev. 36: Garh (Osmaston). 38: Ev. 38: Garh (Osmaston). 39: Chitral (Midar). 46: Sik (Kirsopp). 47: Ev (Denman). 47: Gangotri (Roch). 48: Lhasa (Tucci). 49: Nepal (Tilman). 50: Bandarpunch (Gibson). 50/51: KK. (March).	Technically probably the best of all the Sherpas now working. Is qualified to lead in difficult terrain. Tiger's Badge.
108	Tenzing (Lhakpa)		36: KK (French).	?
D. 12	Tewang		24: Ev. 29: Kanch. 33: Ev. 34: Ev. (Wilson). 35: Ev. 36: Ev.	Went mad, died 1942.
60	Thundu Bhutia		33: Ev. 34: N.P.	Too old now.
154 †	Thundu Sherpa	1915	45-50: Many Sikkim tours.	Excellent cook.
95	Thupden	1918	36: KK (French).	?
	Tillye		39: Garh (Roch).	?
	Tsering		39: K.2.	?
D. 50	Tsering Tarke	1908	29: Kanch. 33: Ev. 35: Ev. 36: Ev.	Died in 1936.
38	Tse Tendrup	1909	36: KK (French). 38: K.2. W K.2.	Too old now.
109	Tsinge Temba		36: KK (French).	?
D. 59	Tsong Dumdu		29: Kanch. 34: Tibet.	Died in 1936.
D. 148	Tuthin Bhutia	1912	38: N.P.	Died in 1942.
123	Wangdi		36: Ev.	?
25	Wangdi Nurbu (Ongdi)		29: Kanch. 30: Kanch. 31: Kamet. 33: Ev. 34: N.P. 36: Ev. 37: Garh (Smythe). 38: Ev. 38: Garh (Austr). 39: Assam (Tilman). 47: Gangotri (Roch).	No longer available. Broke ankle, Gangotri, 1947. Tiger's Badge.

NOTES ON SOME OF THE HIGH-ALTITUDE PORTERS
NOW AVAILABLE

The following three have the highest reputation among the sirdars now available:

ANG THARKAY, aged 41. He gained a high reputation on the Everest Expeditions of 1936 and 1938. Since then he has lost nothing of his mountaineering ability but gained considerably in experience. On many minor expeditions in Sikkim he has acted as a 'guide', in the Swiss sense of the word, finding the route and leading to the top. His great experience enables him to smooth out difficulties with local coolies and make the utmost use of local resources. He is, according to many testimonies, a most pleasant and interesting companion. Angtharkay normally supplies porters and sirdars for the various expeditions.

PASANG DAWA LAMA, or Pasang Dawa Sherpa, aged 39. He reached the summit of Chomolhari with Spencer Chapman in 1937. In 1939 he reached 27,450 feet on K.2, which, if the figures are correct, is the greatest altitude reached by any Sherpa. He has not taken part in any of the big expeditions lately: it is difficult therefore to judge of his present mountaineering ability, though he readied the summit of Chomo Yummo in 1950, together with J. P. Lucas. A word of caution: lie is not above trying to get as much money as he can from his employers.

TENZING BHUTIA, or Tenzing Khumjung, aged 33. He is the most accomplished of the three, and speaks English quite well. In the winter of 1949/50 he was employed as a skiing instructor with the Indian Army in Kashmir. He is a very good climber, well qualified to act as a 'guide'. His work on Bandarpunch in 1950 was highly praised. As he is the youngest of the three a great future is before him.

Of the other Sherpas Dawa Thondup, aged 43, should be especially mentioned. In spite of his age he is still first class. He reached the summit of Abi Gamin in 1950. He is very modest-possibly the reason why he has not acted as sirdar up till now.

Among the younger generation of porters Sarki deserves special mention. His work on Nun Kun was highly praised, and he reached Camp V on Annapurna carrying a heavy load. Several others are also gaining a good reputation. The gap caused by the war seems to be slowly filling up again. Much credit for the training of the younger men goes to the Swiss expeditions. It is to be hoped that future expeditions will always employ one or two of the younger porters (they are normally better at load-carrying) so that they may gain experience.

All the Sherpas and Bhutias of Darjeeling have suffered greatly in the overwhelming landslides of June 1950. Many houses were destroyed, and a great number of them are still living in temporary quarters, or, having found accommodation, are having to pay exorbitant rents.

RULES FOR THE EMPLOYMENT OF SHERPA PORTERS

The following rules have no official authority, but they have been prepared in the light of conditions obtaining at present, and the rates given are based on those now prevailing; as such, they are intended to serve merely as a guide to members.

Rates. For small expeditions and expeditions working mainly below the snow-line: Sirdar, Rs. 5 per day; Porter, Rs. 3 per day. Half-rates for porters returning unladen during the course of small expeditions. For expeditions of longer duration: Sirdar, Rs. 150 to Rs. 175 per month; Porters, Rs. 100 to Rs. 120 per month.

Advances. Rs. 20 to Rs. 25 per month; e.g. for an expedition lasting three months, Rs. 60 to Rs. 75 is the usual advance, which should be paid at least a month beforehand. The amount will not be refunded if the expedition is cancelled within a fortnight of the start. The Hon. Local Secretary in Darjeeling would be prepared to assist leaders of expeditions, but he would require ample notice.

Food. For tours in Sikkim porters provide their own food along bungalow routes, but food must be provided for them off the main routes and above the snow-line. It is customary, also, to provide them with cigarettes.

Equipment. Must be provided by the employer, especially in the case of mountaineering parties. Some small expeditions have found it cheaper to pay porters a hire charge for supplying their own equipment, which is generally good and mainly acquired from large foreign expeditions. The usual hire charge in this case is Rs. 20 per month, payable to each fully-equipped man.

Fares. Third-class railway fares from and to Darjeeling should be paid, plus Rs. 2 per day for food.

It should be noted that members resident in India often complain that foreign expeditions tend to spoil porters by paying enhanced rates, e.g. Rs. 210 per month was paid in 1950 to a sirdar; or by giving them a large 'bakshish' at the end, although this should never be more than 15 per cent, of their wages; or by presenting them with wrist-watches and other such gifts; or by offering them horses to ride during the early marches. The other extreme, however, was recorded when one party expected their porters to carry loads of 70 lb. in addition to their own kit of 10 to 20 lb. Prodigious feats of load-carrying by Sherpa porters have been recorded on occasion, but they are not to be emulated. A porter's normal load should not exceed 50 to 60 lb. and on difficult ground and above the snow-line it should be rather less.

The following revised rates of compensation payable for injury or death to porters were introduced in August 1950 by the Political Officer in Sikkim:

Undertaking to pay Compensation

I hereby undertake to pay any porter, sirdar, or other servant hired by me for the purpose of my tour, or to his dependants, or failing that to his nearest living relative, compensation on the undermentioned scale, in the event of his meeting death or suffering injury while in my employ:

(a) Injury: Partial or whole loss of finger or toe: Rs. 10 per joint or part of a joint lost or damaged, except on the index finger, thumb, or great toe, when the amount shall be doubled.

Partial or total loss of a limb .... Rs. 150

Loss of sight of both eyes .... Rs. 500

Loss of sight of one eye . . . . . Rs. 300

In addition to such compensation a subsistence allowance of Rs. 15 per month will be paid to any porter who is incapacitated from work through accident or frost-bite on an expedition, for a period up to a maximum of twelve months.

(b) Death: Married man .... Rs. 1,000

Single man ...... Rs. 500

Female porter (whether married or single) . Rs. 500

Appendix 6
TIGER BADGES

Note: Reproduced with permission from *The Himalayan Journal*, Archives of The Himalayan Club, Volume 27, 1966, www.himalayanclub.org/hj.

THE COMMITTEE OFTEN RECEIVE REQUESTS for information concerning Tiger Badge Awards. We are recording below the official and minuted roll of awards of the Tiger Badge up to August 31, 1967.

Date of Minute	Name	H/C No.	Expedition	Remarks
	Lewa	46	Everest 1938	Died (year not known)
	Pasang Kikuli*	8	Not known	Died 1939
	Kusang Namgir	9	Not known	Died 1950
	Ang Tharkay	19	Everest 1938	
	Wangdi Norbu	25	Not known	Died 1952
30-5-39	Lakpa Tenzing	30	Everest 1938	
	Renzing	32	Not known	Died 1947
	Tenzing Norgay	48	Everest 1938	
	Dawa Thondup	49	K2 1939	
	Dawa Tsering	53		Died 1939
	Palden	54		Died
	Pasang Dawa Lama	139		

Date of Minute	Name	H/C No.	Expedition	Remarks
30-5-39	Lobsang	144		Died 1945
	Ang Tenzing	3		Died 1949
31-4-40	Ang Tenzing	51		
	Aila	61		
	Gender	91		Reported dead
21-7-53	Ang Tempa III	155	Everest 1953	
	Anullu	170	Everest 1953	
	Ajiba	10	Everest 1952	
	Ang Tsering	36	Everest 1952	
	Sarki	151	Everest 1952	
	Da Namgyal	157	Everest 1952	
21-7-53*	Dawa Tenzing	173	Everest 1953	
	Ang Nima	176	Everest 1953	
	Pasang Phutar	188	Everest 1953	
	Ang Namgyal	190	Everest 1953	
	Gompu	191	Everest 1953	
30-5-56	I-la Tenzing	85	Kanchengjunga 1955	
	Ang Norbu	172	Kanchengjunga 1955	Died
	Tashi I	178	Kanchengjunga 1955	
	Ang Temba IV	179	Kanchengjunga 1955	
	Urken	232	Kanchengjunga	
30-5-56	Gyalzen Nuru	163	Makalu 1955	Died 1961
	Gundin	167	Makalu 1955	
	Ang Phuta	186	Makalu 1955	
	Ang Nima	132	Dhaulagiri 1955	

*Although Pasang Kikuli's name appears in the first batch of awardees, he died before the badges were distributed. Nawang Topgay was awarded the badge for his efforts on the Everest expedition of 1953, but his name does not appear in the list.

Date of Minute	Name	H/C No.	Expedition	Remarks
12-2-60	Sonam Girney	Nil	Everest 1960	
	Ang Norbu	Nil	Everest 1960	
	Da Norbu	193	Everest 1960	
	Pemba Sundar	182	Everest 1960	
27-4-62	Wangdi	Nil	Jannu 1959	
	Da Norbu	161	Jannu 1959	
9-8-62	Mingma Tsering	340	Makalu 1961	
	Pemba Tenzing	341	Makalu 1961	
	Nima Dorje	345	Makalu 1961	
23-7-64	Ang Tshering	203	Everest 1963	
	Choetari	360	Everest 1963	
	Girmin Dorje	229	Everest 1963	
	Nawang Dorje	354	Everest 1963	
	Ang Nyima	355	Everest 1963	
	Phu Dorje	351	Everest 1963	
30-7-65	Dawa Norbu (Darjeeling)	322	Everest 1965	
	Tashi (Darjeeling)	236	Everest 1965	
	Karma (Darjeeling)	326	Everest 1965	Died 1967
	Sona (Darjeeling)	357	Everest 1965	
	Kalden (Gangtok)	309	Everest 1965	
	Tenzing Nendra (Khumjung)	362	Everest 1965	
	Nawang Hilla (Khumjung)	363	Everest 1965	
	Pasang Tendi (Khumjung)	364	Everest 1965	
	Mingma Tshering (Phorche)	365	Everest 1965	
	Tenzing Gyatso (Phorche)	366	Everest 1965	
	Pemba Tharke (Phorche)	367	Everest 1965	
	Nima Tenzing (Pangboche)	368	Everest 1965	
	Dawa Tenzing (Namche)	369	Everest 1965	

Appendix 7
CONTEMPORARY DARJEELING SHERPA CLIMBERS

This is a list of some of the current climbers from Alu Bari Darjeeling. The achievements of these young men are spectacular, though they are generally less well known than their Nepalese counterparts. Their CVs do not include Karakoram peaks because Indian passport holders are prohibited from climbing in Pakistan. Peaks mentioned as "attempts" are often the result of the Sherpas not being offered a chance to summit during an expedition. We have, however, chosen to list such climbs, because the Sherpa participated in these expeditions and contributed to the success of the members who did reach the summit.

Mingma Hapshe Sherpa: Everest, 2012, 2013, 2016 (twice), 2017, 2019; Manasulu, 2015, 2017; Lhotse, 2017; Dhaulagiri, 2018. Born on May 10, 1986, Mingma Sherpa has been climbing since 2000 and by 2019, he had a formidable record of climbs. He has climbed Everest six times, twice in a span of five days in 2016. Apart from Everest and other Nepal 8000ers, he has summitted Kamet, Chaukhamba, Sutarsin, Saser Kangri, Mana, Laxmi, Nun, Kun, Nehru, Kedar Dome, Nanda Devi (East), Kunti Banar, Palak II, Satopanth, Trimukhi Parbat, Indrasen, Trishul, and others, many of them more than once. He was awarded the Garud Medal in 2021.

Samgyal Sherpa: Everest, 2012, 2013, 2014, 2016. Born on October 4, 1970, Samgyal has climbed since 2000, attempting Kangchenjunga twice and Saser Kangri and Momostang Kangri once, and has summitted Rimo,

Kamet three times, and Mrigthuni. He has participated in more expeditions to Everest as well. He was awarded the Garud Medal in 2018.

Nim Dorjee Sherpa: Everest, 2006, 2009, 2010, 2011, 2012 (twice), 2013, 2016 (rescue mission), 2017, 2018, 2019; Manaslu, 2012, 2019. Born on June 4, 1984, Nim Dorjee climbed on Everest in 2004, 2009, and 2015, climbing from the North, South, and Southwest faces. Additionally, he attempted Dhaulagiri in 2018. He was awarded the Garud Medal in 2019.

Passang Phutar Sherpa: Everest, 2007, 2010; Cho Oyu, 1997, 2002; Kangchenjunga, 2011. Passang Phutar Sherpa had participated in more than fifty expeditions between 1990 and 2017, including several attempts on Everest, Dhaulagiri, Kamet, Shishapangma, Ama Dablam, and Nun, and had success on mountains such as Bhrigupanth, Shivling, Manirang, Satopanth, Thalaysagar, and Dharmasura, among others. He was awarded the Garud Medal in 2017.

Tashi Sherpa: Everest, 2013, 2018; Kangchenjunga, 2011, 2014; Lhotse, 2012, 2013; Cho Oyu, 2014; Manaslu, 2016, 2017; Dhaulagiri, 2017; Makalu, 2017; Annapurna, 2019. Born on January 1, 1982, Tashi has an amazing climbing record. Besides the formidable 8000ers that he has climbed, he has also gone to Everest and Dhaulagiri with other expeditions and summitted Ama Dablam and Himlung as well.

Sangay Sherpa: Everest, 2004, 2006, 2013, 2015, 2017; Cho Oyu, 2005; Kangchenjunga, 2008, 2010, 2011, 2018; Lhotse, 2012, 2016; Makalu, 2014, 2019; Manaslu, 2017. Sangay was born on January 7, 1972. His biodata mentions only one time on Everest when he did not summit but reached an altitude of 8,665 meters. He has been on the summit of all the other 8000ers, several more than once.

Pemba Tsering Sherpa: Everest, 2016, 2017, 2018. Born on November 10, 1989, Pemba Tsering seems to have been on fire from 2012 through 2018, participating in twenty expeditions in six years to tough mountains—Thalaysagar, Nandaghunti, Nun, Kun, Gaurichen, Bhagirathi, and Saser Kangri to name a few. All those except Changabang were successful.

Ang Dorjee Sherpa: Everest, 2013. Like several Darjeeling Sherpas, Ang Dorjee, born on October 4, 1986, operates in India and Nepal. India has many tough mountains, but only one 8000er. Apart from an attempt on Everest in 2005, Ang Dorjee has summitted all the mountains he went to, including Indrasan, Thalaysagar, Nun, Kun, and Saser Kangri.

Ang Tashi Sherpa: Everest, 2004. Born on August 18, 1980, Ang Tashi has had mixed results on mountains. He has been on Everest three times but succeeded only once, summitted Kamet twice, and been on several other expeditions.

Dawa Narbu Sherpa: Everest, 2011, 2012, 2013, 2014, 2017, 2018, 2019. Dawa Narbu was born on November 24, 1978. Besides reaching the summit of Everest seven times, he has been on expeditions to Dhaulagiri, Kamet, Kun, Mamostang Kangri, Plateau Peak, and others.

Lakhpa Norbu Sherpa: Everest, 2013, 2018, 2019; Cho Oyu, 2016; Dhaulagiri, 2017. Lakhpa Norbu has been on Everest seven times and returned from the last camp four times (2004, 2012, 2014, and 2015). He climbed on many other Himalayan peaks, including Kamet, Kabru, Menthosa, Kangchenjunga, Satopanth, and Brigupanth.

Lakhpa Tenzing Sherpa: Everest, 2017, 2018. Although Lakhpa Tenzing's career has not led him to many 8000ers, his success on hard technical peaks is impressive. Born on August 31, 1978, he has climbed Mulkila, Menthosa, Bhrigupanth, Saser Kangri, Nanda Kot, Satopanth, and many Indian peaks.

Lobasang Sherpa: Everest, 2019. Born on March 22, 1984, Lobasang, another Everester, has more than twenty-five high-mountain expeditions to his credit. He has climbed Kamet, Shivling, Nanda Devi (East), Trishul, Kamet, and Nandakot, among others.

Mingma Thendu Sherpa: Everest, 2008, 2009, 2011, 2016, 2018, 2019; Lhotse, 2008, 2012; Dhaulagiri, 2017. Mingma Thendu has been on Everest at least ten times and other formidable mountains such as Annapurna, Makalu, Thalaysagar, Kamet, and Chowkhamba. He considers himself a mountain enthusiast who is well aware of the pros and cons of several mountains in India and Nepal.

Mingma Tenzing Sherpa: Everest, 2013, 2016, 2017, 2018, 2019, 2021 (twice), 2022; Lhotse, 2021. Born on October 15, 1986, Mingma Tenzing is another Everest king. He has not bothered to add other expeditions to his résumé.

Mingma Temba Sherpa: Everest, 2009, 2011, 2013, 2017; Dhaulagiri, 2016. Yet another Mingma—yet another Everester. Mingma Temba Sherpa was born on September 20, 1982. His triumphs include several Ladakhi peaks such as Nun, Kun, Saser Kangri, and Rimo, and Uttarakhand peaks such as Satopanth and Kamet.

Nima Thendu Sherpa: Everest, 2016, 2019; Lhotse, 2017, 2018 (twice). Another Alubari Sherpa, Nima, born on September 18, 1987, started climbing 8,000-meter peaks in 2006 when he summitted Mamostang Kangri. Since then, his climbing career has been a continuous journey, including Nun, Kun, Jaonli, Trimukhi Parbat, Jongsong, and Shivling, among others.

Norbu Sherpa: Everest, 2016, 2018. Born in 1989, Norbu has climbed since 2004, covering technical India peaks such as Satopanth, Bhrigupanth, Panchachuli, Kamet, Nun-Kun, and others.

Pasang Tenzing Sherpa: Everest, 2006, 2012. Pasang Tenzing was born on January 15, 1979. Working with the Indo Tibetan Border Police, he supplied a very professional résumé, detailing not only his mountaineering expeditions but other achievements as well. During a career spanning more than two decades, he has completed at least thirty high-mountain expeditions. At age eighteen, he was the youngest person to climb Kamet. In 1999, he stood on Swargarohini as part of the first all-Sherpa mountaineering expedition. That same year, during the Gya expedition, he brought down the body of eminent mountaineer Arun Samant and also evacuated two sick members. He participated in similar rescues on Kangchenjunga and Nanda Devi.

Phurba Sherpa: Everest, 2007, 2009, 2011, 2012, 2013, 2014, 2015, 2016, 2017, 2019, 2023; Cho Oyu, 2014; Manaslu, 2017; Lhotse, 2018. Phurba is one of the highest-achieving Sherpas of Alubari. He has participated in forty-eight expeditions from 1998 to 2023, on forty of which he reached the summit. He has climbed Thalasagar, Nanda Devi, Satopanth, Bhagirathi, Chowkhamba, Kamet, Shivling, and several other peaks with different teams worldwide. His support of Indian mountaineer Chetana Sahoo on Everest saved her life. He began climbing in 1998, and continues climbing and opening routes today. A suave man of the world, Phurba is tech savvy and a local community leader. He has been an invaluable source of information and support in Darjeeling.

NOTES

Chapter 1: Who Is the Sherpa in the Word *Sherpa*?
p. 29 **Pharak:** Pharak, or Ghat, is the area that lies between Solu and Khumbu.

p. 30 **Tantra:** Tantra refers to Hindu/Buddhist practices involving rituals, magic, and incantations.

p. 32 **in India, when lists of scheduled tribes, scheduled castes, and OBCs:** Other Backward Class (OBC) is a collective term used by the government of India to classify communities that are socially or educationally disadvantaged.

p. 33 **there is a story current in the days before the railway a single Bhotia carried a grand piano:** A grand piano can weigh anywhere between 500 and 1,200 pounds (227 to 544 kilograms). Baby grands weigh in around 540 pounds (245 kilograms), and a professional grand piano can weigh between 700 and 1,200 pounds (318 to 544 kilograms), depending on its height.

Chapter 2: Coming to Paradise
p. 39 **Stones that talk to each other:** Subba, "Sabdatitma Tajenglung."

p. 41 **it is solely on account of the climate:** Kennedy, *The Magic Mountains*, p. 22.

p. 42 **The hill station of Darjeeling began life in 1835:** Dozey, *A Concise History of the Darjeeling District since 1835*, p. 54.

p. 42 **this energetic Scotsman:** O'Malley, *Bengal District Gazetteers: Darjeeling*, p. 22.

p. 43 **this merry troupe:** Hooker, *Himalayan Journals*.

p. 44 **By 1895, 186 tea estates covered:** Jules-Dash, *Bengal District Gazetteers—Darjeeling*, p. 114.

p. 45 **a Calcutta resident:** Known as the toy train, the Darjeeling Himalayan Railway now operates only between New Jalpaiguri and Darjeeling, a distance of eighty-eight kilometers. The journey takes seven hours, twenty minutes, with much of the track running on Hill Cart Road and at many points even crisscrossing it.

Chapter 3: The Night Before the Expedition
p. 51 **In 1802, the EIC launched:** "The Great Trigonometrical Survey."

p. 52 **Sikdar was a student:** Kochhar, "Did Radhanath Sikdar Measure the Height of Mount Everest First?"

p. 53 **Once the British government took control of India:** For more information, read Anthony Verrier's *Francis Younghusband and the Great Game*, published by Jonathan Cape in 1991.

p. 54 **The first person who admitted:** Martyn, "The Story of the Himalayan Club, 1928–1978."

p. 55 **These expeditions needed hundreds of porters:** The 1930 expedition to Kangchenjunga, led by Professor Günter Oskar Dyhrenfurth, carried six tons of baggage, and was assembled into 350 porter loads. The team comprised five Germans, three English, two Swiss, and one Austrian—a total of eleven members. Dyhrenfurth opined, "This sounds an enormous quantity but it may be mentioned for comparison that the Vissers, for instance, took on their last expedition 450 porters for half the number of Europeans. For the baggage of the third Everest expedition (which contained the same number of Europeans as ours), 70 porters and 350 animals carrying about 770 coolie loads were required." Dyhrenfurth, "The International Himalayan Expedition."

p. 56 **an extraordinary aptitude for entering:** "In Memoriam, The Hon Charles Granville Bruce."

p. 58 **Yet you can size up a man pretty well:** The image of the superior, benevolent patriarch looking after lesser beings in his care, as he would his animals, is not limited to Ruttledge's book. It is a refrain that runs through most expedition accounts of the first half of the twentieth century.

Chapter 4: The Men with No Names

p. 63 **an ominous sound, sharp, arresting, violent, and yet somehow soft like an explosion of untamped gunpowder:** Bruce, *The Assault on Mount Everest, 1922*, p. 282.

p. 64 **More experience, more knowledge might perhaps have warned us:** Ibid, p. 286.

p. 64 **The regret of all members of the Expedition:** Ibid.

p. 67 **an examination of *The Himalayan Journal's* porter list:** Krenek, "Himalayan Porters," p. 121.

p. 70 **Sherpa Nima Tendrup:** Also known as Nima Thondup (HC no. 67).

Chapter 5: Two Women and a Club

p. 73 **The first half of the 1860s proved:** Band, "150 Years of the Alpine Club."

p. 73 **From the late nineteenth to the first decade of the twentieth century:** See chapter 2.

p. 75 **had to be secured at all costs:** Bauer, *The Seige of Nanga Parbat 1856–1953*, p. 54.

p. 75 **a fascinating footnote:** Conefrey, "Darjeeling Legends: A Fascinating Footnote to Himalayan History."

p. 75 **they meant much more:** Although this chapter recounts the history of The Himalayan Club through the work of two women, the reader must note that the club has retained its importance for ninety-three years as a result of many hardworking volunteers. For more information on its history, visit himalayanclub.org.

p. 78 **about an equal number:** Townend, "Notes on Sherpa Porters."

p. 78 **The tragedy on Nanga Parbat in 1937:** There were two more German expeditions to Nanga Parbat, in 1938 and 1939. They too met with bad weather. Wanting to take no chances with tragedy a third time, the expeditions turned back at different points.

p. 80 **Mrs. Henderson was a very good lady:** Douglas, "The Face of Everest."

p. 80 **I am certain that without:** Braham, "Obituary of Jill Henderson."

p. 81 **By then a big change was on the way:** Braham, "Correspondence."

p. 82 **But now this money:** "Club Proceedings 1959–60."

p. 82 **Within a decade, two other climbing institutions:** See chapter 11.

Chapter 6: Big Little Man: Ang Tharkay

p. 88 **at Tenzing Tharkay's house in Siliguri:** Siliguri is a city in the state of West Bengal situated on the route from Darjeeling to the nearest airport and train station at Bagdogra. Its average elevation is 122 meters, making it a city in the plains.

p. 88 **his autobiography, written in French:** *Ang Thrace, Memoirs d'un Sherpa*: Norton, *Ang Thrace*. Ang Tharkay recounted his story in Nepali to Mohan Lal Mukherjee, who narrated it in English to Basil Norton. Henri Delgove then translated it from English, and published it in French.

p. 88 **an English translation had been published:** Tharkay and Norton, *Sherpa*.

p. 90 *dak* **bungalow:** *Dak* literally translates as "mail," but they were guesthouses the British built in remote areas for officials who were traveling. They were also staging posts for mail, hence their name.

p. 93 **Bangdel explained:** Renowned artist and fellow Nepali Lain Singh Bangdel was a dear friend of the Indian filmmaker Satyajit Ray, and, in 1952, he was enrolled at the École des Beaux-Arts. The French introduced the two almost as soon as Ang Tharkay landed so that the little Sherpa would not feel alone in a strange land.

p. 93 **In 2016, a journalist, Saprina Panday, interviewed:** Panday, "The Journey of a Nepali Sherpa into the Pages of a Tintin Comic Book."

p. 93 **He had cut off the handsome pigtail:** Shipton, *The Six Mountain-Travel Books*, p. 601.

p. 95 **We left the HMI with my four kids:** Ongmu, Ang Tharkay and Ang Yangje's oldest daughter, was already married to climbing Sherpa Pannu. The couple lived in Manali.

p. 96 **an ice cream that cost two *annas*:** Old coinage. Sixteen annas made one rupee.

p. 98 **Ang Tharkay accompanied me:** Braham, "In Memoriam—Ang Tharkay."

Chapter 7: Porter, Tantric, Rogue: Pasang Dawa Lama

p. 101 **a thigh-bone instrument:** This is a trumpet known in Tibetan as a *kangling* (literally, "leg flute"). It is made from a human femur or tibia and is used for specific rituals as well as funerals.

p. 101 **damar:** The *damar* or *damaru* is a small, two-headed drum made of wood and covered with hide on both ends. Its resonators are attached by thongs or twine; a twist of the wrist makes the resonators strike both drum ends.

p. 102 **In 1937, British climber Freddie Spencer Chapman:** Spencer Chapman refers to him as Pasang and as Pasang (Sherpa) when he introduces him in "The Ascent of Chomolhari, 1937."

p. 103 **Pasang Dawa Lama, Pasang Kikuli:** These names are listed in the section on expeditions ("The American Expedition to K2, 1939") and "Himalayan Porters" (by Krenek) in *The Himalayan Journal*.

p. 104 **was one of the first recipients:** Pasang Kikuli was also on the list and would have received the Tiger Badge had he not died on the mountain, just months before they were awarded. Nevertheless, the title Tiger became associated with his name.

p. 106 **Au:** *Au* means "uncle"—a term of respect used for older males.

p. 107 **In the summer of 1954:** There is a film about this tragedy directed by Ignacio Aguirre and Romina Coronel.

p. 109 **A very high mountain:** Tichy, "Cho Oyu 1954."

p. 110 **the expedition report shows:** Goyal, "Neelkantha-Chowkhamba Expedition."

p. 110 **Captain Kohli chose him:** See chapter 16.

p. 111 **The more good in it is:** Pasang Dawa Lama's poem was published in Kohli, *Sherpas: The Himalayan Legends*, p. 113.

Chapter 8: Family Man: Ang Tsering

p. 113 **During our first visit:** See chapter 2.

p. 114 **When journalist Ed Douglas asked:** Douglas, "The Face of Everest."

p. 115 **Hugh Ruttledge, the expedition leader, wrote:** Ruttledge, "The Mount Everest Expedition of 1933."

p. 115 **except for a shaky account of the infamous German attempt:** Bechtold, "The German Himalayan Expedition to Nanga Parbat 1934."

p. 117 **The list of Himalayan porters:** Krenek, "Himalayan Porters," p. 123.

p. 119 **by the *Anandabazar Patrika* newspaper:** *Anandabazar Patrika* is a Bengali-language newspaper and part of the ABP media conglomerate headquartered in Kolkata, West Bengal. The newspaper has been an ardent supporter of Indian mountaineering and has financed several expeditions, going back to the 1950s. They launched a subscription after Tenzing Norgay climbed Everest in 1953 that collected enough funds to build him a new house, with some left over to put into a fund for the welfare of climbing Sherpas. To learn more, see chapter 10.

p. 120 **Tenzing's first wife, Dawa Phuti:** See the epilogue for more about Sherpa clans.

p. 121 **Ang Tsering was born in Nepal:** Douglas, "The Face of Everest."

Chapter 9: Those Magnificent Men and Women

p. 127 **As he told us, "My father's name:** Three Ang Tserings were recorded as working at the same time.

p. 127 ***The Himalayan Journal* porter list:** Krenek, "Himalayan Porters," p. 123.

p. 130 **Soli Mehta, editor of *The Himalayan Journal*, later wrote:** Mehta, "Obituary, Ajeeba and Wangdi."

p. 134 **Dawa gets special mention:** Krenek, "Himalayan Porters," p. 123.

p. 135 **Da Thondup was married earlier:** Da Thondup's first wife was the daughter of Kitar (HC no. 35). See chapter 8.

Chapter 10: Bedrock: Tenzing Norgay

p. 138 **Tenzing laid bare his life:** Ullman's *Man of Everest*, as told to Malcolm Barnes.

p. 143 **like the ill-fated Maurice Wilson:** Maurice Wilson was an eccentric who, despite a lack of mountaineering or flying experience, succeeded in 1934 in flying from Britain to India, surreptitiously entering Tibet and climbing to around 7,000 meters on Everest.

However, he died on the slopes, and a British expedition found his body the following year.

p. 143 **Tenzing admitted that anyone else:** Denman returned in 1948 with money and equipment, but again no permit. This time no one agreed to go with him, so he left the country, giving his equipment to Tenzing. Interestingly, Denman also wrote a book titled *Alone to Everest*. Microsoft computer scientist and designer, as well as a mountain climber and researcher, Bill Bruxton observed, "He might be the only person on the planet who would consider himself alone when accompanied by Tenzing Norgay."

p. 143 **Sardar Wangdi Norbu's accident:** For more about Wangdi Norbu, see chapter 5.

p. 144 **With the Swiss, he experienced a sense:** The status-conscious British never shared such camaraderie with the Sherpas.

p. 145 **like Ravi Mitra:** Rabindranath (Ravi) Mitra was the owner and publisher of a Nepali newspaper. More importantly, he was the friend of and guide to Sherpas, particularly Tenzing. He was instrumental in giving Tenzing the tricolor to place atop Everest, an act that changed Tenzing's fortune forever. Later on, Mitra taught Tenzing how to sign his name and also helped with translation for his first autobiography.

p. 152 **In early May 1986, PemPem visited her father:** These are all Tenzing's children; see appendix 3, "Family Trees," for more information.

Chapter 11: The Gang's All Here: The Himalayan Mountaineering Institute

p. 155 **New Delhi / 15 November, 1954. / My dear Chief Minister:** Nehru, Letters to Chief Ministers.

p. 157 **Laying the foundation stone, Nehru said:** All cited quotations are from Nehru's inaugural speech, "Origin and Growth."

p. 157 **Sonam Doma:** Sonam Doma is the daughter of Tenzing Norgay's older sister and is married to Dorjee Lhatoo.

p. 157 **Phu Lhamu:** Phu Lhamu was the daughter of Tenzing's oldest brother, Kesang. Much older than Sonam Doma, she was a porter on the 1953 Everest expedition.

p. 158 **In *Alpine Journal* in 1994, Harish Kapadia:** Kapadia, "The Himalayan Mountaineering Institute, Darjeeling."

Chapter 12: Heart of Gold: Nawang Gombu

p. 162 **My father sent me there:** Oral history transcripts shared by Mick Conefrey.

p. 163 **I am carrying two oxygen cylinders:** Douglas, "Nawang Gombu Obituary."

p. 164 **Brig. Khullar:** Brigadier Darshan Kumar Khullar was the leader of the contentious 1984 Everest expedition that put the first woman, Bachendri Pal, on the summit. Rita Gombu was also part of this expedition. See chapter 16.

p. 165 **Selected as a candidate for the 1984 Indian Everest expedition:** See chapter 16.

p. 165 **Pasang Phutar:** Pasang Phutar "Jockey" was a famous climber and equestrian. He was also Rita Gombu's maternal uncle.

p. 167 **RMI guide Dave Hahn's 2011 tribute to Gombu:** Hahn, "Dave Hahn's Memories of Nawang Gombu Sherpa."

Chapter 13: More Tales from Darjeeling

p. 175 [the nearby villages of] Rimbik, others to Sonada: Rimbik is roughly sixty kilometers from Darjeeling, bordering Nepal; several trek routes start in Rimbik. Sonada is roughly seventeen kilometers before Darjeeling town on the Siliguri–Darjeeling route, and is famous for its magnificent monastery.

p. 175 Cho Oyu that same year with Herbert Tichy: See chapter 7.

p. 175 I well remember him: Mehta, "Obituary, Ajeeba and Wangdi."

p. 179 [She] became to all intents and purposes: Chari, *Mountain Memories*, p. 98.

Chapter 14: The Last Tigers: Nawang Topgay and Sona "King Kong"

p. 184 Da Tsering: Da Tsering, although featuring in the porter list of 1950–51, has no porter number against his name.

p. 184 At a committee meeting: Notes, "The Grading of Sherpa and Bhotia Porters."

p. 184 A grand total of sixty-four badges: See appendix 6 for the complete list of Tiger Badge awardees.

p. 185 As first Sirdar, Lewa: Bechtold, "The German Himalayan Expedition to Nanga Parbat 1934."

p. 185 Mr. Kydd: J. W. Kydd was the local secretary of The Himalayan Club from 1936 to 1937.

p. 187 We were tied together: Dubin, "Tigers of the Snow: Three Generations of Great Climbing Sherpas."

p. 192 to recover a lost CIA nuclear spy device: See chapter 16.

Chapter 15: Renaissance Man: Dorjee Lhatoo

p. 196 *dhotis:* A *dhoti* is a long piece of unstitched cloth draped in such a way as to form loose trousers for men.

p. 198 Potala: Potala in Lhasa, the winter palace of the Dalai Lamas from 1649 to 1959, was declared a UNESCO World Heritage Site in 1994.

p. 201 With a ration card: Ration cards are government-issued cards that listed the members of a household and allowed them to buy subsidized essentials at government-approved shops.

p. 202 Chong Rinzing: Chong Rinzing, son of a prominent Sherpa and Dorjee Lhatoo's childhood friend, was introduced in chapter 1.

p. 204 My sister now lives in Delhi: Lhatoo's sister passed away in 2018; he did not attend her funeral. (The interview would have been conducted in 2014.)

p. 204 [the Gurkha Regimental Recruiting Center] Katapahar: The Gurkha Regimental Recruiting Centre of Katapahar was situated on one of the ridges above Darjeeling.

p. 206 Premchand, Thondu Sherpa, Santosh Arora, and I got to the top: Chachu, a Bhutanese member, was to have been the fifth summiteer, but he panicked on the summit ridge, just one hour below the top, and refused to go farther.

p. 208 Dorjee Lhatoo climbed Everest in 1984: See chapter 16.

Chapter 16: The Great Indian Dream

p. 213 Fortunately, its first Headmaster, Arthur Foot: Jayal, "Early Years of Indian Mountaineering," p. 152.

p. 213 **The hills have claimed:** Ibid.

p. 214 **Gasping for breath, [Roy] Greenwood:** Kohli, *Mountaineering in India*, p. 17.

p. 214 **A failed first attempt was followed:** Ibid, p. 29.

p. 215 **The flamboyant Pasang Dawa Lama:** See chapter 7.

p. 215 **On the way to basecamp, he collapsed:** Nandu Jayal died in 1958 of pulmonary edema caused by overexertion. His Sherpas believed, however, that he died of heartbreak. Jayal had promised his friend Tenzing Norgay that he would deliver the latter's niece and her newborn baby to her village in Nepal on his way to the Cho Oyu basecamp. The new mother, however, had not quite recovered from the trauma of childbirth, and died just as they crossed into Nepal. Jayal cared for the baby tenderly until it could be handed over to its family, but he was ridden with guilt and died just days later.

p. 217 **one reached the top:** Nawang Gombu and Ang Kami were full team members, while Phu Dorjee was a high-altitude Sherpa. In all, three Sherpas stood atop Everest in 1965.

p. 217 **How honoured and privileged I feel:** Kohli, "Nine atop Everest," p. 19.

p. 218 **by 1984, 101 expeditions were recorded:** Kohli, *Mountaineering in India*, p. 84.

p. 218 **"a gentleman climber":** Khullar, *The Call of Everest*, p. 17.

p. 218 **We now had two dead men:** Khullar, "Indian Everest Expedition, 1984," p. 21.

Chapter 17: The Lost Legacy

p. 223 **The nationalistic attitude generated:** Sengupta, "Vertical Limit."

p. 224 **At present we are 27 Climbing Sherpas:** Lhatoo, "The Climbing Sherpas of Darjeeling," p. 271.

p. 225 **Nawang Gombu was director:** When Gombu climbed Everest twice, the post of deputy director of field training was created as a reward in recognition of his achievements. When Tenzing retired, Gombu was promoted to director of field training, and the role of deputy director was given to Nima Tashi. An additional post of deputy director was later created for Dorjee Lhatoo, who was designated deputy director B while Nima Tashi was deputy director A. After Dorjee Lhatoo left the HMI, no one else was given the post, and all three posts—director of field training, deputy director A, and deputy director B—were scrapped.

p. 227 **Two sweater sellers and:** Kapadia, "Memories," p. 155. Photo republished; caption mentioned in text.

p. 227 **the alleged failure of the Himalayan Mountaineering Institute:** Gombu and Lohani, *Nawang Gombu*, p. 19.

p. 227 **Last year, the institute, with a glorious legacy:** Ibid, p. 22.

Chapter 18: New Men in Town

p. 231 **people from the area translate:** Das, *The Long Walk from Darkness to Light*, p. 4.

p. 233 **josh:** Best conveyed in English as "energy" or "enthusiasm."

p. 235 **where he rose through the ranks:** See chapter 11.

p. 235 **Not [possible to climb] K2 on an Indian passport:** As India and Pakistan have poor diplomatic relations, given their history and an ongoing war in the Siachen area of the Karakoram, Pakistan's government does not grant Indian passport holders visas to climb in Pakistan. Even regular visitor visas are hard to come by. The reverse is true for Pakistanis who wish to visit or climb in India as well.

p. 237 **There are very few Sherpa instructors:** In 2022, Pasang Tenzing was the only Sherpa instructor remaining among the permanent teaching staff at the HMI.

Chapter 19: Shadows on the Mountain

p. 240 **that Pasang Phutar and his younger brother Pemba Chorty:** Sengupta, "Vertical Limit."

p. 243 **Dada:** A term of respect, *dada* means "brother" in Hindi.

Chapter 20: In Every Home an Everester

p. 253 **a board game called *A Nice Cup of Tea:*** Alubari, boardgamegeek.com.

p. 254 **The brothers Samgyal, Nim Dorjee:** The brothers Samgyal, Nim Dorjee, and Mingma Hapshe are all recipients of the Garud Award. Refer to chapter 19 to learn more about Mingma Hapshe.

Epilogue: Lunch at Glenary's

p. 264 **there are a total of eighteen Sherpa clans:** See appendix 2 for a list of Sherpa clans.

p. 265 **Tenzing Norgay brought Doma:** See chapter 10.

p. 265 **The expedition ended in disaster:** See chapter 9.

p. 266 **Two climbers—Michael Groom:** See appendix 3 for Tenzing Norgay's family tree.

p. 268 **The body was brought down:** Pasang Phutar was one of the Sherpas who brought Lobsang Tshering's body down from Everest. See chapter 19.

RESOURCES

Books

Amir, Ali, ed. *For Hills to Climb*. New Delhi: The Doon School Old Boys Society, 2001.

Bauer, Paul. *The Siege of Nanga Parbat 1856–1953*. London: Rupert Hart-Davis, 1956.

Bhanja, K. C. *History of Darjeeling and Sikkim Himalaya*. New Delhi: Gyan Publishing House, 2011.

Bruce, Charles Granville. *The Assault on Mount Everest, 1922*. New York: Longmans, Green & Co.; London: Edward Arnold & Co., 1923.

Bryn, Alf B. *Peaks and Bandits*. Sheffield: Vertebrate Publishing, 2021.

Chari, Lalit. *Everest 1953: The Epic Story of the First Ascent*. London: One World Publications, 2012.

———. *Mountain Memories*. Mumbai: Malvika Chari, 1995.

Das, Susanta Kumar. *The Long Walk from Darkness to Light: An Autobiography of Kusang Dorjee*. Darjeeling: Susanta Kumar, 2018.

Davis, Wade. *Into the Silence*. London: Vintage, 2012.

District Census Handbook, Calcutta, Vol–II, West Bengal—Census 1961. https://new.census.gov.in/nada/index.php/catalog/28973.

Dittert, Rene, Gabriel Chevally, and Raymond Lambert. *Forerunners to Everest—The Story of the Two Swiss Expeditions of 1952*. London: George, Allen & Unwin Ltd., 1954.

Douglas, Ed. *Tenzing: Hero of Everest*. Washington, DC: National Geographic Society, 2003.

Dozey, E. C. *A Concise History of the Darjeeling District since 1835*. Kolkata: Bibliophile, 2012.

Ellsworth, Scott. *The World beneath Their Feet—The British, the Americans, the Nazis, and the Mountaineering Race to Summit the Himalayas*. London: John Murray, 2020.

Finch, George I. *Climbing Mount Everest*. London: George Philip & Son Ltd., 1930.

Fisher, James F. *Sherpas: Reflections on Change in Himalayan Nepal*. Berkeley: University of California Press, 1990.

Gombu, Ongmo, and Lokesh Lohani. *Nawang Gombu: His Life and Times through Media Clippings*. New Delhi: Highlanders Design Services, 2007.

Hansen, Peter H. *The Summits of Modern Man: Mountaineering after the Enlightenment.* Cambridge: Harvard University Press, 2013.

Herzog, Maurice. *Annapurna: Conquest of the First 8000-Metre Peaks.* London: Triad Paladin, Grafton Books, 1986.

Hooker, Joseph Dalton. *Himalayan Journals, or Notes of a Naturalist in Bengal, the Sikkim, Nepal Himalayas, the Khasia Mountains, etc.* London: John Murray, 1854.

Hunt, John. *The Ascent of Everest.* London: Hodder & Stoughton, 1953.

Jules-Dash, Arthur. *Bengal District Gazetteers—Darjeeling.* Alipore, Bengal: Bengal Alipore Press, 1947.

Kapadia, Harish, ed. *A Passage to Himalaya.* Mumbai: The Himalayan Club, 2001.

——. *Across Peaks and Passes in Darjeeling and Sikkim.* New Delhi: Indus Publishing Company, 2002.

Kennedy, Dane. *The Magic Mountains: Hill Stations and the British Raj.* Berkeley: University of California Press, 1996.

Khullar, Darshan Kumar. *The Call of Everest: First Ascent by an Indian Woman.* New Delhi: Vision Books, 1992.

Koehler, Jeff. *Darjeeling: A History of the World's Greatest Tea.* New Delhi: Bloomsbury Publishing India, 2015.

Kohli, Mohan Singh. *Mountaineering in India.* New Delhi: Vikas Publishing House Pvt. Ltd., 1989.

——. *Nine Atop Everest—Spectacular Indian Ascent.* New Delhi: Indus Publishing, 2000.

——. *Sherpas: The Himalayan Legends.* New Delhi: UBS Publishers' Distributors Pvt. Ltd., 2003.

——, and Kevin Conboy. *Spies in the Himalayas.* Lawrence: University Press of Kansas, 2003.

Mallory, George L. *Climbing Everest—The Complete Writings of George Leigh Mallory.* Islington: Gibson Square, 2012.

Mason, K. *Abode of Snow—A History of Himalayan Exploration and Mountaineering.* London: Rupert Hart-Davis, 1955.

McDonald, Bernadette. *I'll Call You in Kathmandu: The Elizabeth Hawley Story.* Seattle: Mountaineers Books, 2005.

McKinnon, Lyn. *Only Two for Everest: How a First Ascent by Riddiford and Cotter Shaped Climbing History.* Dunedin: Otago University Press, 2016.

Mitchell, Ian R., and George W. Rodway. *Prelude to Everest: Alexander Kellas, Himalayan Mountaineer.* Edinburgh: Luath Press, 2011.

Morin, Micheline. *Everest—From the First Attempt to the Final Victory.* Varanasi: Pilgrims Publishing, 2011.

Morris, Jan. *Coronation Everest.* London: Boxtree Ltd., 1958.

National Classification of Occupations, 2015. Volume I. Ministry of Labour & Employment, Government of India. https://www.ncs.gov.in/Documents/National%20 Classification%20of%20Occupations%20_Vol%20I-%202015.pdf.

Neale, Jonathan. *Tigers of the Snow: How One Fateful Climb Made the Sherpas Mountaineering Legends.* New York: Thomas Dunne Books, 2002.

Nehru, Jawaharlal. *Letters for a Nation: From Jawaharlal Nehru to His Chief Ministers 1947–1963*. New Delhi: Penguin Allen Lane, 2014.

Norgay, Jamling, with Coburn Broughton. *Touching My Father's Soul: In the Footsteps of Sherpa Tenzing*. London: Random House, 2001.

Norgay, Tenzing, as told to Malcolm Barnes. *After Everest—An Autobiography by Tenzing Norgay Sherpa*. New Delhi: Vikas Publishing House Pvt. Ltd., 1977.

Norgay, Tenzing, as told to James Ramsay Ullman. *Man of Everest—An Autobiography of Tenzing*. Varanasi: Pilgrims Publishing, 2005.

Norton, Christopher. *Everest Revealed: The Private Diaries and Sketches of Edward Norton, 1922–24*. London: The History Press, 2014.

Norton, Basil. *Ang Thrace: Memoirs d'un Sherpa*. Paris: Amiot Dumont, 1954.

Norton, Edward Felix, ed. *The Fight for Everest 1924*. Varanasi: Pilgrims Publishing, 2002.

O'Malley, L. S. S. *Bengal District Gazetteers: Darjeeling*. New Delhi: Logos Press, 1985.

Ortner, Sherry B. *High Religion: A Cultural and Political History of Sherpa Buddhism*. New Delhi: Motilal Banarsidas Publishers, 1992.

——. *Life and Death on Mount Everest—Sherpas and Himalayan Mountaineering*. New Delhi: Oxford University Press, 2000.

Pares, Bip. *Himalayan Honeymoon*. London: Hodder & Stoughton, 1940.

Perrin, Jim. *Shipton & Tilman: The Great Decade of Himalayan Exploration*. London: Hutchinson, 2013.

Ruttledge, Hugh. *Attack on Everest*. New York: National Travel Club, 1935.

Shastry, Padma. *Sherpas—The Brave Mountaineers*. Darjeeling: Himalayan Mountaineering Institute, 1991.

Shipton, Eric. *The Six Mountain-Travel Books*. Seattle: Mountaineers Books, 2010.

Smeeton, M. *A Taste of the Hills*. London: Rupert Hart-Davis, 1961.

Smythe, Frank S. *The Six Alpine/Himalayan Climbing Books*. Seattle: Mountaineers Books, 2000.

——. *The Spirit of the Hills*. London: Hodder & Stoughton, 1935.

Smythe, Tony. *My Father, Frank—Unresting Spirit of Everest*. Sheffield: Baton Wicks, 2013. Published by Mountaineers Books in Legends & Lore series in 2015.

Stevens, Stanley F. *Claiming the High Ground: Sherpas, Subsistence, and Environmental Change in the Highest Himalaya*. Berkeley: University of California Press, 1993.

Tenzing, Judy, and Tashi Tenzing. *Tenzing and the Sherpas of Everest*. New Delhi: HarperCollins Publishers, 2002.

Tharkay, Ang, with Basil P. Norton. *Sherpa: The Memoir of Ang Tharkay*. Seattle: Mountaineers Books, 2016.

Tilman, H. W. *Mount Everest, 1938*. Cambridge, UK: Cambridge University Press, 1948.

Ullman, James Ramsay. *Man of Everest: The Autobiography of Tenzing*. London: G. G. Harrap, 1955.

Verrier, Anthony. *Francis Younghusband and the Great Game*. London: Jonathan Cape, 1991.

von Fürer-Haimendorf, Christoph. *The Sherpas of Nepal—Buddhist Highlanders*. Kolkata: Oxford Book Co., 1964.

Younghusband, Sir Francis. *Everest—The Challenge*. Varanasi: Pilgrims Publishing, 2004.

———. *The Epic of Mount Everest*. Varanasi: Pilgrims Publishing, 2002.

Articles and Papers

Brown, Chip. "Sorrow on the Mountain." *The National Geographic Magazine* (2014): 57.

Climbing Club Bulletins. Various issues.

"Alubari: A Nice Cup of Tea." Board Game Geek 2019. boardgamegeek.com/boardgame/228959/alubari-nice-cup-tea.

Band, George. "150 Years of the Alpine Club." *The Himalayan Journal* 64 (2008): 193.

Bechtold, Fritz. "The German Himalayan Expedition to Nanga Parbat 1934." *The Himalayan Journal* 7 (1935): 27.

Biddle, Pipa. "Why It's Better to Carry Weight on Your Head." *The Atlantic*, August 18, 2017. www.theatlantic.com/technology/archive/2017/08/tumplines/537306/.

Braham, Trevor. "Correspondence." *The Himalayan Journal* 56 (2000): 265.

———. "In Memoriam—Ang Tharkay." *The Himalayan Journal* 39 (1983): 222–223.

———. "Obituary of Jill Henderson." *The Himalayan Journal* 49 (1993): 270.

Chakraborty, Subhasish. "The Darjeeling Himalayas—A Paradise in Peril." *The Hans India*, January 9, 2014. www.thehansindia.com/posts/index/Life-Style/2014-01-09/Darjeeling-Himalayas-A-paradise-in-peril/81878.

Chapman, Spencer. "The Ascent of Chomolhari, 1937." *The Himalayan Journal* 10 (1938): 126.

"Club Proceedings 1959–60." *The Himalayan Journal* 22 (1960): 177.

Conefrey, Mick. "Darjeeling Legends: A Fascinating Footnote to Himalayan History." *Mick Conefrey* (blog), June 2020. https://www.mickconefrey.co.uk/articles/darjeeling-legends.

Douglas, Ed. "The Face of Everest." *The Guardian*, April 23, 2001. theguardian.com/education/2001/apr/23/artsandhumanities.highereducation.

———. "Nawang Gombu Obituary." *The Guardian*, May 24, 2011. theguardian.com/world/2011/may/24/nawang-gombu-obituary.

Dubin, Jenny. "Tigers of the Snow: Three Generations of Great Climbing Sherpas." *Outside Magazine*, April 1, 2003. www.outsideonline.com/adventure-travel/destinations/asia/tigers-snow.

Dyhrenfurth, G. O. "The International Himalayan Expedition." *The Himalayan Journal* 3 (1930): 79–80.

Georgiou, Mark. "Everest Olympic Medal Pledge Set to Be Honoured." *BBC News*, March 26, 2012. www.bbc.com/news/uk-17493939.

Goyal, Commodore S. N. "Neelkantha-Chowkhamba Expedition." *The Himalayan Journal* 23 (1961): 100.

"The Great Trigonometrical Survey: RSTV Life and Culture" Sansad TV, March 30, 2020. https://www.youtube.com/watch?v=S6v8PGd0CSc.

Hahn, Dave. "Dave Hahn's Memories of Nawang Gombu Sherpa." Rainier Mountaineering Institute, July 17, 2011. rmiguides.com/blog/2011/07/17/dave_hahns_memories_of_nawang_gombu_sherpa.

Handwerk, Brian. "The Sherpas of Mount Everest." *The National Geographic Magazine*, 2010

Herge [Georges Prosper Remi]. "Tintin in Tibet." *The Adventures of Tintin*. Great Britain: Methuen and Company, Ltd., 1962.

Horell, Mark. "10 Great Sherpa Mountaineers." *Mark Horell* (blog), March 19, 2014. www.markhorrell.com/blog/2014/10-great-sherpa-mountaineers.

———. "Footsteps on a Mountain—An Early History of the 8000m Peaks: The Sherpa Contribution." *Mark Horrell* (blog), February 24, 2016. www.markhorrell.com/blog/2016/an-early-history-of-the-8000m-peaks-the-sherpa-contribution.

"In Memoriam: The Hon Charles Granville Bruce." *The Himalayan Journal* 12 (1940): 132.

Jayal, N. D. "Early Years of Indian Mountaineering." *The Himalayan Journal* 62 (2006): 152.

Kapadia, Harish. "The Himalayan Mountaineering Institute, Darjeeling." *The Alpine Journal* (1994): 225.

———. "Memories—Training, Sherpas, and Friends—1964." *The Himalayan Journal* 75 (2020): 155.

Khullar, Darshan Kumar. "Indian Everest Expedition, 1984." *The Himalayan Journal* 41 (1984): 21.

Kochhar, Rajesh. "Did Radhanath Sikdar Measure the Height of Mount Everest First?" *The Wire*, August 10, 2021. science.thewire.in/the-sciences/radhanath -sikdar-measure-height-mount-everest-first/.

Kohli, Mohan Singh. "Nine Atop Everest," *The Himalayan Journal* 26 (1965): 19.

Krenek, Ludwig, "Himalayan Porters" *The Himalayan Journal* 16 (1951): 121.

Lhatoo, Dorjee. "The Climbing Sherpas of Darjeeling." *Himalayan Journal* 35 (1976–78): 271.

LJT. "The Grading of Sherpa and Bhotia Porters." *The Himalayan Journal* 12 (1940): 140–141.

Martyn, John. "The Story of the Himalayan Club, 1928–1978." *The Himalayan Journal* 35 (1979): 3.

Mason, Kenneth. "Himalayan Accidents in 1939." *The Himalayan Journal* 12 (1940).

Mason, K., ed. "The American Expedition to K2, 1939." *The Himalayan Journal* 12 (1940): 123.

Mehta, Soli. "Obituary, Ajeeba and Wangdi." *The Himalayan Journal* 33 (1975): 225.

Miller, Robert. "High Altitude Mountaineering Cash Economy and the Sherpa." *Human Organization, Society for Applied Anthropology* 24, no. 3 (1965): 244–249. www.jstor.org/stable/44125136.

Nehru, Jawarhalal. *Letters to Chief Ministers*. Vol. 4, 1947. Accessed 2019. archive.org /details/in.ernet.dli.2015.54646.

———. "Origin and Growth." Himalayan Mountaineering Institute. Accessed 2018. hmidarjeeling.com/origin-and-growth.

Ortner, Sherry. "Who Shapes the Text? Sherpas and Sahibs on Mount Everest." Ann Arbor: University of Michigan, 1990.

Panday, Saprina. "The Journey of a Nepali Sherpa into the Pages of a Tintin Comic Book." *Scroll*, May 29, 2016. scroll.in/article/807276/the-journey-of-a-nepali-sherpa-into-the-pages-of-a-tintin-comic-book.

Rand, Christopher. "The Story of the First Sherpa to Climb to the Top of Mount Everest." *The New Yorker*, May 28, 1954. www.newyorker.com/magazine/1954/06/05/tenzing-of-everest.

Ruttledge, Hugh. "The Mount Everest Expedition of 1933." *The Himalayan Journal* 6 (1934): 39.

Salkeld, Audrey, and Liesl Clark. "Sherpas on Everest." *Everest Online*. www.pbs.org/wgbh/nova/everest/history/sherpason.html.

Schaffer, Grayson. "The Disposable Man: A Western History of Sherpas on Everest." *Outside Magazine*, July 10, 2013. www.outsideonline.com/outdoor-adventure/climbing/disposable-man-western-history-sherpas-everest.

———. "The Value of a Sherpa Life." *Outside Magazine*, April 18, 2014. www.outsideonline.com/outdoor-adventure/climbing/value-sherpa-life/.

Sengupta, Rudraneil, "Vertical Limit," *Mint*, May 4, 2012. livemint.com/Leisure/zuN1zWTaYTsyJze1Us4rHP/Vertical-limit.html.

Subba, S. "Sabdatitma Tajenglung." *Yuma Manghim Udghatan Samaroha Smarika*. Darjeeling: Limbu/Subba Tribal Society, 2017.

Tichy, H. "Cho Oyu 1954." *Alpine Journal* 60 (1955): 247.

———. "Cho Oyu 26,750 Feet," *The Himalayan Journal* 19 (1956).

Townend, Joan. "Notes on Sherpa Porters." *The Himalayan Journal* 16 (1947): 86.

"Triumph on Everest." I: Siege and Assault by Sir John Hunt; II: The Conquest by Sir Edmund Hillary. *The National Geographic Magazine* 106 (1954).

Films and Websites

Aguirre, Ignacio, and Romina Coronel. *Dhaulagiri 1954—Argentinos en Himalaya*. Caprichos Visuales, 2004. www.mntnfilm.com/en/film/dhaulagiri-1954-argentinos-en-himalaya-2004.

Alpine Journals, www.alpinejournal.org.uk.

Bill Buxton's "Books on History and Exploration," with a focus on Central Asia: the territories of and around the Greater Himalaya, Tibet, Afghanistan, India, Pamirs, Hindu-Kush, and High Tartary; "The History of Climbing and Mountaineering," especially in the Himalaya and Karakoram Ranges, 2022. www.billbuxton.com/climbing.html.

The Himalayan Club Newsletters, www.himalayanclub.org/publications/e-letter.

The Himalayan Journals, Volumes 1–76, www.himalayanclub.org/publications/the-himalayan-journal

The Himalayan Mountaineering Institute, hmidarjeeling.com

The Indian Mountaineer, www.indmount.org

United Sherpa Association, www.sherpakyidug.org

INDEX

ABOUT THE AUTHORS

Deepa Balsavar (left) and Nandini Purandare (right) *(Photo by Azra Bhagat)*

Nandini Purandare is editor of the internationally renowned *Himalayan Journal (THJ)*. Purandare is a writer and editor for the Avehi-Abacus Project, which develops educational materials for schools across India. An economist by training, Purandare has worked as a consultant with several organizations and research centers. She is a devout reader of mountain literature and avid trekker and traveller in the Himalaya.

Deepa Balsavar has written and illustrated more than thirty books for children. As a consultant with UNICEF on the Meena Project in South Asia, Balsavar wrote scripts and trained animation houses in Bangladesh. She has also developed communication material on HIV/AIDS, sexuality and gender education, mental health, and women's studies. Balsavar teaches communication design at the Industrial Design Centre, IIT Bombay, and was a core team member of the Avehi-Abacus Project for two decades.

Purandare and Balsavar founded **The Sherpa Project** to record oral histories through in-depth interviews with the climbing Sherpa community, friends, associates, and contemporary climbers in Darjeeling, as well as in other Indian cities and abroad. The project has nearly 150 audiovisual recordings and a rich bank of research material, including material from the archives of project sponsor The Himalayan Club. Purandare and Balsavar have uncovered a wealth of untold stories that offer a unique perspective on this important but unsung community. Their advisors include eminent Darjeeling Sherpa Dorjee Lhatoo, noted Himalayan explorer and Royal Geographic Society member Harish Kapadia, and before his death, legendary British mountaineer Doug Scott.

Purandare and Balsavar both reside in Mumbai.

recreation • lifestyle • conservation

MOUNTAINEERS BOOKS, including its two imprints, Skipstone and Braided River, is a leading publisher of quality outdoor recreation, sustainability, and conservation titles. As a 501(c)(3) nonprofit, we are committed to supporting the environmental and educational goals of our organization by providing expert information on human-powered adventure, sustainable practices at home and on the trail, and preservation of wilderness.

Our publications are made possible through the generosity of donors, and through sales of 700 titles on outdoor recreation, sustainable lifestyle, and conservation. To donate, purchase books, or learn more, visit us online:

MOUNTAINEERS BOOKS

1001 SW Klickitat Way, Suite 201 • Seattle, WA 98134
800-553-4453 • mbooks@mountaineersbooks.org • www.mountaineersbooks.org
An independent nonprofit publisher since 1960

YOU MAY ALSO LIKE:

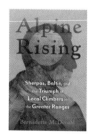   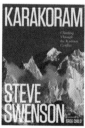